American Book Company's

PASSING THE

GEORGIA END OF COURSE TEST

IN

AMERICAN LITERATURE AND COMPOSITION

WRITTEN TO THE GPS STANDARDS

Zuzana Urbanek
Margaret DuPree
Sara Hinton

Dr. Frank J. Pintozzi, Project Director

American Book Company
PO Box 2638
Woodstock, GA 30188-1383
Toll Free: 1 (888) 264-5877   Phone: (770) 928-2834
Fax: (770) 928-7483   Toll Free Fax: 1 (866) 827-3240
www.americanbookcompany.com

ACKNOWLEDGEMENTS

The authors would like to gratefully acknowledge the formatting and technical contributions of Marsha Torrens.

We also acknowledge the assistance of Yvonne Benson in the preparation of this book for publication.

This product/publication includes images from CorelDRAW 9 and 11 which are protected by the copyright laws of the United States, Canada, and elsewhere. Used under license.

This publication follows the conventions of *The Chicago Manual of Style*.

Table of Contents

Chapter 6   The Writing Process   139

Chapter 7   The Research Process   163

Chapter 8   Using Standard American English   179

Georgia End of Course Test in American Literature and Composition
Preface

Passing the Georgia End of Course Test in American Literature and Composition will help students who are learning or reviewing GPS standards and strands for the Reading Comprehension, Writing, and Conventions sections of the **Georgia End of Courst Test in American Literature and Composition**. The materials in this book are based on the GPS Learning standards and strands as published by the Georgia Department of Education.

This book contains several sections:

    1) General information about the book itself

    2) A diagnostic test

    3) An evaluation chart

    4) Nine chapters that teach the concepts and skills needed for test readiness

    5) Two practice tests

Standards are posted at the beginning of each chapter, in the diagnostic and practice tests as well as in a chart included in the answer manual.

We welcome comments and suggestions about this book. Please contact the authors at

American Book Company
PO Box 2638
Woodstock, GA 30188-1383

Call Toll Free: (888) 264-5877
Phone: (770) 928-2834
Toll Free Fax: 1 (866) 827-3240

Visit us online at
www.americanbookcompany.com

About the Authors:

Margaret DuPree has a B.A. in English from the University of Georgia and is completing her M.A. She has tutored college students in literature and composition as well as children with learning disabilities to improve their reading and comprehension skills.

Sara Hinton has a B.A. from Columbia University and an M.A. in The Teaching of English from Teachers College, Columbia University. She taught middle school Language Arts and college courses in writing, grammar, and literature for several years.

Zuzana Urbanek serves as ELA Curriculum Coordinator for American Book Company. She is a professional writer with 25 years of experience in education, business, and publishing. She has taught English abroad as a foreign language, and in the United States to native speakers and as a second language. Her M.A. is from Arizona State University.

About the Project Director:

Dr. Frank J. Pintozzi is a former professor of Education at Kennesaw (GA) State University. For over 28 years, he has taught English and reading at the high school and college levels as well as in teacher preparation courses in language arts and social studies. In addition to writing and editing state standard-specific texts for high school exit and end of course exams, he has edited and written numerous college textbooks.

American Book Company produces best-selling books and software for learning standards based on state curriculums and for passing exit and end of grade exams in Alabama, Arizona, California, Florida, Georgia, Indiana, Louisiana, Maryland, Minnesota, Mississippi, Nevada, New Jersey, North Carolina, Ohio, South Carolina, Tennessee, and Texas.

GA EOCT American Literature and Composition Diagnostic Test

The purpose of this diagnostic test is to measure your knowledge of American Literature and composition. This diagnostic test is based on the Georgia GPS standards for American Literature and Composition and adheres to the sample question format provided by the Georgia Department of Education.

General Directions:

1. Read all directions carefully.

2. Read each question or sample. Then choose the best answer.

3. Choose only one answer for each question. If you change an answer, be sure to erase your original answer completely.

4. After taking the test, you or your instructor should score it using the evaluation chart following the test. This will enable you to determine your strengths and weaknesses.

Standards covered by each question are indicated next to the question. For standard ELAALRL1, a letter follows the standard number, indicating F = fiction, NF= nonfiction, P = poetry, or D = drama.

SECTION 1

excerpt from Franklin D. Roosevelt's first Fireside Chat, Washington, D.C., March 12, 1933

Following is an excerpt of a speech given by FDR while he was President of the United States. It was near the end of the Great Depression, and he was urging people to be brave as the country recovered. Because of his education, position, and experience Roosevelt's information about banking is reliable and valid.

After all, there is an element in the readjustment of our financial system more important than currency, more important than gold, and that is the confidence of the people. Confidence and courage are the essentials of success in carrying out our plan.

You people must have faith; you must not be stampeded by rumors or guesses. Let us unite in banishing fear. We have provided the machinery to restore our financial system; it is up to you to support and make it work. It is your problem no less than it is mine. Together we cannot fail.

1 Which of the following BEST explains the author's tone in the passage? ELAALRL4 ELA11W1

A angry

B encouraging

C taunting

D relieved

2 Knowing that this speech was given near the end of the Great Depression, which of the following BEST explains the speech's importance? ELAALRL1, NF ELAALRL3

A The people needed a renewed sense of hope and responsibility after such difficult times.

B The people caused the depression with irresponsibility; FDR wanted to make sure that didn't happen again.

C The people needed to feel that the president was their friend as much as their leader.

D The people wanted to be reassured that the depression was really over.

3 The word *readjustment,* as it is used in the passage, suggests that the financial system was being adjusted ELAALRC3

A for the first time.

B again.

C for the last time.

D indefinitely.

4 This passage BEST exemplifies what purpose for writing? ELA11W2

A narrative

B expository

C persuasive

D technical

excerpt from Cotton Mather's Memorable Providences, Relating to Witchcrafts and Possessions

About Midsummer, in the year 1688, the Eldest of these Children, who is a Daughter, saw cause to examine their Washerwoman, upon their missing of some Linnen [linens] which twas fear'd she had stollen from them; and of what use this linnen might bee to serve the Witchcraft intended, the Theef's Tempter knows! This Laundress was the Daughter of an ignorant and a scandalous old Woman in the Neighbourhood; whose miserable Husband before he died, had sometimes complained of her, that she was undoubtedly a Witch, and that whenever his Head was laid, she would quickly arrive unto the punishments due to such an one. This Woman in her daughters Defence bestow'd very bad Language upon the Girl that put her to the Question; immediately upon which, the poor child became variously indisposed in her health, and visited with strange Fits, beyond those that attend an Epilepsy or a Catalepsy, or those that they call The Diseases of Astonishment.

Cotton Mather was one of the judges in the Salem Witch Trials. In this passage, he describes an accused witch this way:

> This Laundress was the Daughter of an ignorant and a scandalous old Woman in the Neighbourhood; whose miserable Husband before he died, had sometimes complained of her, that she was undoubtedly a Witch…

5 Why would he use this type of strong language? ELAALRL4 ELAALRL3 ELAALRC4

A to persuade his readers the right person was on trial

B to teach his readers about the physical appearance of witches

C to force a confession from the condemned thief

D to explain why the accuser of the washerwoman took ill with fits

6 Mather writes about the girl becoming "variously indisposed in her health." In this context, what does *indisposed* mean? ELAALRL5 ELAALRC4

A unwilling   C unwell

B reluctant   D wary

7 This work was written in the late 17th century, while American English was still in its formation and strongly influenced by other languages. What is the MOST striking difference in conventions that a reader sees in this passage? ELA11C1

A The lack of organization makes it hard to read.

B There no consistency of verb tense as we use now.

C Different punctuation marks are used than we use today.

D We no longer capitalize most nouns, only proper nouns.

8 This nonfiction description of society and its persecution of those who did not conform to its norms later became a theme explored by what novelist?

ELAALRL1, NF
ELAALRL2
ELAALRL3

A Anne Bradstreet, in "To My Dear and Loving Husband"

B Benjamin Franklin, in *Poor Richard's Almanac*

C Nathanial Hawthorne, in *The Scarlet Letter*

D James Fenimore Cooper, in *Leatherstocking Tales*

9 What type of figurative language is used in the following sentence?

ELAALRL1, P

The horse's long, lithe legs looked lovely.

A analogy

B alliteration

C euphemism

D personification

10 To which literary period does writing of the Harlem Renaissance belong?

ELAALRL3

A Romanticism

B Realism

C Modernism

D Postmodernism

11 What type of figurative language is used in the following sentence?

ELAALRL1, P

The wind howled outside her bedroom window.

A paradox   C simile

B metaphor   D onomatopoeia

Questions 12–23 are based on the following two passages:

The following passages consider the ways movies reflected popular moods at two points in the 20th century. The first relates to films in the 1930s; the second to films in the 1970s.

Passage 1:

1 By the height of the Great Depression in 1933, more Americans were flocking to movies than ever before, eager to escape the crushing poverty and pervading sense of hopelessness that massive unemployment and growing debt brought on a seemingly daily basis. **2** Because tickets cost only pennies and offered hours of diversion, they existed for millions of Americans as a cheap way to fill the hours of the day. **3** Moreover, movies had yet to escape the public perception as a "working class" medium—fit not for the cultured, educated elite but for the lower, blue collar people of little, if any, secondary or high school education. **4** Hollywood responded by making films that both appealed to peoples' yearnings for release from economic want and attacking the government and social systems that produced the Depression and the economic collapse that caused it.

5 A great example of the films that both exploited and glamorized financial security were the hugely popular "Thin Man" series starring Willam Powell and Myrna Loy as Nick and Nora Charles, rich socialites who solved murders among New York's elite society. **6** Set in luxurious homes and expensive nightclubs, the murders always revolved around the idle rich and were motivated by petty greed and vanity. **7** Powell's Nick, a former working-class gumshoe, uses common sense and a street-wise attitude to see through the affectations and snobbery of the socialites. **8** In every example, his unpretentious logic won out over the treachery of the idle rich, standing up for justice regardless of economic station.

9 Similarly, the "gangster" films that became prominent during this period portrayed the modern-day outlaws of that era, individuals who defied the systems responsible for the Depression and made their own way in an uncaring environment. **10** Films like *The Public Enemy* and *Angels with Dirty Faces* showed working class men and women clawing their way to riches despite the police and judges who stood in their way—representatives of the same systems that many working class people held responsible for the Depression. **11** That the criminals died violent, untimely deaths was almost beside the point to audiences who devoured these films; the gangster heroes won out, no matter the cost.

Passage 2:

12 By the 1970s, anxiety regarding the nation's direction and identity became reflected in popular entertainment, as a new generation of writers and directors—products of the social conscience of the previous decade—exerted their influence on the entertainment mainstream. **13** In the aftermath of the Vietnam War and the growing Watergate scandal, American film audiences entered into a renewed romance with the Western genre, albeit a new strain that served as social allegory. **14** In these New Westerns, the heroes were frequently lawbreakers and outcasts who rejected social convention and morality in order to make a life for themselves on the American Frontier. **15** Films such as *Butch Cassidy and the Sundance Kid* and *Jeremiah Johnson* resonated deeply with audiences worried about confining government and technological structures; *The Outlaw Josie Wales*, about a Confederate solider looking to lead a productive life in the West, spoke to the post-Vietnam yearning for individual redemption. **16** Similarly, the brutal violence of vigilante films such as *Dirty Harry* and *Taxi Driver* enthralled audiences facing skyrocketing crime rates and a weakened justice system. **17** In both types of films, the recurring theme is "don't trust governments or economies; you're on your own." **18** The theme continued throughout the decade, spiraling into urban political drama (*Serpico*), science fiction (*The Omega Man*), and even romance (*Love Story*). **19** While by the start of the '80s the pessimism had thawed somewhat, the '70s spirit of individualism influenced the next generation of filmmakers who came of age in the 1990s, crafting such anti-establishment works as *The Shawshank Redemption*, *Traffic*, and *The Matrix*.

12 Which of the following is an overarching theme of both passages?   ELAALRL2

   A   Movies remained violent for 60 years.

   B   Movies both reflect and comfort the social anxieties of their audience.

   C   People seem to be drawn to violent movies.

   D   Filmmakers of the '90s were influenced by films of the '30s.

13 Sentence 11, "That the criminals died..." indicates that   ELAALRL1, NF

   A   people continued to cheer for movie gangsters, despite a film's moral.

   B   people realized gangsters were bad.

   C   moviegoers wanted to be gangsters.

   D   authorities insisted that movie gangsters must die at the end of the movie.

14 In sentence 10, "clawing" MOST nearly means   ELAALRL5 ELAALRC3

   A   lazing around.

   B   using fingernails.

   C   swiping at.

   D   struggling.

15 In sentence 19, "thawed" MOST nearly means   ELAALRL5 ELAALRC3

   A   remained cynical.

   B   fell deeply in love.

   C   quickly become soured.

   D   slowly became more positive.

16 In passage 1, the author's attitude towards the gangster movies is one of   ELA11W2 ELA11LSV2

   A   open affection.

   B   objective curiosity.

C   measured disdain.

D   vague worry.

17 **In sentence 13, the author** ELAALRL1, F
writes that a new strain
of films "served as social allegory."
What is the BEST definition of the genre
of allegory?

A   a representation of ideas and
principles through a story

B   giving human qualities to animals,
objects, and other non-human things

C   using something that designates one
thing to designate another, creating a
comparison

D   a figure of speech in which a part is
used for the whole or the specific
indicates the general

18 **It can be inferred from sen-** ELA11W1
tence 3 that the author ELA11LSV2

A   thinks that rich people didn't
normally attend movies in the 1930s.

B   believes gangster movies superior to
other types of movies.

C   wants to be a filmmaker.

D   has never seen a gangster film.

19 **Compared to the passage 1,** ELAALRL1,NF
passage 2 shows a greater
concern about the

A   number of movies being released.

B   limited availability of movies dealing with social concerns.

C   problems faced by people in a given
decade.

D   creation of dialogue between filmgo-
ers and moviemakers.

20 **Passage 1 links the popularity** ELAALRL3
of gangster films primarily
with

A   public eagerness to see violence
onscreen.

B   the public's hunger to see individuals
revolt against the system.

C   new advances in movie technology.

D   society's outrage about police
incompetence and ineffectiveness.

21 **The statement in sentence 17,** ELAALRL2
"don't trust to governments
or economies; you're on your own,"
MOST indicates that the author believes
that

A   films of the 1970s reflected the deep
suspicion of society.

B   filmmakers were too obsessed with
"message" in their movies.

C   films of the 1970s weren't socially
conscious enough.

D   films of the 1970s were socially conscious to a fault.

22 **What situation is reflected in** ELAALRL3
the atmosphere of both
decades discussed in these passages?

A   Films failed to reflect the society of
their viewers.

B   Filmmakers forced their ideas on
audiences.

C   Audiences welcomed their social
concerns expressed on film.

D   Studios had a political agenda in
making crime films.

23 **The author of passage 1** ELAALRL3
would MOST likely view the
vigilante films of the 1970s as

A   a passing fad.

B   nostalgic memories of earlier films.

C   the logical descendent of the gangster
film.

D   part of a long tradition of social relevance in film.

Excerpt from *The Song of Hiawatha*

by Henry Wadsworth Longfellow

At the stern sat Hiawatha,
With his fishing-line of cedar;
In his plumes the breeze of morning
Played as in the hemlock branches;
On the bows, with tail erected,
Sat the squirrel, Adjidaumo;
In his fur the breeze of morning
Played as in the prairie grasses.

On the white sand of the bottom
Lay the monster Mishe-Nahma,
Lay the sturgeon, King of Fishes;
Through his gills he breathed the water,
With his fins he fanned and winnowed,
With his tail he swept the sand-floor.

There he lay in all his armor;
On each side a shield to guard him,
Plates of bone upon his forehead,
Down his sides and back and shoulders
Plates of bone with spines projecting
Painted was he with his war-paints,
Stripes of yellow, red, and azure,
Spots of brown and spots of sable;
And he lay there on the bottom,
Fanning with his fins of purple,
As above him Hiawatha
In his birch canoe came sailing,
With his fishing-line of cedar.

"Take my bait," cried Hiawatha,
Dawn into the depths beneath him,
"Take my bait, O Sturgeon, Nahma!
Come up from below the water,
Let us see which is the stronger!"
And he dropped his line of cedar
Through the clear, transparent water,
Waited vainly for an answer,
Long sat waiting for an answer,
And repeating loud and louder,
"Take my bait, O King of Fishes!"

Quiet lay the sturgeon, Nahma,
Fanning slowly in the water,
Looking up at Hiawatha,
Listening to his call and clamor,
His unnecessary tumult,
Till he wearied of the shouting;
And he said to the Kenozha,
To the pike, the Maskenozha,
"Take the bait of this rude fellow,
Break the line of Hiawatha!"

24 **This selection could BEST be described as** ELAALRL1, P

   A   an epic.

   B   a lyric.

   C   a narrative poem.

   D   a heroic couplet.

25 **The main conflict in the selection is between** ELAALRL1, P

   A   Hiawatha and the squirrel.

   B   Hiawatha and the King of Fishes.

   C   the various fish in the river.

   D   the fisherman and his fishing equipment.

26 The fish speaking to one another is an example of what literary device?

ELAALRL1, P

- **A** irony
- **B** metaphor
- **C** onomatopoeia
- **D** personification

27 All the lines of this passage contain similar, simple-sentence structure, creating a distinct

ELAALRL1, P

- **A** rhyme.
- **B** rhythm.
- **C** diction.
- **D** organization.

28 This passage is an example from which era in American literature?

ELAALRL1, P
ELAALRL3

- **A** Nationalism
- **B** Romanticism
- **C** Transcendentalism
- **D** Naturalism

Read this passage about Postmodernist literature and answer questions 29–40.

A country going through a large-scale war changes its society in many ways. Such changes are reflected in the nation's literature. This was true of post-World War II America, a time of revelation about atrocities committed: the atomic bombs dropped on Hiroshima and Nagasaki, the Holocaust, the bombing of Dresden and of Tokyo, and the internment of Japanese-Americans. Its no small coincidence that these violations of basic human rights ushered in the American Civil Rights Movement, a major phase of feminism, and new ways for all Americans to view the world. Postmodern literature, continuing through today, expresses these new views.

As a literary era, Postmodernism is hard to pin down. According to historian Hans-Peter Wagner, "Postmodernism, then, can be used at least in two ways—firstly, to give a label to the period … and secondly, to describe the highly experimental literature produced by writers beginning with Lawrence Durrell and John Fowles in the 1960s and reaching to the breathless works of Martin Amis and the "Chemical (Scottish) Generation" of the fin-de-siècle [end of the century]." Postmodernism started as both a reaction to Modernism, with its themes of alienation and disillusionment, and an extension of it. Both modern and postmodern authors worked with a new subjective point of view. Rather than telling a story through an objective, disconnected narrator, writers employed the limited and biased realities of individual characters.

An excellent example of Postmodernism is the poetry of Alan Ginsberg, famous American Beat Poet. He is best known for the 1956 long poem *Howl*, a commentary about the destructive forces of materialism and conformity in America. Another example of the identity-seeking theme come in these last lines of his 1986 poem, "Is About": "Who cares what it's all about?/I do! Edgar Allen Poe cares! Shelly cares! Beethoven & Dylan care./Do

you care? What are you about/or are you a human being with 10 fingers and two eyes?" The poem also refers to America's rising fear and suspicions about fascism and communism. Today, the political aims of fascism and communism have been defeated, but new threats arise every day.

The stories told through Postmodern literature represent responses to such things as living under nuclear threat, witnessing incredible growth in communications and mass media, and dealing with the growing melting pot of cultures and belief systems. Basically, it's a reaction to the world moving extremely fast. Representing this movement are works by authors like Thomas Pynchon, Don DeLillo, Joyce Carol Oates, Toni Morrison, Chuck Palahniuk, and Carl Hiaasen. For example, Morrison's novel *Song of Solomon* is about Macon "Milkman" Dead III, who is trying to figure out his slave ancestry, the relationships of his family, and finally his own identity. It mirrors many of the nagging questions of the modern era such as, "Where did I come from?" and "What's my role in all of this?"

Postmodern authors are keenly aware of criticisms against American politics, culture, and history and are concerned with how these affect individuals. The stories they tell often seem to be celebrations of Americana, containing theme parks, fast food, TV shows, and plastic surgery. But they also look at these phenomena with satire and some embarrassment. Overall, Postmodern authors explore how modern life, especially mass media and popular culture, affect the average American.

29 This passage can be BEST described as   ELA11W2

A a narrative story.

B a persuasive essay.

C an expository work.

D a technical document.

30 What is the thesis or controlling idea of this passage?   ELA11W2

A "A country going through a large-scale war changes its society in many ways."

B "As a literary era, Postmodernism is hard to pin down."

C "An excellent example of Postmodernism is the epic poem *The Waste Land* by T.S. Eliot."

D "Postmodern authors deal with how modern life, especially mass media and popular culture, affect the average American."

31 Which of the following is the BEST way to combine the first two sentences of this passage?   ELA11W4

A A country going through a large-scale war changes its society and such changes are reflected in the nation's literature.

B In many ways a country going through a large-scale war changes its society, which reflects in the nation's literature.

C A country going through a large-scale war changes its society in many ways, and this is reflected in the nation's literature.

D A nation's literature reflects the country going through a large-scale war, which also changes its society in many ways.

32 Which of the following would   ELA11W3
be LEAST helpful for a
research paper about Postmodernist literature?

   A   an encyclopedia

   B   a story by Joyce Carol Oates

   C   an interview with Toni Morrison

   D   a blog about writing short stories

33 According to the information   ELAALRL2
in this passage, what universal theme BEST applies to many works
of postmodern literature?

   A   Cultural diversity makes a nation stronger.

   B   Pulling together in time of war brings rewards afterwards.

   C   When leaders enter into conflicts, they bring entire nations into them.

   D   No matter how strong a government is, it cannot protect all of its people.

34 The writer of the text needs to   ELA11C1
do some revision and editing.
Which paragraph is not coherent
because the ideas do not flow well as
part of the passage?

   A   paragraph 2

   B   paragraph 3

   C   paragraph 4

   D   paragraph 5

35 Which paragraph contains   ELA11W3
information that needs a citation?

   A   paragraph 1

   B   paragraph 2

   C   paragraph 3

   D   paragraph 4

36 Read the second sentence of   ELA11C1
paragraph 2. What, if any,
errors in punctuation has the writer
made?

> According to historian Hans-Peter Wagner, "Postmodernism, then, can be used at least in two ways—firstly, to give a label to the period … and secondly, to describe the highly experimental literature produced by writers beginning with Lawrence Durrell and John Fowles in the 1960s and reaching to the breathless works of Martin Amis and the "Chemical (Scottish) Generation" of the fin-de-siècle [end of the century]."

   A   correct as is

   B   remove the comma after *Wagner*: According to historian Hans-Peter Wagner "Postmodernism…

   C   substitute single quotation marks around *Chemical (Scottish) Generation*: …and the 'Chemical (Scottish) Generation' of the…

   D   move the end quotation marks after *fin-de-siècle*: …of the fin-de-siècle [end of the century]."

37 In paragraph 1, should any   ELA11C1
punctuation corrections be
made?

   A   correct as is

   B   change the colon to a semicolon after *committed*

   C   add an apostrophe to *Its*: It's no small coincidence…

   D   change the period to a question mark on the last sentence

38 What would be the BEST   ELA11C1
transition to use at the beginning of paragraph 4?

   A   However,   **C**   Therefore,

   B   Meanwhile,   **D**   Furthermore,

GO ON

In the fourth paragraph, the author uses two forms of the word grow while making a point. They are underlined below.

The stories told through Postmodern literature represent responses to such things as living under nuclear threat, witnessing incredible growth in communications and mass media, and dealing with the growing melting pot of cultures and belief systems.

39 What would be the BEST resource in which to find another word to avoid this unintentional repetition?   ELA11W3

   A   dictionary

   B   thesaurus

   C   encyclopedia

   D   English textbook

40 If the author of this passage was about to hand it in as a research paper for English class, what would he or she need to do first?   ELA11C2

   A   add a title and the author's name

   B   double-space the body of the paper

   C   add a bibliography or works-cited page

   D   all of the above

STOP

SECTION 2

DO NOT TURN PAGE UNTIL INSTRUCTED TO DO SO

"The First Moccasins"

A Plains Indian Story

There was once a great chief of the Plains who had very tender feet. Other mighty chiefs laughed at him; little chiefs only smiled as he hobbled past; and though they did not dare to smile, the people of the tribe also enjoyed the big chief's discomfort. All of them were in the same canoe, having no horses and only bare feet, but luckily very few of them had tender feet. The unhappy medicine man who was advisor to the Chief-of-the-Tender-Feet was afraid and troubled. Each time he was called before the chief, he was asked, "What are you going to do about it?" The "it" meant the chief's tender feet.

Forced by fear, the medicine man at last hit upon a plan. Though he knew that it was not the real answer to the chief's foot problem, nevertheless it was a good makeshift. The medicine man had some women of the tribe weave a long, narrow mat of reeds, and when the big chief had to go anywhere, four braves unrolled the mat in front of him so that he walked in comfort. One day, the braves were worn out from seeing that the chief's feet were not worn out. They carelessly unrolled the mat over a place where flint arrowheads had been chipped. The arrowheads had long ago taken flight, but the needle-sharp chips remained. When the big chief's tender feet were wounded by these chips, he uttered a series of whoops which made the nearby aspen tree leaves quiver so hard that they have been trembling ever since.

That night the poor medicine man was given an impossible task by the angry chief: "Cover the whole earth with mats so thick that my feet will not suffer. If you fail, you will die when the moon is round."

The frightened maker of magic crept back to his lodge. He did not wish to be put to death on the night of the full moon, but he could think of no way to avoid it. Suddenly, he saw the hide of an elk which he had killed pegged to the ground, with two women busily scraping the hair from the hide, and an idea flashed into his groping mind. He sent out many hunters; many women were busy for many days; many braves with hunting knives cut, and women sewed with bone needles and rawhide sinews.

On the day before the moon was round, the medicine man went to the chief and told him that he had covered as much of the earth as was possible in so short a time. When the chief looked from the door of his lodge, he saw many paths of skin stretching as far as he could see. Long strips which could be moved from place to place connected the main leather paths. Even the chief thought that this time the magic of the medicine man had solved tenderfoot transportation for all time—but this was not to be!

One day, as the big chief was walking along one of his smooth, tough leather paths, he saw a pretty maiden of the tribe gliding ahead of him, walking on the hard earth on one side of the chief's pathway. She glanced back when she heard the pitter-patter of his feet on the elk hide pathway and seemed to smile. The chief set off on the run to catch up with her, his eyes fixed on the back of She-Who-Smiled, and so his feet strayed from the narrow path and landed in a bunch of needle-sharp thorns! The girl ran for her life when she heard the hideous howls of the chief, and Indians in the distant village thought that they were being attacked by wildcats.

Two suns later, when the chief was calm enough to speak again, he had his medicine man brought before him and told the unhappy man that next day, when the sun was high, he would be sent with all speed to the land of shadows.

That night, the medicine man climbed to the top of a high hill in search of advice from friendly spirits on how to cover the entire earth with leather. He slept, and, in a dream vision, he was shown the answer to his problem. Amid vivid flashes of lightning, he tore down the steep hillside, howling louder than the big chief as jagged rocks wounded his bare feet and legs. He did not stop until he was safely inside his lodge. He worked all night and until the warriors who were to send him on the shadow trail came for him, just before noon the next day. He was surrounded by the guards armed with war-clubs. He was clutching close to his heart something tightly rolled in a piece of deerskin. His cheerful smile surprised those who saw him pass. "Wah, he is brave!" said the men of the tribe. "He is very brave!" said the women of the tribe.

The big chief was waiting just outside his lodge. He gave the guards swift, stern orders. Before the maker of magic could be led away, he asked leave to say a few words to the chief. "Speak!" said the chief, sorry to lose a clever medicine man who was very good at most kinds of magic. Even the chief knew that covering the entire earth with leather was an impossible task.

The medicine man quickly knelt beside the chief, unrolled the two objects which he took from his bundle, and slipped one of them on each foot of the chief. The chief seemed to be wearing a pair of bear's hairless feet, instead of bare feet, and he was puzzled at first as he looked at the elk hide handicraft of his medicine man. "Big chief," the medicine man exclaimed joyfully, "I have found the way to cover the earth with leather! For you, O chief, from now on the earth will always be covered with leather." And so it was.

41 In the first paragraph, ELAALRL1, F
what does the author mean
by *in the same canoe*?

   A   Everyone in the tribe was literally all
in a large canoe.

   B   Everyone in the tribe was in the same
situation.

   C   Everyone in the tribe owned the same
kind of canoe.

   D   Everyone in the tribe wore little
canoes on their feet.

Read this sentence form the story:

> He uttered a series of whoops which made the
> nearby aspen tree leaves quiver so hard they
> have been trembling ever since.

42 Why would an author use ELAALRL4
exaggeration of the type
found in the sentence above?

   A   to explain why something happens

   B   to describe how something looks

   C   to frighten readers about something

   D   to set the mood for the scene

Read this sentence from the fourth paragraph.

> Suddenly, he saw the hide of an elk which he
> had killed pegged to the ground, with two
> women busily scraping the hair from the hide,
> and an idea flashed into his groping mind.

43 What is the meaning of ELAALRL5
groping? ELA11RC3

   A   inquiring   **C**   fumbling

   B   nosy   **D**   cautious

44 Which is the main conflict ELAALRL1, F
in this story?

   A   chief vs. medicine man

   B   chief vs. tribe

   C   chief vs. nature

   D   medicine man vs. chief's feet

Read the following statement from the story:

> Two suns later, when the chief was calm
> enough to speak again…

45 What does *two suns* mean? ELAALRL5
ELA11RC3

   A   two years

   B   two months

   C   two weeks

   D   two days

46 This selection is an example of ELA11W2

   A   narrative writing.

   B   expository writing.

   C   persuasive writing.

   D   technical writing.

Read this sentence from paragraph 2.

> One day, the braves were worn out from seeing
> that the chief's feet were not worn out.

47 Which, if any, of these rhetori- ELA11W4
cal strategies does the author
use?

   A   analogy

   B   parallelism

   C   repetition

   D   none of the above

48 If you were writing a research paper about Native American stories, this text would be an example of what kind of material? ELA11W3

   A   anecdotal scripting

   B   annotated bibliography

   C   primary source

   D   secondary source

49 What is the main purpose of this passage? ELA11W1

   A   to convey a sense of adventure about the American frontier

   B   to elicit an emotional response about relationships in the tribe

   C   to describe various members of the Plains Indian tribe

   D   to recount a myth about how moccasins were invented

Read this sentence from the last paragraph:

> The medicine man quickly knelt beside the chief, unrolled the two objects which he took from his bundle, and slipped one of them on each foot of the chief.

50 The way in which the phrases are linked together and similar in tense and number is called ELA11C1

   A   parallel sentence structure.

   B   subordinating clauses.

   C   verb tense consistency.

   D   subject-verb agreement.

Read the following prompt and the essay that a student wrote in response to it. Then answer questions 51 through 59.

Writing prompt

Have you ever read a book that made you look at life a little differently, or made you think about the people around you differently? Think about the last book that made a difference in your views and describe how the book made this happen for you. Use as many examples and details as you can from the book.

Student Essay

Literature can change readers' perspectives on life drawing them into characters' inner thoughts and the events in their lives. Readers can sympathize with a character and begin to see life through the eyes of that character. One of the books that changed my perception was *I Know Why the Caged Bird Sings*. It's Maya Angelou's autobiography about her childhood in the South. It was a really neat book.

When Maya's parents divorce, she and her brother are sent to live with their grandmother in rural Stamps, Arkansas. The children observe and are subjected to the cruelties of the racism rampant at that time. Maya and her brother are sent to live with their mother in St. Louis. Life in St. Louis is different but not better for the children. Her mother's boyfriend molests and eventually rapes Maya, inflicting physical and emotional damage on the child. Before the boyfriend can be tried in court, he is sentenced to death by a less merciful and more swift lady Justice. The young Maya feels personally responsible for the man's death and decides to stop speaking to everyone, except her brother, Bailey.

The children's mother sends them back to their grandmother in Stamps where Maya is introduced to literature through Mrs. Bertha Flowers. The power of literature breaks through Maya's long-held silence. One evening, after spending several hours reading Mrs. Flowers' books, Maya returns to her grandmother's house full of things to say. In her excitement, she casually turns to Bailey and says, "By the way…" Before she can finish her sentence, she is punished for taking the Lord's name in vain. (The Lord is the Way, thus "by the way" is blasphemy.) Maya returns to her silence.

It is this part of the book that most affected my ways of seeing the importance of literature and words. This incident made me think about the positive and negative power of words on a child's delicate perception of the world. A victim of abuse and racism, Maya needs escape. She can enjoy, through the authors' eyes, parts of the world and experiences she may never see. She can learn things she may never learn in school.

Words can carry several meanings. Idiomatic phrases and slang can often be misconstrued by someone who is not familiar with the current language. A popular example is the phrase "get outa here" to mean that something is unbelievable. Someone who is unfamiliar with the phrase might actually leave the room. Maya's grandmother, who is deeply religious, feels that "the way" is God, and saying "by the way" is saying "by God." To her grandmother, this was blasphemy. To Maya, the phrase was a casual way of saying, "Oh, I almost forgot…" In this way, a simple phrase may take on two different meanings depending on who hears it.

The power of words is the caged bird's song and has become the theme of Maya Angelou's life story. When Maya stops speaking, it is because she believes that her words in court brought about a man's death. Her speech is brought back through literature and stifled again by her grandmother's religious fervor. *I Know Why the Caged Bird Sings* became a reminder to me to watch what I say because my words can be more powerful than I intend them to be. It also reminds me to be precise and weigh my words carefully so that what others hear is what I intend to say.

51 Where in this essay would the following sentence BEST fit? ELA11W1

> Literature provides her with the means to escape her world into another where she may have some control.

A	paragraph 2	**C**	paragraph 4
B	paragraph 3	**D**	paragraph 5

52 What is the correct way to write the first sentence? ELA11C1

A Literature can change readers perspectives on life drawing them into characters inner thoughts and the events in their lives.

B Literature can change readers' perspectives on life by drawing them into characters' inner thoughts and the events in their lives.

C Literature can change readers' perspectives on life; drawing them into characters' inner thoughts and the events in their lives.

D Literature can change readers' perspectives on life: drawing them into characters' inner thoughts and the events in their lives.

53 Review paragraph 2 of the essay. Which would be the BEST transition to add to the following sentence: ELA11C1

> Maya and her brother are sent to live with their mother in St. Louis.

- **A** Later,
- **B** Sometimes,
- **C** However,
- **D** In addition,

54 Which sentence from paragraph 1 is too informal for this passage? ELA11W4

- **A** Readers can sympathize with a character and begin to see life through the eyes of that character.
- **B** One of the books that changed my perception was *I Know Why the Caged Bird Sings*.
- **C** It's Maya Angelou's autobiography about her childhood in the South.
- **D** It was a really neat book.

55 Which of the following is NOT a correct way to combine these sentences from paragraph 5? ELA11C1

> Words can carry several meanings. Idiomatic phrases and slang can often be misconstrued by someone who is not familiar with the current language.

- **A** Words can carry several meanings; idiomatic phrases and slang can often be misconstrued by someone who is not familiar with the current language.
- **B** Whereas words can carry several meanings, idiomatic phrases and slang can often be misconstrued by someone who is not familiar with the current language.
- **C** Words can carry several meanings, and idiomatic phrases and slang can often be misconstrued by someone who is not familiar with the current language.
- **D** Since words can carry several meanings, idiomatic phrases and slang can often be misconstrued by someone who is not familiar with the current language.

56 What is the BEST way to organize this essay? ELA11W1

- **A** leave as is
- **B** paragraph 1, 4, 2, 3, 5, 6
- **C** paragraph 1, 2, 3, 5, 4, 6
- **D** paragraph 1, 6, 3, 2, 5, 4

57 Which word from paragraph 2 has an error in capitalization? ELA11C1

- **A** grandmother
- **B** Stamps
- **C** court
- **D** Justice

Read this sentence from paragraph 3.

> One evening, after <u>spending several hours reading</u> Mrs. Flowers' books, Maya returns to her grandmother's house full of things to say.

58 **Identify the underlined part of the sentence.** ELA11C1

   A   main clause

   B   infinitive phrase

   C   participial phrase

   D   gerund phrase

59 **If the student who wrote this essay had to do a presentation about it, which audio-visual support would MOST help the audience's understanding?** ELA11LSV2

   A   a photograph of Maya Angelou

   B   a copy of *I Know Why the Caged Bird Sings*

   C   a handout of idioms and their meanings

   D   a map of the places where Maya lived

60 **Unless the teacher instructs otherwise, the standard margins for an essay that you are handing in should be how wide?** ELA11C2

   A   one-half inch on all sides

   B   one inch on all sides

   C   one-half inch on the sides and one inch at top and bottom

   D   It depends on the type of essay it is.

61 **When you are required to list works cited for a research paper, what kinds of sources should be included?** ELA11C2

   A   all the works you looked at to get information

   B   all resources used, with a brief explanation of each

   C   all the works that appear in citations in the essay

   D   only the works that are considered primary sources

62 **If a research paper assignment calls for a title page, what should that page typically include?** ELA11C2

   A   just the title of the paper

   B   the title and the name of the teacher

   C   the title, the author's name, and the class for which the paper is written

   D   the title, the author's and the teacher's names, the date, and the works cited listing

63 **If you were giving an oral report about the growth of literature along the American frontier, which would be the MOST helpful prop to have?** ELA11LSV2

   A   a map of the United States

   B   a recording of the Gettysburg Address

   C   a flag representing the original thirteen colonies

   D   a reproduction of the Declaration of Independence

Read this excerpt from the play *The Climbers* by Clyde Fitch (1865–1909), the first American playwright to publish his plays. Then answer questions 64–70.

In this scene, the women talking have just returned from the funeral of George Hunter, Mrs. Hunter's husband and the brother of Ruth. They are having afternoon tea, including sandwiches, and Mrs. Hunter has the opinion that, except for the children, those in mourning should not have an appetite.

RUTH. Oh! You're having tea!

[*Glad that they are.*]

MRS. HUNTER. [*Taking a second cup.*] I thought the children *ought* to.

RUTH. Of course they ought and so ought you, if you haven't.

MRS. HUNTER. Oh, I've *trifled* with something

JESSICA. Sit here, Aunt Ruth.

BLANCHE. Will you have a cup, Aunt Ruth?

RUTH. Yes, dear, I'm feeling *very* hungry.

[*Sitting on the sofa beside* JESSICA *and pressing her hand as she does so*.]

MRS. HUNTER. Hungry! How can you!

RUTH. Because I'm not a hypocrite!

MRS. HUNTER. [*Whimpering.*] I suppose that's a slur at me!

RUTH. If the slipper fits! But I confess I haven't eaten much for several days; I couldn't touch anything this morning, and I begin to feel exhausted; I must have food and, thank Heaven, I want it. Thank you.

[*To* BLANCHE, *taking the cup from her.*]

MRS. HUNTER. I think it's awful, Ruth, and I feel I have a right to say it—I think you owed it to my feelings to have worn a long veil; people will think you didn't love your brother.

RUTH. [*Dryly.*] Will they? Let them! You know as well as I do that George loathed the very idea of crêpe and all display of mourning.

MRS. HUNTER. [*Feeling out of her element, changes the subject.*] You stayed behind?

RUTH. Yes. I wanted to be the last there. [*Her voice chokes; she tries to control herself.*] Ah! You see my nerves are all gone to pieces. I *won't* cry any more!

MRS. HUNTER. I don't see how you could bear it—staying; but you never had any heart, Ruth.

RUTH. [*Mechanically, biting her lips hard to keep the tears back.*] Haven't I?

MRS. HUNTER. My darling husband always felt that defect in you.

RUTH. George?

MRS. HUNTER. He resented your treatment of me, and often said so.

RUTH. [*Very quietly, but with determination.*] Please be careful. Don't talk to me like this about my brother, Florence—or you'll make me say something I shall be sorry for.

MRS. HUNTER. I don't care! It wore on him, the way you treated me. I put up with it for his sake, but it helped undermine his health.

RUTH. Florence, stop!

MRS. HUNTER. [*In foolish anger, the resentment of years bursting out.*] I *won't* stop! I'm alone now, and the least you can do is to see that people who've fought shy of me take me up and give me my due. You've been a cruel, selfish sister-in-law, and your own brother saw and hated you for it!

64 Which life experience would MOST improve a reader's ability to identify with the characters in this excerpt?   ELA11RC4

  A   being familiar with having tea in the afternoon

  B   disagreeing with loved ones about situations

  C   feeling hungry at the wrong time

  D   having been to a funeral

65 To learn more about the afternoon tea meal (which was routine for the American upper class during this period but is not commonplace anymore), where would be the BEST place seek information?   ELAALRC4

  A   an encyclopedia article about tea

  B   the chapter "Teas and Other Afternoon Parties" in Emily Post's book, *Etiquette* (1922)

  C   a film that shows high society having a tea meal

  D   the Web site "Best Places to Visit for Afternoon Tea" from the United Kindom's Tea Council

66 In the fourth line of dialogue, when Mrs. Hunter says that she has *trifled* with something, what exactly does she mean? ELA11RC3

   A She played with her food.

   B She teased the cook about the sandwiches.

   C She briefly considered sitting down.

   D She thought about eating but decided against it.

Read the following section, especially the speech Ruth makes in reaction to Mrs. Hunter being offended.

> **RUTH.** Because I'm not a hypocrite!
>
> **MRS. HUNTER.** [*Whimpering.*] I suppose that's a slur at me!
>
> **RUTH.** If the slipper fits! But I confess I haven't eaten much for several days; I couldn't touch anything this morning, and I begin to feel exhausted; I must have food and, thank Heaven, I want it. Thank you.

67 What is the meaning of the expression *if the slipper fits*? ELA11RC3

   A It figuratively conveys that if you act like a hypocrite, you are one.

   B It is a literal complaint by Ruth that nothing fits her when she eats too much.

   C She is making an allusion to Cinderella and the magic glass slipper.

   D She is saying that Mrs. Hunter should wear shoes that fit her.

68 *The Climbers* was published in 1905. Which of these probably had the MOST effect on Fitcher on as he wrote this play? ELAALRL1, D,F / ELAALRL3 / ELAALRL4

   A the aftermath of the Civil War

   B American social life of the period

   C a growing lack of trust in government

   D the beginning of the Feminist Movement

Toward the middle of the play, Mrs. Hunter says the following:

> **MRS. HUNTER.** I think it's awful, Ruth, and I feel I have a right to say it—I think you owed it to my feelings to have worn a long veil; people will think you didn't love your brother.

69 Which part of this speech is an example of synecdoche (when a part of something is used to represent the whole)? ELAALRL1, D

   A "…I feel I have a right to say it…"

   B "…you owed it to my feelings…"

   C "…to have worn a long veil…"

   D "… people will think you didn't love your brother."

70 Reading this play by Clyde Fitch might be good to do if you were doing a research paper about ELAALRL1, D / ELAALRL3 / ELA11W3

   A Transcendentalism.

   B Realism.

   C Naturalism.

   D Modernism.

Read the following paragraph. Then answer questions 71 to 80.

1) "You seem to be in a real catch 22 my friend." **2)** Chances are that you understand what this phrase means. **3)** These words were first published in the novel *Catch-22* by Joseph Heller in 1961. **4)** Since then, the phrase "catch 22" has come to mean any no-win situation. **5)** The story of Yossarian, a World War II bombardier afraid to die for the war, is best known for its dark humor and satire of bureaucracy. **6)** The idiom and the book's title come from a fictitious military regulation described in the novel, which basically prevents anyone from avoiding combat missions. **7)** "Orr was crazy and could be grounded. **8)** All he had to do was ask; and as soon as he did, he would no longer be crazy and would have to fly more missions. **9)** Orr would be crazy to fly more missions and sane if he didn't, but if he was sane he had to fly them. **10)** If he flew them he was crazy and didn't have to; but if he didn't want to he was sane and had to. **11)** Yossarian was moved very deeply by the absolute simplicity of this clause of Catch-22 and let out a respectful whistle." **12)** The story has become an allegory for any irreconcilable situation.

71 This paragraph would fit BEST in an essay about   ELAALRL5

   A   post-WWII writers.

   B   depictions of wars in novels.

   C   idioms that originated in literature.

   D   changes in the meanings of words over time.

72 What correction, if any, is needed in the first sentence?   ELA11C1

   A   no correction needed

   B   change *real* to *really*

   C   place double quotation marks around *catch 22*

   D   place a comma after *catch 22*

73 Which is the BEST way to combine sentences 3 and 4?   ELA11C1

   A   The words "catch 22" were first published in the novel *Catch-22* by Joseph Heller in 1961; however, the phrase has come to mean any no-win situation.

   B   Since these words were first published in the novel *Catch-22* by Joseph Heller in 1961, the phrase "catch 22" has come to mean any no-win situation.

   C   The phrase "catch 22" has come to mean any no-win situation, and these words were first published in the novel *Catch-22* by Joseph Heller in 1961.

   D   These words were first published in the novel *Catch-22* by Joseph Heller in 1961, coming to mean any no-win situation since then.

74 To properly cite the quote in this paragraph, where should the in-text citation be placed?   ELA11W3

   A   after sentence 6, before the quote begins

   B   at the beginning of sentence 7

   C   at the end of sentence 11

   D   at the end of the paragraph

75 Which is the BEST way to revise sentence 6?   ELA11C1

A   Leave the sentence as it is.

B   The idion and the book's title come from a fictitious military regulation (which basically prevents anyone from avoiding combat missions) described in the novel.

C   Described in the novel, the idiom and the book's title come from a fictitious military regulation which basically prevents anyone from avoiding combat missions.

D   Basically preventing anyone from avoiding combat missions, a fictitious military regulation described in the novel is where the idiom and the book's title come from.

76 Which is the closest synonym for the word *irreconcilable* as it is used in the last sentence?   ELAALRL5 ELA11RC3

A   contradictory

B   hostile

C   inflexible

D   volatile

77 What would be the BEST transition statement to add between sentences 6 and 7?   ELA11W1 ELA11W4

A   This is how catch 22 comes about as a phrase, because this regulation is called the Catch-22 regulation.

B   It's described by the narrator.

C   The narrator describes Yossarian's first encounter with the rule regarding a fellow bombardier.

D   The Catch-22 regulation is complicated.

78 Which description of the book, *Catch-22*, provides the BEST clues to the theme of this novel?   ELAALRL2

A   "The story of Yossarian, a World War II bombardier afraid to die for the war..."

B   "...best known for its dark humor and satire of bureaucracy."

C   "The idiom and the book's title come from a fictitious military regulation..."

D   "...the absolute simplicity of this clause of Catch-22..."

79 The author of *Catch-22* was probably MOST influenced by   ELAALRL1, F ELAALRL4

A   a dreadful fear of flying.

B   having been in the army.

C   his hatred of bureaucrats.

D   man's search for identity.

80 The logic of the Catch-22 regulation is an example of   ELAALRL1, F,P

A   metaphor.

B   hyperbole.

C   imagery.

D   paradox.

EVALUATION CHART FOR GEORGIA EOCT IN AMERICAN LITERATURE AND COMPOSITION DIAGNOSTIC TEST

Directions: On the following chart, circle the question numbers that you answered incorrectly, and evaluate the results. These questions are based on the *GPS Standards*. Then turn to the appropriate chapters, read the explanations, and complete the exercises. Review other chapters as needed. Finally, complete the Practice tests to assess your progress and further prepare you for the **Georgia End of Courst Test in American Literature and Composition.**

Note: Some question numbers will appear under multiple chapters because those questions require demonstration of multiple skills.

Chapter	Diagnostic Test Question(s)
Chapter 1: A Brief History of American Literature	2, 8, 10, 28, 33, 68, 78
Chapter 2: Literary Structure: American Fiction and Nonfiction	1, 2, 5, 8, 12, 13, 17, 19, 20, 21, 22, 23, 25, 41, 42, 44, 71, 78, 79, 80
Chapter 3: Literary Structure: American Poetry and Drama	9, 11, 24, 25, 26, 27, 64, 68, 69
Chapter 4: Word Meanings	3, 5, 6, 14, 15, 45, 64, 65, 66, 67, 76
Chapter 5: Understanding Mass Media	16, 18, 19, 20, 43, 59, 63
Chapter 6: The Writing Process	1, 4, 29, 30, 31, 32, 35, 46, 47, 49, 51, 54, 56, 71, 74, 77
Chapter 7: The Research Process	39, 48, 61, 62, 65, 70, 74
Chapter 8: Using Standard American English	7, 31, 34, 36, 37, 38, 50, 52, 53, 55, 57, 58, 60, 72, 73, 75
Chapter 9: Paragraph Structure and Manuscript Formatting	34, 35, 38, 40, 53, 56, 74

Chapter 1
A Brief History of American Literature

This chapter covers the following Georgia standard.

ELAALRL1	Trace the history of the development of American fiction.
	Trace the historical development of poetic styles and forms in American literature.

INTRODUCTION

The literary tradition of the United States stretches back five centuries and includes the writing of some of the earliest inhabitants as well as later explorers and settlers of the North American continent. As the country grew in both size and power, successive generations of American writers contributed significant works to the body of world literature, often redefining the forms and genres in which they wrote.

The following summary of American literature mentions only the most important characteristics and works of each given period. To further understand American literature, review recommended reading selections found throughout this chapter. Most of these selections can be found in American literature textbooks or on the Internet at www.gutenberg.org or www.classicreader.com.

This chapter is arranged by general historical period. These historical periods sometimes, but not always, correspond to generally recognized **literary movements** in American Literature. These movements are included in the following chart, with a brief definition and approximate time period for each. Note that some movements overlap one another. Different sources sometimes give varying time periods for the movements.

MAJOR MOMENTS IN AMERICAN LITERATURE

Movement	Time Period	Emphasis	Notable Authors
Colonialism	1620 to 1770s	history, religion, the New World	Benjamin Franklin, Cotton Mather, Anne Bradstreet
Revolutionary	1750s to 1800	great documents of American revolution and independence	Thomas Paine, Thomas Jefferson, Benjamin Franklin
Nationalism	1770s to 1820s	authentic American settings and characters	Washington Irving, James Fenimore Cooper, Edgar Allan Poe
Romanticism	1780s to 1880s	emotion and imagination over logic and scientific thought	Nathanial Hawthorne, Herman Melville, Henry Wadsworth Longfellow
Transcendentalism	1830s to 1850s	self-reliance, independence from modern innovations	Ralph Waldo Emerson, Henry David Thoreau, Walt Whitman
Realism	1850s to 1900	simpler style, everyday concerns	Henry James, William Dean Howells, Mark Twain, Kate Chopin
Naturalism	1880s to 1940s	heredity and environment control people	Stephen Crane, Frank Norris, Jack London, Theodore Dreiser
Modernism	1900 to 1950 (some say continues through present)	alienation, reaction to modern life	T.S. Eliot, Ernest Hemingway, Sinclair Lewis, Willa Cather, John Steinbeck
The Lost Generation	1914 to 1930s	post-WWI disillusionment	F. Scott Fitzgerald, Ernest Hemingway, Ezra Pound
Harlem Renaissance	1920s	African-American literary movement	Langston Hughes, Zora Neale Hurston
Southern Agrarians	1930s	Southern American poets return to metrical verse and narrative	John Crowe Ransom, Robert Penn Warren
New York School	1940s to 1960s	urban, alternative lifestyles, leftist	Frank O'Hara, John Ashbery, Barbara Guest
Beat Generation	1950s and 1960s	anti-establishment	Jack Kerouac, Allen Ginsberg, William S. Burroughs, Ken Kesey, Hunter S. Thompson
Confessional Poets	1950s and 1960s	self-exploration, often brutal	Robert Lowell, Sylvia Plath
Postmodernism	1950 to present	post-WWII skepticism about absolutes, embracing of diversity, irony, and word play	Thomas Pynchon, Kurt Vonnegut, Joyce Carol Oates

EARLY AMERICAN LITERATURE 1400–1600

Native Americans were the earliest known inhabitants of what is now the United States. Their reverence for nature and the universe strongly influenced the literature they created. Only a few tribes had a written language, so many of their myths, songs, and stories were preserved in oral traditions. Early European settlers often clashed with the Native Americans, which sometimes resulted in the loss of culture as tribes scattered or died out due to imported diseases.

Bartolome de las Casas

In the Spanish colonies, several writers produced diaries, journals, and histories about their experiences in the New World. Among them was a Spanish priest named Bartolome de las Casas (1474–1566). In his *Brief Account of the Destruction of the Indies* (1552), de las Casas criticizes the Spanish conquistadores for their enslavement of native peoples. He also points out the many atrocities the Spanish committed as they destroyed lives and confiscated properties of Native Americans.

What would become part of today's USA originally took shape as a series of colonies of Great Britain during the 17th and 18th centuries. Britain exported much of its culture to the colonies. As a result, our earliest literature can be seen as a direct extension of the English literature of that period. With a 600-year head start, Europe cast a shadow over American literature that proved difficult to escape, eclipsing or dismissing American literary efforts until the mid-19th century. Nevertheless, American literature did find its own unique direction.

THE EARLY COLONIAL PERIOD: 1600–1700

Some of the earliest American writing includes pamphlets of explorers and merchants encouraging English citizens to colonize the New World. Captain John Smith (1580?–1631), the founder of the Jamestown colony of Virginia, wrote many pamphlets that both defended the colony's existence and rallied support for its cause. William Penn (1644–1718), the founder of Pennsylvania, and James Edward Oglethorpe (1696–1785), the founder of Georgia, also wrote numerous essays, brochures, and **broadsides** (public bulletin boards) promoting their respective colonies.

Religion also played a crucial role in early American literature. The Puritan founders of New England sought freedom of worship in New England and believed that living a simple and strict life would restrain the forces of evil in the world. The teachings of the Bible and hard work would bring prosperity to believers in this world and an eternal reward in the next world. In his *Ecclesiastical History of New England* (1702), the famous Puritan preacher, Cotton Mather (1663–1728) showed how the success of New England and its leaders was foreshadowed in events in the Bible. Another colonial writer, John Eliot (1604–1690), translated the Bible into the native tongue of the Algonquin Indian nation.

The debates over freedom of worship that were sweeping 17th-century Europe appeared in much of the writing about and from the New World. John Winthrop (1587–1649), the first governor of Massachusetts, kept a journal describing the colony's Puritan foundations. Some writers, like Roger Williams (1603–1683) of Rhode Island, wrote articles that fiercely argued for separation of church and state.

John Winthrop

Scholars and explorers recorded experiences with the local Indians. Mary Rowlandson (1637–1711), a Massachusetts woman held captive by local tribes for three months, published *A Narrative of the Captivity and Restoration of Mrs. Mary Rowlandson* in 1682. The work was a huge success in both the colonies and Europe, spawning an entire genre of **captivity narratives** which described close encounters between Europeans and Native Americans. The captivity narrative lasted decades and was the first uniquely American literary genre.

Poetry, while not commonplace during the Colonial Period, enjoyed several successes. Anne Bradstreet (1612–1672), the first published American poet, released "The Tenth Muse Lately Sprung Up in America" in 1647. Michael Wigglesworth (1631–1705) wrote about the end of the world in his best selling poem "The Day of Doom" published in 1662.

European audiences were slow to recognize American authors. Snobbery and a European perception of the colonies as uncultured hinterlands worked against Colonial writers and poets. In fact, American literature would not be taken truly seriously until the last years of the 19th century.

Recommended Reading
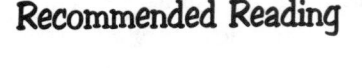

- Michael Wigglesworth, "The Day of Doom"

- John Smith, *The Generall Historie of Virginia, New England, and the Summer Isles*

- Mary Rowlandson *A Narrative of the Captivity and Restoration of Mrs. Mary Rowlandson*

- Cotton Mather, *Ecclesiastical History of New England*

THE COLONIAL PERIOD AND THE AMERICAN REVOLUTION: 1620–1800

In the Colonial Period, important writers made contributions beyond New England into the Middle and Southern Colonies. Large plantations devoted to agriculture became the norm. Nobility and the "leisurely life of the gentleman" were the ideal. A unique kind of American humor sprinkled with wit and satire emerged in the writings of William Byrd II (1674–1744) and Robert Beverly (1673–1722). Byrd's *History of the Dividing Line* is a humorous account of his adventures while surveying the border between North Carolina and Virginia.

As plantations developed, planters used African slaves for their crops, as servants, and for maintenance of their large holdings. The experience of slavery soon became a subject for literature as well. These **slave narratives** often described the loss of homeland, family, and dignity as well as the cruel treatment of slaves on plantations. One of the most famous of these slave narratives is *The Interesting Life of Olaudah Equiano, or Gustavus Vassa, the Africa* (1789).

With the approach of the American Revolution, emphasis shifted away from matters of religion and exploration towards fierce discussions of political rights and freedoms. Patriots like Samuel Adams (1722–1803) and Josiah Quincy (1744–1775) wrote passionate essays and pamphlets calling for greater liberties. Benjamin Franklin's annual *Poor Richard's Almanac* (1732–1757) contained practical advice and amusing situations that helped shape the notion of American identity.

One of the most famous publications of the Revolutionary Period (1776–1783) was Thomas Paine's *The American Crisis* (1776). In a few short paragraphs, Paine rallies support for the rebellion using vivid language and references to epic events. Here is an excerpt from "The Crisis No. 1":

"These are the times that try men's souls. The summer soldier and the sunshine patriot will, in this crisis, shrink from the service of their country; but he that stands it now deserves the love and thanks of man and woman. Tyranny, like hell, is not easily conquered; yet we have this consolation with us, that the harder the conflict, the more glorious the triumph. What we obtain too cheap, we esteem too lightly: it is dearness only that gives every thing its value.

The issue of taxation by England of American colonies became an epic conflict between good and evil. Not surprisingly, the essay was highly effective in getting colonists to rise up in revolution.

Recommended Reading

- William Byrd, *History of the Dividing Line*
- Thomas Paine, *American Crisis*
- Benjamin Franklin, *Poor Richard's Almanac*
- Olaudah Equiano, *The Interesting Life of Olaudah Equiano, or Gustavus Vassa, the Africa*

Practice 1: Early American Literature

1. What did the earliest American literary works reflect about the authors' beliefs?

    A.   the colonists' longing to return to the "Old World"
    B.   appeals for the deportation of the Native Americans, so-called "Indians"
    C.   the right of the colonies to exist and a desire for more emigrants to join them
    D.   commentaries on the colonists' harsh living conditions and lack of adequate food

2. How did many Europeans respond to colonial authors and their works?

    A.   They applauded the colonists' refreshing and experimental literary forms.
    B.   They urged European authors to imitate colonial efforts to please their readers.
    C.   They reacted with snobbery, regarding the colonies as uncultured hinterlands.
    D.   They regarded colonial publications as threats to traditional European literature.

3. What did Thomas Paine seek to achieve with his publication of *The American Crisis*?

    A.   rally support for Americas' rebellion against British tyranny and colonial taxation
    B.   help Europeans understand colonial Americans' hearty response to deprivation
    C.   appeal to the British for defense against marauding Native Americans
    D.   shape American identity as distinctly different from European influence

4. What was the first uniquely American literary genre?

    A.   historic colonial diaries   C.   captivity narratives
    B.   the new American novel   D.   "broadsides"

5. One of the main themes of early Native American stories was
   A. conflict with settlers.
   B. reverence for nature.
   C. loss of culture.
   D. cure for disease.

6. Of the following, who MOST believed in working hard and living a strict life from the Bible?
   A. Benjamin Franklin
   B. Spanish explorers
   C. James Oglethorpe
   D. Puritans

7. Which of the following BEST describes the main difference between the writings of Cotton Mather and William Byrd?
   A. Mather was interested in justifying the Puritan settlements in New England while Byrd focused on exploration of new territory in the rural South.
   B. Mather believed in following God's ways while Byrd ignored any belief in God.
   C. Mather defended the rights of slaves to be free in the New World while Byrd bought and kept slaves on his plantation in Virginia.
   D. Mather argued for strong, Godly leaders that would expand the Puritan colonies while Byrd advocated that one wise leader be chosen to govern the colonies.

8. Which of the following authors were similar in their outlook on American independence?
   A. Anne Bradstreet and Mary Rowlandson
   B. Roger Williams and Cotton Mather
   C. William Byrd and Mary Rowlandson
   D. Thomas Paine and Samuel Adams

9. What literary form was effective in getting colonists to rise up in revolution?
   A. poetry
   B. the novels
   C. the essay
   D. broadsides

10. Stories that related the experiences of African-Americans on plantations were called
   A. captivity narratives.
   B. pamphlets.
   C. slave narratives.
   D. broadsides.

A NEW NATION FINDS ITS VOICE: 1800–1850

Following the American Revolution, the United States entered into an uneasy peace with Great Britain, and its literature continued mostly to imitate English and European styles. Following America's rematch with England in the War of 1812, a series of gifted writers struggled to find a uniquely American voice.

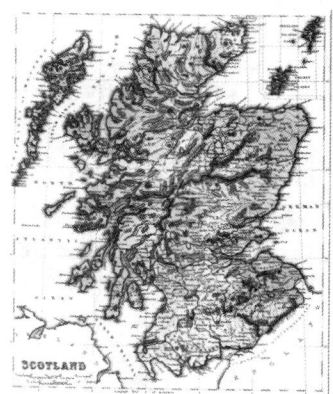

Great Britain

Modern literary historians consider Washington Irving (1783–1859), best known for "The Legend of Sleepy Hollow" (1819), as the first to develop an engaging, humorous style directly traceable to the American experience. He wrote about characters and events from his New York childhood, adding elements of local legends. Another of his works includes "The Legend of Rip Van Winkle*"* (1819).

James Fenimore Cooper's (1789–1851) *Leatherstocking Tales* novels (including *The Last of the Mohicans*) were a commercial success both in the United States and abroad when published between 1823 and 1841. Cooper composed thrilling adventure stories about life on the American frontier, which at the time stopped just short of the Midwest. His main character, Natty Bumppo, is a staunch individualist who overcomes adversity much like the cowboys of the later Wild West. Like Irving's work, Cooper's books nevertheless failed to secure America a solid literary reputation abroad.

The works of Edgar Allan Poe (1809–1849) quickly established him as a master of both the literary essay and the short story. Poe was among the first to use the **short story** as a narrative device, producing such deeply psychological works as "The Murders in the Rue Morgue" (1841) and "The Cask of Amontillado" (1846). Those original two stories established the **detective story** genre, which would gain enormous popularity a century later. Moreover, Poe energized the short story as a literary form, laying the groundwork for much of 20th century literature in the United States and Europe. Poe also wrote mesmerizing poetry that is still appreciated today. The eerily vivid style of his often macabre tales can be seen in the following excerpt from "The Fall of the House of Usher" (1845):

Edgar Allan Poe

> During the whole of a dull, dark, and soundless day in the autumn of the year, when the clouds hung oppressively low in the heavens, I had been passing alone, on horseback, through a singularly dreary tract of country; and at length found myself, as the shades of the evening drew on, within view of the melancholy House of Usher. I know not how it was—but, with the first glimpse of the building, a sense of insufferable gloom pervaded my spirit.

As the United States advanced across the continent, some writers began to explore nature as the source of truth and beauty in the world, encouraging others to follow a more spiritual path to happiness. Ralph Waldo Emerson (1803–1882), in his 1836 book *Nature*, laid the groundwork for the movement known as **Transcendentalism**. Transcendentalists believed that nature was a unifying force between God and human beings. Knowledge of the truth could be achieved only through an individual's intuition and feelings rather than the intellect and the ideas of the past. Emerson's student, Henry David Thoreau (1817–1862), published the memoir *Walden* in 1854, furthering the ideas of nature as a guide to peace and self knowledge. For example:

> A lake is the landscape's most beautiful and expressive feature.
> It is Earth's eye; looking into which the beholder measures
> the depth of his own nature.

During this period, a group of writers known as the **Fireside Poets**, including William Cullen Bryant (1794–1878) and Henry Wadsworth Longfellow (1807–1882), created original poetry based on American historical events. Longfellow's epic poems *Evangeline* (1847) and *The Song of Hiawatha* (1855) and Bryant's "Thanatopsis" (1811) remain landmarks in poetic history.

REBELLION, ROMANCE, REDEDICATION: 1850–1900

Harriet Beecher Stowe

By the mid-19th century, the heated debate over slavery threatened to erupt into full-blown rebellion. In a desperate attempt to draw sympathy from the cities of the north, **abolitionist** (anti-slavery) writers including Frederick Douglass (1817–1895) and Harriet Beecher Stowe (1811–1896) published works about the injustice and inhumanity of slavery. Douglass' autobiographical *Narrative of the Life of Frederick Douglass, An American Slave* debuted in 1845, described his bondage and freedom and provoked heated debate across the nation. Six years later, Stowe's *Uncle Tom's Cabin* (1851) brought the slavery issue into open conflict. The book was so controversial that, years later when the author met President Abraham Lincoln during the Civil War, Lincoln reportedly called her "the little woman who made this great war." Abolitionist essays and pamphlets found audiences through the 1850s and for the duration of the war.

American fiction authors were at last coming into their own, creating novels and short stories of profound texture, significance, and symbolism. Released in 1851, *Moby-Dick* by Herman Melville (1819–1891) is considered by many to be the finest American novel ever written. Inspired in part by a true story, the narrative follows the crew of the doomed ship *Pequod* as it stalks the albino whale that maimed its pursuer, Captain Ahab, years before. For the obsessed Ahab, the whale symbolizes fate, and striking it down represents a blow for individual freedom.

> That inscrutable thing is chiefly what I hate; and be the white whale agent, or be the white whale principal, I will wreak that hate upon him. Talk not to me of blasphemy, man; I'd strike the sun if it insulted me.

Meanwhile, a Massachusetts writer named Nathaniel Hawthorne was publishing short stories and novels concerning guilt, repression, and rigidity in New England. His quasi-allegorical masterpiece *The Scarlet Letter* (1850), about a woman cast out from her township for the sin of committing adultery, best demonstrates his belief that the individual's desires are routinely constrained by the rules of an unforgiving society. Hawthorne often criticized his Puritan ancestors for their narrow, dogmatic beliefs.

American poets also continued to thrive. Walt Whitman (1819–1892) published his landmark *Leaves of Grass* collection in 1855. Abandoning rhymed, metrical verse, Whitman wrote in free verse that was conversational in style. His unrestrained optimism and individualism link him to the Transcendentalists; his vivid images and everyday language reveal the realism in his poetry. Emily Dickinson (1830–1886), among the most famous poets anywhere, wrote elegantly crafted meditations on life, death, and freedom. Though her work would not gain widespread popularity for another 40 years, she wrote her best poems during the Civil War period (1861–1865). Her brief poems use unusual capitalization, frequent dashes, and a lyric style that is easily recognizable.

The speech that Abraham Lincoln (1809–1865) gave following the hideously costly Battle of Gettysburg in 1863 is so eloquent and has proven so memorable it is considered by many a work of art. This excerpt captures his command of English prose:

> It is rather for us to be here dedicated to the great task remaining before us—that from these honored dead we take increased devotion to that cause for which they gave the last full measure of devotion—that we here highly resolve that these dead shall not have died in vain—that this nation, under God, shall have a new birth of freedom—and that government of the people, by the people, for the people, shall not perish from the earth.

Many historians and literary scholars believe that Lincoln's speech rededicated the country after the war, giving it the same unifying sense of purpose that the Declaration of Independence had created 87 years earlier. That new sense of purpose would heavily influence America's rapid expansion into the West and inspire a new of generation of writers not only from the East Coast but also from the heart of the frontier.

Westward Expansion and Regional Awareness: 1850–1890

As United States settlement expanded, authors and poets arose from the frontier and the new states of the Midwest. The first major American novelist born away from the East Coast was Samuel Clemens (1835–1910), whose pen name was Mark Twain.

Mark Twain

A former riverboat pilot and newspaper writer, Twain introduced the technique of **vernacular** into American fiction in such works as *Life on the Mississippi* (1883) and *The Adventures of Huckleberry Finn* (1884). Vernacular is the technique of writing dialogue to reflect the way people of a certain region actually talk. It includes the slang and speech patterns that make up local speech, like those along the Mississippi River, who populated Twain's books. Later, novelists like William Faulkner, Flannery O'Connor, and Edith Wharton would adapt this style to illustrate the customs and speech of their own native areas. Read the following excerpt from *The Adventures of Huckleberry Finn*. Notice how the speech of the text resembles someone talking in everyday conversation, complete with dialect and non-grammatical construction.

> At first I hated the school, but by-and-by I got so I could stand it. Whenever I got uncommon tired I played hooky, and the hiding [whipping] I got next day done me good and cheered me up. So the longer I went to school the easier it got to be. I was getting sort of used to the widow's ways, too, and they warn't so raspy on me.

Other writers explored regional culture and customs using vernacular. Bret Harte (1836–1902) introduced Wild West stories of lowlife characters like gunslingers, rustlers, and gamblers to American readers. Set in the western mining frontier, stories like "The Outcasts of Poker Flat" contain local dialect and engaging dialogue that brings this era to life. Other notable examples include the Creole stories of George Washington Cable (1844–1925) and the stories of Tennessee mountain people by Mary Noailles Murfree (1850–1922). Joel Chandler Harris (1848–1908), a Georgia writer, began publishing the Uncle Remus stories in 1881. Br'er Rabbit, one of the main characters, appears as the trickster who often outwits his animal friends. These collections and adaptations of African-American folklore and dialect were hugely popular at their time but have since become mired in controversy. Nonetheless, they brought Southern culture in general and African-American narrative in particular to a wide audience.

Uncle Remus

At about this time, a New York-born writer named Henry James (1843–1916) was achieving the long-sought respect of European audiences and critics. James, who came from a wealthy New York family of intellectuals (his brother William was a pioneer in the field of psychology) spent much of his life in England and France. His works, most notably *The American* (1877) and *The Ambassadors* (1903), relate the tension between Old World sensuality and New World idealism. To James, the ancient decadence of Europe was almost toxic to the new breed of self-made American, and only through clinging to one's values could an American hope to remain uncorrupted. A generation later, this idea would bear a direct influence on the works of F. Scott Fitzgerald and Ernest Hemingway, two of the most famous American authors of the 20th century.

Twain, Cable, Harris, Murfee, Harte, and James came to be known as writers of **Realism** because they explored many facets of daily life using common people speaking the real language of the day. Unlike the idealized and virtuous characters of the romantic era, Realists portrayed characters with both vices and virtues that reflected the actual world of a more urban, industrialized society.

Recommended Reading

- Washington Irving, "The Legend of Sleepy Hollow"
- Edgar Allan Poe, "The Fall of the House of Usher"
- Henry David Thoreau, *Walden*
- William Cullen Bryant, "Thanatopsis"
- Frederick Douglass, *Narrative of the Life of Frederick Douglass, An American Slave*
- Herman Melville, "Bartleby the Scrivener"
- Nathaniel Hawthorne, "Young Goodman Brown"
- Mark Twain, "The Celebrated Jumping Frog of Calaveras County"
- Emily Dickinson, "Hope"; "Because I would not stop for Death
- Henry James, "Daisy Miller"; *The Turn of the Screw.*

Practice 2: New Voices in a New Nation

1. For what popular literary form is Edgar Allan Poe BEST remembered?

   A. novel   B. literary essay   C. drama   D. short story

2. What conflict marked Abraham Lincoln's presidency, and whom did he call its "maker"?

   A. the South's discriminatory treatment of Negroes / Frederick Douglass
   B. the American Revolution / Thomas Jefferson.
   C. the American Civil War / Harriet Beecher Stowe
   D. the War of 1812 / Admiral David Farragut

3. What belief held by Nathaniel Hawthorne does his novel, *The Scarlet Letter*, demonstrate?

   A. society's swift punishment for illegitimacy
   B. individuals' desires are constrained by the rules of society
   C. women are naturally superior to men
   D. society punishes those who exhibit individualism

4. What would you select as a definite characteristic of Transcendentalism?

   A. pessimism   B. optimism   C. indifference   D. restriction

5. Which of the following works is written in a venacular style?

   A. Uncle Remus tales   C. *Walden*
   B. "The Murders in the Rue Morgue"   D. *The Last of the Mohicans*

6. How would you improve your understanding of Transcendentalism?

   A. Read the works of Henry James.
   B. Research the life of Samuel Clemens.
   C. Read Thoreau's *Walden*.
   D. Research Natty Bumppo's adventures on the American frontier.

7. Why were Poe's works different from the writings of earlier American authors?

   A. Early American authors avoided themes of horror and decline.
   B. Poe wrote only short stories at a time when most authors produced novels.
   C. Earlier writers like Irving and Cooper described their characters as uneducated yet full of common sense.
   D. Poe's short stories and poems were original and influential.

8. How does Walt Whitman's poetry mirror Transcendental viewpoints?

   A. His poetry promotes individualism in thought and action.
   B. Whitman uses images from the real world around him.
   C. The *Leaves of Grass* was published the middle of the 19th century.
   D. Whitman avoided rhyme and rhythm in his poetry.

9. "The wretchedness of slavery and the blessedness of freedom were perpetually before me. It was life and death with me." These words most likely reflect the feelings of which of the following abolitionist writers?

A. Mark Twain
B. Harriet Beecher Stowe
C. Ralph Waldo Emerson
D. Frederick Douglass

10. The novels of Henry James often suggest that Europe's impact on American life was
A. positive.
B. minimal.
C. negative.
D. beneficial.

UPHEAVAL, REALISM, AND THE CLOSING OF AN AGE: 1890–1920

The Industrial Revolution of the 1890s brought sweeping changes to America, as its cities filled with both immigrants and people from smaller towns searching for a better life. A new era of **Naturalism** produced writers who renounced the optimism of the post-Civil War period and revealed instead the sometimes-ugly realities of industrialization. In response, a new breed of journalists, called **muckrakers**, published books calling attention to the abuses of large corporations and the plight of the urban poor. Read this excerpt from the most famous muckraking book, *The Jungle* (1906), by Upton Sinclair, which resulted in public outrage over conditions in the Chicago meat packing industry:

> This is no fairy story and no joke; the meat will be shoveled into carts and the man who did the shoveling will not trouble to lift out a rat even when he saw one.

Other noteworthy muckraking books include Lincoln Steffans' *The Shame of the Cities* (1904), about government corruption; and Ida Tarbell's *The History of the Standard Oil Company* (1904). Muckraking pieces were successful partly because they appeared in widely circulated magazines such as *McClure's*, *The Independent*, and *Cosmopolitan*. In doing so, they reached audiences who read magazines for entertainment but that typically did not read literature.

The new sense of social awareness was seen in fiction, as well. Writers who had come of age after the Civil War rejected the restrictions of Victorian behavior and instead explored its contradictions and hypocrisies. Naturalists often exposed social problems and the darker sides of American life. Stephen Crane's (1871–1900) *The Red Badge of Courage* (1895) depicted the violence and misery of warfare, separating it from the romantic idealism of earlier war stories. Sherwood Anderson's (1876–1941) *Winesburg, Ohio* (1919) revolutionized both the treatment of small-town America and the novel structure itself. A collection of interrelated short stories, the book lays bare the desperation beneath the surface of a small Midwestern town. Extremely controversial at the time of its publication, it had a direct influence on the next generation of American writers.

Women were increasingly a powerful force in literature during this period. Edith Wharton (1862–1937), one of the first American women writers to receive critical acclaim, published novels exposing the flaws of the idle New York social elite. *The Age of Innocence* (1920) and *The House of Mirth* (1905) both call attention to the tragedy of upper-middle-class women confined by social convention. Another notable author of the period was Willa Cather (1873–1947), who published *My Antonia* in 1918 as a remembrance of the American frontier. She describes the quiet dignity of pioneers in Nebraska and the Southwest. Finally, Kate

Chopin (1851–1904) pushed the boundaries of women's equality with her novel *The Awakening* (1899). In this novel, Chopin explores a young married woman's frustrated attempt to escape her family and establish a new identity.

This period was the so-called Gilded Age of great wealth but also desperate poverty. Its writers were often revolutionary in bringing to light the overwhelming disparity of the era. The generation that followed them would go even further, changing the very nature of literature and its purpose. In retrospect, a world war and its aftermath seemed to leave them no choice.

Recommended Reading

- Sherwood Anderson, "Hands"
- Stephen Crane, *The Red Badge of Courage*
- Edith Wharton, "Sanctuary"
- Kate Chopin, "The Story of an Hour"

THE LOST GENERATION: 1920–1930

World War I (1914–1918) had been waged with the noblest of ideals and ended in unprecedented loss of life and human suffering. American writers of the 1920s and 1930s, perhaps because of the nation's previously untarnished idealism, took the bitterness of the war's aftermath to heart. Their disillusionment showed in their work, with its themes of alienation and techniques like **stream of consciousness** that mirrored the individual's search for identity. Gertrude Stein (1874–1946), an American poet living in Paris, lamented that the artists of the WWI generation were unable to live normal lives because of their experiences, naming them "The Lost Generation." Stein, Ezra Pound (1885–1972), T.S. Eliot (1888–1965), and other American poets living in Europe experimented with the form and structure of poems, creating work that was often confrontational and unsettling. Eliot's epic poem *The Waste Land* (1922), about the postwar world, was probably the most influential poem to arise from this period:

> What are the roots that clutch, what branches grow
>
> Out of this stony rubbish? Son of man,
>
> You cannot say, or guess, for you know only
>
> A heap of broken images, where the sun beats,
>
> And the dead tree gives no shelter, the cricket no relief,
>
> And the dry stone no sound of water.

At the same time, Robert Frost (1874–1963), one of America's best known poets, was producing traditional rhymed poetry. It appealed to a wide audience, as most people could easily relate to subjects such as walking down country roads or observing the cycle of nature. While deceptively simple, his poems often suggest deeper meanings. For example, the last stanza of "Stopping by Woods on a Snowy Evening" (1923) is not just about a sleigh ride in the snow but also about the inevitability of death.

Robert Frost

> The woods are lovely, dark and deep,
>
> But I have promises to keep,
>
> And miles to go before I sleep,
>
> And miles to go before I sleep.

Frost's contemporary, William Carlos Williams (1883–1963), excelled at a relaxed, natural poetry that mirrored the colloquial speech and rhythms of ordinary working people. His poems are like photographs reflecting the spontaneous patterns of everyday experience. His poetry is a link between the free verse of Whitman and the later Beat and confessional poets of the 1950s and '60s.

Recommended Reading

- Gertrude Stein, *Three Lives*
- T.S. Eliot, *The Waste Land*
- Ezra Pound, *The Cantos*
- Robert Frost, "The Road Not Taken"

Ernest Hemingway

Ernest Hemingway (1899–1961), an ambulance driver during the World War I, believed most abstract language was by its nature false and misleading. He crafted a style of simple, concrete, and straightforward prose that, nearly a century later, continues to find imitators the world over. Hemingway's most important works specifically concerning World War I and its aftermath include *The Sun Also Rises* (1926) and *A Farewell to Arms* (1929). Hemingway's short story collection, *In Our Time* (1925), addresses attempts by WWI veterans to readjust to normal life in the Midwest.

Another veteran, William Faulkner (1897–1962), would rival Hemingway in influence and critical reception, if not in popular appeal. Faulkner adapted the loose, free-flowing narrative style crafted by the Irish novelist James Joyce and melded it with a Southern vernacular similar to that of Mark Twain. The result was an intense, deeply psychological narrative style that appeared spontaneous even on the printed page. Faulkner's works almost exclusively dealt with the people of Yoknapatawpha County, a semi-fictional region of rural Mississippi.

Recommended Reading

- Hemingway, *In Our Time*; *A Farewell To Arms*; *The Sun Also Rises*
- Faulkner, *The Sound and the Fury*; *As I Lay Dying*; "A Rose for Emily"; "The Bear"

F. Scott Fitzgerald (1896–1940), though himself not a war veteran, nevertheless wrote novels and many short stories depicting the restless, anxious lives of the Lost Generation. His "Jazz Age" novels include *This Side of Paradise* (1920), which made him a popular sensation at the age of 23; and of course *The Great Gatsby* (1925), considered by some to be the greatest American novel. In his lifetime, Fitzgerald was known primarily as a short story writer, earning huge sums for his work from such magazines as *Esquire*, *The Saturday Evening Post*, and *McClure's*. His later work, much like that of Henry James, tries to reconcile the differences between European and American values.

Hemingway, Stein, and to a lesser extent Fitzgerald and Faulkner were typical of an emerging class of American writers and artists living in Paris in the 1920s. This "Lost Generation" was not limited to American novelists, short story writers, and poets, but also included artists and playwrights. Other notable members of this group include the publisher Sylvia Beach, the journalists Djuna Barnes and Dorothy Parker, and the novelist and dramatist Sinclair Lewis, who became the first American to win the Nobel Prize in Literature. His novel, *Main Street* (1920), satirized the complacency and staleness of small town life.

Recommended Reading

- F. Scott Fitzgerald, "Babylon Revisited"; "The Lost Decade"; *Tender Is the Night*
- Djuna Barnes, *Nightwood*
- Sinclair Lewis, *Babbitt*

African-American literature also underwent a watershed event during this period, with an explosion of creative works coming out of Harlem, New York. This **Harlem Renaissance** lasted from approximately 1919 to 1936 and was an unprecedented show of talent in literature, drama, and visual arts. Noted poets of this period include Langston Hughes, whose meditation on the diminished hopes of black Americans in the poem "A Dreamed Deferred" (1951) has become synonymous with the black struggle:

> What happens to a dream deferred?
> Does it dry up
> like a raisin in the sun?
> Or fester like a sore—
> And then run?

Countee Cullen (1903–1946) and Jean Toomer (1894–1967) wrote traditionally rhymed poetry that explored yet transcended race through such universal themes as the struggle for identity and the security of a community. Richard Wright's (1908–1960) novel, *Native Son* (1945), depicts the main character, Bigger Thomas, living in a poor, segregated neighborhood which leads him to commit murder and face punishment for his crime. Zora Neale Hurston (1903–1960) wrote stories and novels evoking the daily rhythms of African-American life in the rural South, strongly influencing later African-American women writers.

Recommended Reading

- Langston Hughes and Zora Neale Hurston, *The Mule-Bone: A Comedy of Negro Life in Three Acts*
- Jean Toomer, *Cane*
- Richard Wright, *Black Boy*
- Langston Hughes, "A Dream Deferred"

THE GREAT DEPRESSION: 1930–1945

The restlessness and exuberance of the 1920s came to a sudden halt with the stock market crash of October 1929. As the nation sank into a decade-long economic depression, American literature attempted to redefine itself by addressing the suffering of those victimized by hardship.

Probably the most famous novel of the Great Depression is John Steinbeck's *The Grapes of Wrath*. Published in 1939, it relates the trials of the Joad family seeking a better life in California. Heavily influenced by both the New Testament and American folklore, the novel and its 1940 film version deeply resonated with the American public. Steinbeck is more or less the "voice" of the Great Depression in American literature, having also published *Of Mice and Men* (1937), *In Dubious Battle* (1936), and *The Pearl* (1947), all dealing with the struggles of the working class trying to survive.

Other significant writers of the 1930s include Nathanial West, author of *Miss Lonelyhearts* (1933), a novel about a male newspaper reporter who answers questions from readers suffering from loneliness and economic deprivation during the Great Depression. John Fante (1909–1983), author of *Ask the Dust* (1939), captures the mood and culture of Los Angeles by telling the story of a Depression-era struggling writer and his romance with a Mexican waitress.

Recommended Reading

- John Steinbeck, "The Chrysanthemums"; *Of Mice and Men*
- John Fante, *Ask the Dust*
- Nathaniel West, *Miss Lonleyhearts*

Additionally, a new kind of novel appeared during the Depression that came to define much of 20th century American culture. Cheaply produced and quickly written, **pulp fiction** appeared in magazines and "dime novels" that generally revolved around detectives, private investigators, or policemen attempting to solve complex and frequently lurid mysteries. Part of pulp's appeal was its "hardboiled" narrative voice, which ranged from bitterly witty to sadly poetic. A great example of this is spoken by Raymond Chandler's (1888–1959) hero Philip Marlowe, a private investigator in Los Angeles:

> I'm a romantic... I hear voices crying in the night and I go to see what's the matter. You don't make a dime that way. . . No percentage in it at all. No nothing, except sometimes I get my face pushed in, or get tossed in the can, or get threatened by some fast-money boy.

> –from *The Big Sleep*, 1939

Though dismissed as commercial tripe when they were published, these novels—particularly those by Chandler and Dashiell Hammett (1894–1961)—are now considered by many scholars to be a legitimate literary genre. Their influence runs through 20th century film, television, video games, and other media. Most private investigators and policemen in modern novels, films, and television are to some extent descendants from characters in pulp novels.

Recommended Reading

- Raymond Chandler, *The Big Sleep* (1939)
- Dashiell Hammett, *The Maltese Falcon* (1930)

THE RISE OF AMERICAN DRAMA 1920–1950

Until the early 20th century, English, French and Italian drama dominated theater in the United States. Most American plays were mediocre and unoriginal.

This changed with Eugene O'Neill (1888–1953), the greatest American playwright of the 20th century. His original vision, emotional depth, and theatrical innovations resulted in remarkable plays that are still performed today. Borrowing from Freud and his own personal background, he wrote a number of plays that explore the tensions and passions hidden in families, working class people, and the wealthy. With O'Neill's special light and sound effects, *Desire under the Elms* (1924) and *Strange Interlude* (1928) reveal the primitive emotions just under the surface of his characters' lives. The autobiographical *Long Day's Journey into Night* (1956) deals with his own family's emotional and physical collapse. In 1936, O'Neill won the Nobel Prize for Literature.

Other prominent dramatists include Thornton Wilder (1897–1975), who presented the redeeming values of American life in his classic play, *Our Town* (1938). Using innovative elements such as time shifts, ghosts, and audience input, he creates the typical American small town with its mix of joy, sorrow, and nostalgia. The Southern playwright Tennessee Williams (1911–1983) wrote many plays contrasting past and present, illusion and reality. His troubled family was the inspiration for many of his plays, and he won the New York Drama Critics Circle Award for Best Play of the Season for *The Glass Menagerie* (1945) and the Pulitzer Prize for *A Streetcar Named Desire* (1947). His plays often deal with the fantasies people create to escape the bitter realities of the present. In several cases, his characters cannot deal with the demise of romantic Old South values when confronted with the realities of a new urban industrial society.

Arthur Miller (1915–2005) wrote *Death of a Salesman*, a landmark work of American drama in 1949. In this play, Miller describes a common salesman's search for self worth in the face of failure in his life. Miller won a Pulitzer Prize for this play and went on to write others, including *The Crucible* (1953) about the Salem Witch Trials during the Puritan Era in New England.

AFTER WORLD WAR II: THE LITERATURE OF UNCERTAINTY 1945–1970

As did post-WWI writers a generation before, the writers of the World War II era and through the 1950s found themselves at a loss to understand meaning and purpose in the world. Material prosperity and peace came after the war, but the resulting conformity also bred alienation and discontent. In his novel, *The Catcher in the Rye* (1951), J.D. Salinger portrayed the disillusionment and phoniness of the era in the person of Holden Caulfield, a sensitive 16-year-old who drops out of an elite boarding school.

In the 1950s, James Baldwin (1924–1987) and Ralph Ellison (1914–1994) conveyed the frustrations and uncertainties of African Americans. Racial segregation and life in the black community led these authors to write about their experiences. Baldwin's autobiographical *Go Tell It on the Mountain* (1953) looks at the role of the Church in the African-American community as both a unifying force and one of hypocrisy. In Ellison's *Invisible Man* (1952), a black man living in a hole recalls his disappointing experiences going to a prejudiced college and observing the corruption in his own community.

Such uncertainty fueled new experimentation in the use of the novel to communicate not only narrative but also thoughts and sensations. Kurt Vonnegut's (1922–2007) *Slaughterhouse Five* (1969), about a WWII soldier reliving his wartime experiences while a prisoner on the alien planet of Tralfamadore, blended the genres of science fiction, realism, and mystery to new and often shocking effect. Joseph Heller's (1923–1999) *Catch-22* (1961) satirizes the Allied war effort in Italy with black, witty humor. In a different vein, James Jones attempted to fuse ideas of spirituality and honor on the modern battlefront in books such as *The Thin Red Line* (1962) and *From Here to Eternity* (1951).

Recommended Reading

- Kurt Vonnegut, "Harrison Bergeron"
- James Jones, *The Thin Red Line*
- Eugene O'Neill, *Desire Under the Elms*
- Thornton Wilder, *Our Town*
- Arthur Miller, *Death of a Salesman*
- Ralph Ellison, *Invisible Man*

Also coming to prominence during this period were the writers and artists of the Beat Generation, named for their efforts to incorporate jazz rhythms and structures into their writing. To the Beats, post-war society had exhausted itself of ideas and only new sensations and travel would ease the crushing sense of desolation. The most famous of these writers was the novelist Jack Kerouac (1922–1969), whose novel *On the Road* (1957) best sums up that sense of restlessness:

> Oh, man," said Dean to me as we stood in front of a bar, "… Sal, we got to go and never stop 'til we get there."
>
> "Where are we going, man?"
>
> "I don't know, but we gotta go."

Also notable was Beat poet Allen Ginsburg (1926–1997), who composed long, intricate verse that confronted issues of social inequality and spiritual devastation. The first lines of his epic poem *Howl* (1956) summarize the tone and mood of much of his work:

> I saw the best minds of my generation destroyed by madness, starving hysterical naked,
>
> dragging themselves through the negro streets at dawn looking for an angry fix

The Beat Generation movement lasted through the 1950s and early 60s, until roughly the assassination of President John F. Kennedy in 1963. It was soon absorbed into the growing counterculture movement of the 1960s, the "Beatniks" becoming, by and large, "hippies."

Recommended Reading

- Jack Kerouac, *On The Road*
- Allen Ginsburg, *Howl*
- William S. Burroughs, *Naked Lunch*

From 1960 to 1970, several poets practiced more open forms of poetry. Among these were the **Confessional Poets**. These poets bared their most tormented personal problems in a direct and honest style. This new experimental verse arose out of the Beat poetry of the 1950s and the improvised poetry of William Carlos Williams. For example, Robert Lowell (1917–1977), a respected traditional poet, heard Beat poetry with jazz accompaniment. His *Life Studies* (1959) signaled a dramatic change in his past formal poetry and influenced other younger confessional poets. Among these poets were Sylvia Plath (1932–1963) and Anne Sexton (1928–1974). Plath's later poems share her conflicts between her role as good wife and mother and her career as a poet. Sexton's poems exhibit powerful emotions about being a woman and her concerns about madness and death.

POSTMODERNISM, METAFICTION, AND REGIONALISM 1970–PRESENT

By the dawn of the 1970s—following the social and cultural upheaval of WWII, the Civil Rights Movement (1950s to 1970s), the Vietnam War (1954–1975), feminism, and the Cold War (1945–1990—American culture was beginning to show signs of fatigue. American literature, however, continued to plunge forward, evaluating human experience and reexamining the meaning of narrative and text itself. These so-called **Postmodernists** (as compared with the **Modernists** that had occupied much of earlier 20th century literature) sought to push past the readers' expectations of what constituted story and even what determined narrative voice. For Postmodernists, the media, popular culture, and technology affect their outlooks, writing styles, and voices. No deep spiritual meanings exist in art; only words and images from everyday life matter. Fantasy, inner consciousness, and fragmentation in literature are preferred. Their highly experimental work often calls attention to the fact that the text itself was in fact *simply a text*, and not a story that existed in the reader's mind.

A classic example of the Postmodern style appears at the beginning of John Barth's story "Lost in the Funhouse" (1968):

> For whom is the funhouse fun? Perhaps for lovers. For Ambrose it is a *place of fear and confusion.* He has come to the seashore with his family for the holiday, *the occasion of their visit is Independence Day, the most important secular holiday of the United States of America.* A single straight underline is the manuscript mark for italic type, *which in turn* is the printed equivalent to oral emphasis of words and phrases as well as the customary type for titles of complete works, not to mention. Italics are also employed, in fiction stories especially, for "outside," intrusive, or artificial voices, such as radio announcements, the texts of telegrams and newspaper articles, et cetera.

Postmodernism was often savagely attacked by critics who felt its ideas and forms were contrived and self-conscious at the same time. Raymond Carver (1938–1988), a modernist writer, criticized it as a shortcut for novice writers unskilled in traditional storytelling. Nonetheless, its influence continues in the work of such present-day writers as Michael Chabon (1963–), author of *Wonder Boys* (1995) and *The Amazing Adventures of Cavalier and Clay* (2000), and Dave Eggers (1970–), author of *You Shall Know Our Velocity* (2002).

Thomas Pynchon (1937–), a reclusive, award-winning fiction writer, uses images from pop culture, film, advertising, and popular songs as well as learned references from science, history, math, and religion. His novel *Gravity's Rainbow* (1973) is a WWII fantasy that combines violence and comedy in which none of the characters are aware of the historical events unfolding, while the readers are.

Another postmodern writer of novels and plays is Don DeLillo (1936–). His novel *White Noise* (1985) exposes the heavy consumerism, violence, family disintegration, and shallow mass media that dominate American society. For this novel, DeLillo won the National Book Award.

Cyberpunk, a form of late 20th century science fiction, centers on the bewildering intrusion of technology on the individual. Cyberpunk characters are marginalized loners experiencing dramatic mental and physical changes due to the impact of computers, media, and technology. Their mission is to overcome these challenges to save humanity and preserve their lives. The highly popular Matrix trilogy contains cyberpunk elements starting with the first Matrix film release in 1999.

In his novel *Necromancer* (1984), William Gibson (1948–) creates Case, a cyberspace cowboy who must complete a dangerous task if he is to rid his body of deadly toxins. Virtual reality and bioengineering are challenges in *Idoru* (1996), a novel about a man's love quest for a virtual media star in 21st century Japan.

Other movements in the late 20th century include traditional and regional styles of writing, **metafiction** (the blending of fiction and nonfiction), and other innovative techniques. Another name for metafiction is **new journalism**. Truman Capote (1924–1984) blended fiction and nonfiction in his story of a real mass murder in Kansas (*In Cold Blood*, 1966). Actual facts from the US space program formed the basis for Tom Wolfe's (1931–) bestseller, *The Right Stuff* (1979). Hunter S. Thompson, the purveyor of "Gonzo Journalism," in which the reporter becomes the central figure in the story. Thompson also wrote several books, including *Fear and Loathing in Las Vegas* (1972).

In the 1980s, **regional realism** returned with innovative structures such as flashbacks, stories within stories, and a focus on specific locales and characters. Critical of postmodernist ambiguity, John Gardner (1933–1982) wrote novels praising clear, universal messages about family, duty, and personal integrity in such books as *October Light* (1976) and *Mickelson's Ghosts* (1982).

Author Toni Morrison, who won the Nobel Prize for Literature in 1993, uses unique storytelling to convey the multifaceted relationships in African-American communities. *Song of Solomon* (1977) chronicles the life of a black man from birth to adulthood. Her fellow novelist, Alice Walker (1944–) wrote *The Color Purple* (1982) in an epistolary style (series of letters) that recounts an abusive relationship in black dialect. Ishmael Reed (1938–), an African-American novelist, essayist, and poet, opposes cultural and political oppression in contemporary America. Set in 1920s New York, his novel *Mumbo Jumbo* (1972) combines conspiracy theory and voodoo as a way for the protagonist to carry a strange virus spreading jazz, polytheism, and freedom. Other women writers include Flannery O'Connor (1925–1964) and Eudora Welty (1909–2001), both of whom wrote well-crafted short stories exploring the personal lives of heroes and misfits in the rural South.

Writers from the Northeast and Midwest captured the loneliness and anxiety of affluent people. The characters of John Cheever (1912–1982) search for happiness in the business world. In his four Rabbit Angstom books, John Updike (1932–) traces the life of his protagonist over four decades. Nobel Prize-winner Saul Bellow (1976) wrote fiction about people trying to overcome alienation and loneliness, like *Herzog* (1964), the story of a man in midlife crisis searching for purpose and identity in modern life.

Regional novels resurfaced again in the 1990s including *Very Old Bones* (1992) by William Kennedy (1928–). His marginalized characters seek happiness in localized, sometimes grotesque settings. Charles Frazier's (1950–) Civil War novel *Cold Mountain* (1997) takes place in the mountains of North Carolina. Many of Stephen King's (1947–) horror stories occur in his home state of Maine. King, one of the most prolific authors of this generation, is influenced in his horror work by writers like Edgar Allan Poe, but he also writes lyrically crafted coming-of-age stories ("The Body," 1982) and tales of personal struggle and triumph ("Rita Hayworth and the Shawshank Redemption," 1983; *Delores Claiborne*, 1992; *Lisey's Story*, 2006).

CONTEMPORARY NATIVE-AMERICAN, HISPANIC, AND ASIAN-AMERICAN WRITERS

With their ancient oral tradition, Native American stories, myths, and poems continue to be collected and published. In the 1960s and 70s, Native American literature gained a wider audience through the writings of N. Scott Momaday (1984–) and Leslie Marmon Silko (1948–). Their "chant novels" provide insight into Native-American culture and history. Awarded the Pulitzer Prize, Momaday's *House Made of Dawn* (1969) features Abel's struggle and final triumph to fully embrace his native culture in New Mexico. Silko's novel *Ceremony* (1977) reveals how connecting to native culture can lead to healing of past hurts.

Hispanic American writers also express cultural themes. Sandra Cisneros (1954–) wrote the widely praised *The House on Mango Street* in 1984. This coming of age story is told in the dialect of a Mexican teenager living in Chicago. New Mexico is the setting for Rudolfo Anaya's (1937–) novel *Bless Me, Ultima* (1972), in which a young boy must resolve conflict between old and new ways of doing things. Oscar Hijuelos (1951–) was the first Hispanic American to win the Pulitzer Prize for Fiction for his novel *The Mambo Kings Play Songs of Love* (1989). The story revolves around the lives of two Cuban brothers who immigrate to New York City in the 1950s.

Recent themes in Asian American literature focus on ethnicity, gender roles, and assimilation into American society. Maxine Hong Kingston (1940–) wrote *Woman Warrior* (1976) to express views on her Chinese American heritage. In *The Joy Luck Club* (1989), Amy Tan (1952–) explores mother-daughter relationships and the conflicts between her Chinese background and life in the United States.

You may not have read all of the books mentioned, but you probably recognized many titles from films. Filmmakers often choose classics, popular books, or innovative texts as material for movies. However, don't equate seeing a film based on a book with reading the book itself. Even a well-made adaptation can never fully show you what an author wrote. First, the text is interpreted for you; only by reading the text can you know what the author wrote and evaluate it for yourself. Second, due to constraints of time and considerations of audience reaction, the theme and plot of a book often are changed to fit its new medium. And finally, the crafted words of narration and description do not translate to the big screen. They are replaced by a score and scenery—which can be wonderful but offer a different experience altogether from reading the book.

The literary history of the United States is rich and varied. From the earliest Native-American songs and explorers' narratives to the postmodern and cyberpunk novels of today, American literature reflects the key values and ideals of a proud and free nation. By reviewing this brief history, you will gain a better understanding of major periods, characteristics, and authors and their works.

Practice 3: American Literature Grows Strong

1. How did Henry James' fiction say Americans could be saved from Old World corruption?

    A.   by avoiding travel to Europe
    B.   through spiritual rebirth and regular worship
    C.   by reading only wholesome novels and short stories
    D.   through clinging to one's better values

2. Who were the *muckrakers*?

    A.   early cowboys   C.   journalists
    B.   stable boys   D.   industrialists

3. To whom did Gertrude Stein's "The Lost Generation" refer?

    A.   American "ex patriots" who disappeared in Europe
    B.   her parents' generation of wealthy patricians
    C.   unemployed young Americans living in Europe
    D.   World War I era artists whose experiences hurt them

4. Depression-era novelist John Steinbeck is widely regarded as

    A.   a brilliant communist.
    B.   an example of a "rags to riches" story.
    C.   the "voice" of the Great Depression.
    D.   the Depression's "great detractor."

5. What form of writing does Joseph Heller's novel *Catch-22* demonstrate?
    A.   muckraking   B.   pulp novel   C.   realism   D.   satire

6. What did the post-war "Beat Generation" rely on MOST to ease its sense of desolation?
   A. drugs
   B. music
   C. new sensations and travel
   D. literary experimentation

7. Which of the following is the most common characteristic of Postmodernists?
   A. structured narrative
   B. fragmented text
   C. strong characters
   D. deep spiritualism

8. Which of the following authors shares similar styles and themes?
   A. Toni Morrison and William Gibson
   B. Edgar Allan Poe and Stephen King
   C. Allen Ginsberg and Robert Frost
   D. Emily Dickinson and Edith Wharton

9. How does the Matrix film trilogy relate to the fiction of William Gibson?
   A. references to the US space program
   B. comedy and humorous episodes
   C. cyberpunk themes and characters
   D. scenes from the Middle Ages

10. Stories and books written in such genres as science fiction, fantasy, and horror often can convey genuine points about life through
    A. simile.
    B. allusion.
    C. imagery.
    D. allegory.

11. Which of the following is a common theme in today's Hispanic, Asian, and Native American literature?
    A. isolation from American values
    B. conflict between traditional culture and modern society
    C. horror and violence in American cities
    D. clash between personal values and the need to learn and use English

12. Toni Morrison and Alice Waller share a focus on
    A. the challenges of family relationships.
    B. overcoming black dialect.
    C. the importance of music in the black community.
    D. the lack of political representation.

CHAPTER 1 SUMMARY

American literary tradition began more than 400 years ago and includes the writing of Native Americans, early explorers, colonists, and settlers of the North American continent. It took until the mid-19th century for American authors to be taken seriously. Uniquely American genres include captivity narratives, transcendentalism, and the detective story. Literary inventions introduced by American authors include use of vernacular and pulp fiction.

Events leading up to and following the American Revolution (1776) set a tone of rebellion followed by nationalism for American literature. Following the War of 1812, American writers including Washington Irving, James Fennimore Cooper, and Edgar Allen Poe found a distinctly American voice and established new genres (like the short story and the detective story).

In the early 1800s, as the nation expanded, Transcendentalism explored nature as the source of truth and beauty. The heated mid-19th century debate over slavery brought the introduction of abolitionist literature. Later in the century, Realism began to thrive. As America pushed farther west, Mark Twain became the nation's first major not born on the East Coast. He used vernacular to introduce readers to the dialect and slang of a region, and this technique was picked up by other authors.

The work of Henry James related the tension between the Old World and New World, ushering in the idea of self-made, independent Americans, which would be echoed a generation later in the works of F. Scott Fitzgerald and Ernest Hemingway. Bridging the close of the 19th century and opening of the 20th, increasing social awareness encouraged muckraker journalism. Women authors like Edith Wharton, Willa Cather, and Kate Chopin became an increasingly strong force.

The end of WWI brought the Lost Generation of the 1920s and '30s, a group of expatriate writers and poets disillusioned by the state of the world. Ezra Pound and T. S. Elliot experimented with the form and structure of poetry. Ernest Hemingway, an ambulance driver during World War I, crafted a style of simple, straightforward prose that has stood the test of time, remaining distinctly readable today. William Faulkner, another WWI veteran, adopted a loose, free-flowing narrative style. F. Scott Fitzgerald wrote novels and short stories depicting the restless, anxious lives of the Lost Generation.

The life-shattering stock market crash of 1929 preceded America's Great Depression, and American literature attempted to redefine itself by addressing the suffering due to economic hardships. John Steinbeck's novel *The Grapes of Wrath* has been called the "voice" of the Great Depression. A new kind of novel appeared during the Depression—the pulp novel—that came to define much of 20th century American culture and even today influences film, television, video games, and other media.

Once again, uncertainty about the meaning and purpose of life besieged writers following the end of World War II (1945). Works by Kurt Vonnegut and Joseph Heller—ostensibly war-themed novels—employed satire, black humor, science fiction, realism, and mystery to ponder these questions. The Beat Generation of the 1950s and '60s followed, incorporating jazz rhythms and structures into writing. Jack Kerouac and Allen Ginsburg characterized this era of social dislocation and literary experimentation.

Postmodernism of the '70s and early '80s followed the Civil Rights Movement and the Viet Nam War as American culture was showing signs of fatigue. Postmodern writers turned established writing forms inside out and challenged readers' expectations.

CHAPTER 1 REVIEW

1. The American literary tradition began in the

   A. 1400s   B. 1500s   C. 1600s   D. 1700s

2. Early American literature includes works by
   A. Native Americans.
   B. colonists.
   C. settlers.
   D. all of the above.

3. American writers' works have included a wide variety of literary forms including
   A. pamphlets.
   B. broadsides.
   C. classics.
   D. all of the above.

4. Which of these is a uniquely American literary genre?
   A. the historical novel
   B. creation myth
   C. the detective story
   D. autobiography

5. Who is the early 19th-century writer said to have established the first truly American genre of writing?
   A. Edgar Allan Poe
   B. James Fenimore Cooper
   C. Washington Irving
   D. Ralph Waldo Emerson

6. Frederick Douglass and Harriett Beecher Stowe are known as what kind of authors?

   A. Puritan   B. Transcendentalist   C. abolitionist   D. racist

7. Whom did President Abraham Lincoln call the "little woman who made this great war"?
   A. Emily Dickenson
   B. Mary Rowlands
   C. Harriet Beecher Stowe
   D. Edith Wharton

8. The Georgia author BEST remembered for his Uncle Remus stories is
   A. Frederick Douglass.
   B. Joel Chandler Harris.
   C. Samuel Clemens.
   D. Henry James.

9. Henry David Thoreau, a student of Ralph Waldo Emerson, BEST demonstrates what in the following excerpt?

   > A lake is the landscape's most beautiful and expressive feature
   > It is Earth's eye, looking into which the beholder measures
   > the depth of his own nature.

   A. humanism   B. fantasy   C. naturalism   D. transcendentalism

10. During the late 19th to early 20th century, _____ became a new force in American literature.
    A. novelists   B. dramatists   C. women   D. poets

11. What characteristics of muckraking found expression in contemporary fiction?
    A. its sense of realism and social awareness
    B. its demoralizing influence on the poor
    C. its appeal to the uneducated
    D. its profound indifference

12. Which of the following literary works exposed unhealthy conditions in the meat packing industry?
    A. *The Red Badge of Courage*   C. *The Shame of the Cities*
    B. *Slaughterhouse Five*   D. *The Jungle*

13. Some writers, poets, and other artists of the 1920s and '30s are called "The _____ Generation."
    A. Lost   B. Beat   C. Rock   D. Hippie

14. Pulp fiction, dismissed as faddish upon its first appearance, is now considered to be what?
    A. a legitimate literary genre   C. hardboiled Americana
    B. excellent reading   D. one of the most violent genres

15. Much of the literature of the Great Depression deals with
    A. the effects of the stock market crash on New York businessmen.
    B. the struggles of the working class to survive economic hardship.
    C. the migration of workers from the East Coast to the West Coast.
    D. the average citizen's disillusionment and search for identity.

16. Which of these is another American invention that would go on to influence modern novels, films, and television?
    A. slave narratives   C. the pulp novel
    B. the tall tale   D. Beat poetry

17. Authors like Truman Capote, Tom Wolfe, and Hunter S. Thompson blended journalism and fiction in a style called
    A. muckraking.   B. metafiction.   C. new fiction.   D. pulp fiction.

18. Writers during post-World War II expressed _____ about the meaning of life and the world.
    A. uncertainty   B. assurance   C. foolishness   D. premonitions

19. The Harlem Renaissance was a movement that
    A. diminished the hopes of many African-Americans.
    B. brought music into literature for the first time in history.
    C. was limited to Harlem, a neglected area of New York City.
    D. showcased talent among African-American writers and artists.

20. Critics of this literary movement said that its form was contrived and self-conscious, and that it was practiced by novices.
    A. Transcendentalism
    B. Modernism
    C. Postmodernism
    D. Realism

21. Why did outstanding American drama take so long to develop?
    A. American plays were inferior to the European plays performed in the United States.
    B. Actors and actresses were so poorly paid that they could not make a decent living.
    C. The playwright Eugene O'Neill was just beginning to write his plays for the theater.
    D. Americans rarely attended the theater to see plays except during special holidays.

22. A common theme of stories and novels by immigrants or authors descended from non-Caucasian races is
    A. the struggle of assimilating into American culture.
    B. the difficulty of maintaining one's native tongue.
    C. the longing to return home to one's native land.
    D. the lack of opportunity in the United States.

23. Which statement is NOT true about Native-American literature?
    A. Many Native American stories were lost because they were never written down.
    B. Native American myths and poems continue to be collected and published.
    C. Authors from Native American tribes were the first Americans to be published.
    D. Modern Native American writing often deals with reconciling past injustices.

24. Which of the following is the MOST compelling reason to read a story or book rather than just seeing a movie made from it?
    A. It takes longer to read the book, so it's more memorable.
    B. The theme of a book never comes across well in a movie.
    C. A film can never fully convey what an author has written.
    D. A movie has to be two hours long, so many scenes are cut.

25. Taking American literature as a whole, what does the entire body of work <u>most</u> reflect about Americans at all points in our history?
    A. Americans are seldom satisfied with what's going on in the word at any given time.
    B. Entertainment is more important to Americans than social responsibility.
    C. Americans are free thinkers who examine the human condition.*
    D. Authors in America always want to be the best in the world.

Chapter 2
Literary Structure: American Fiction and Nonfiction

This chapter covers the following Georgia standard(s) relating to **fiction**.

ELAALRL1	Identify, analyze, and apply knowledge of literary structures and elements of American fiction..
ELAALRL2	Identify, analyze, and apply knowledge of theme.
ELAALRL3	Relate literature to its context and historical background as well as to works from other time periods.
ELAALRL4	Use a variety of writing genres to demonstrate a grasp of ideas in literature.
ELAALRL5	Identify literal and figurative language, patterns of word change, and allusions using reference books to increase learning.

This chapter covers the following Georgia standard relating to **nonfiction.**

ELAALRL1	Identify, analyze, and apply knowledge of the purpose, structure, and elements of nonfiction and/or informational materials.
	Analyze and evaluate logic and evidence in an author's argument.
	Analyze and evaluate author's use of
	language, style, syntax, and rhetorical strategies for specific purposes.

These standards encompass the content of Domain I: Reading and American Literature. On the EOCT in American literature and composition, questions in this domain will ask you to demonstrate your understanding of cultural and historical influences on American literature as well as your understanding and analysis of significant literary structures, devices, and concepts.

As you learned in chapter 1, American Literature has a rich history. In addition to tracing the development of American fiction and nonfiction, it is also important to understand the structures and elements that authors have used in their writing. In this chapter, we will explore, analyze, and apply knowledge about American fiction and nonfiction. American poetry and drama will be discussed in chapter 3.

FICTION

Fiction tells a story of people, events, and ideas. An author uses her imagination to create fiction. Fiction can entertain the reader by exposing him to new experiences, or fiction can explore experiences people have in common. Fiction can be a **novel**, like Ernest Hemingway's *The Sun Also Rises,* or it can be a **short story** like Jack London's "To Build a Fire."

Within fiction, there are many **genres:** recognizable categories of fiction that use specific form or technique . Major literary genres in fiction include fantasy, romance, satire, science fiction, allegory, fable, folk tale, legend, and myth.

BUST OF HOMER.

American literature, like the writing of other cultures, is influenced by the literature that came before it. Widely-read texts such as Greek myths, the Bible, and epic poems like *The Odyssey* are often referenced in American literature. Having some knowledge of **classic literature,** like these texts, can help us better understand American literature. We can also use our knowledge of **history** to help us understand literature. American literature spans several hundred years and includes writing from such periods as the colonial era, the Civil War, and the Depression. Knowing the period in American history into which literature fits can give us a better understanding of the literature.

Looking for such connections between literature and the world and understanding the devices authors use to create meaning is called **literary analysis**. Thinking about how and why an author writes enriches our experience with literature. When writing a piece of fiction, an author makes many choices about how he will tell the story. What will happen in the story? When will the story take place? Who will tell the story? What is the point of the story? What emotions should the reader experience? An author considers questions such as these when writing a piece of fiction and makes choices based on how he wants readers to respond.

When analyzing literature, we can see deeper meaning and universal connections between writing and how it relates to society and humanity. As you will see in the following sections, looking for and thinking about literary elements such as **character development**, **theme**, **literary devices**, and **language and style** help us get more out of a story.

LITERARY ELEMENTS

SETTING

Setting is the time and place in which a story occurs. For example, the setting of Margaret Mitchell's *Gone with the Wind* is Georgia during the Civil War and Reconstruction. Setting affects other aspects of the story, such as plot, characters, and theme. A story about a farmer set in colonial America would be quite different from a story about a farmer set during the Great Depression.

PLOT

Plot is the sequence of events in a narrative. For example, the plot of Flannery O'Conner's "A Good Man is Hard to Find" is the adventures of a Georgia family on the way to Florida. An author can use events in the plot to build her theme, constructing the action in such a way that it illustrates her beliefs about life.

There are four steps to developing a plot. The structure of the plot depends on the type of story.

Exposition	the information needed to understand a story
Complication	the problem that begins the conflict
Climax	the turning point as the characters resolve the complication
Resolution	the final events that close the story

Plots do not always progress in this order. In a mystery, for instance, the author will save certain details of plot to reveal at the end of the story. Regardless of order, a complete plot includes all four elements.

TIME AND SEQUENCE

Structure is the way a literary work is organized. The way an author structures his story can provide insight into the characters, action, and theme. An author can arrange the **time** and **sequence** in his novel in different ways to best tell his story.

Here are some ways an author can use time and sequence:

chronological order	events are told in the order they happen, in time order from first event to last
flashback	an interruption in the story that shows the reader something that happened earlier
epistolary narrative	the story is told in a series of letters
in medias res	the narrative starts in the middle of the story rather than from the beginning
foreshadowing	clues suggest events that will happen later in the story
frame narrative	a story within a story; the "frame" is the story that begins and ends the tale, with another story being told in between.

Read the excerpt below and answer the question that follows.

> *Edgar Allan Poe uses foreshadowing in "The Cask of Amontillado." Read the excerpt below then discuss the questions that follow with a classmate. Then share your answers with the class.*

Speaker 1: "Enough," he said; "The cough is a mere nothing; it will not kill me. I shall not die of a cough."

Speaker 2: "True—true," I replied.

How could Speaker 2 know that Speaker 1 will not die of a cough?

What do you predict will happen to Speaker 1?

POINT OF VIEW

Who is telling a story affects the information given. Imagine that you are babysitting two brothers, and you find them fighting in the kitchen, one holding a piece torn out of the other's shirt. Ask each boy what happened, and you will likely get two different stories.

One of the decisions an author makes when writing is from whose **point of view** the story will be told. Who is telling the story? How much information do they have? Point of view affects the story details a reader gets and how and when they get those details.

The most common points of view are:

first person	the narrator uses "I" to tell the story.
third person	the narrator uses "he," "she," or "they" to tell the story and does not participate in the action.
• **third person omniscient**	the narrator knows the thoughts of all characters.
• **third person limited**	the narrator has limited access to the thoughts of the character.

Once a reader knows from whose point of view the story is told, she gets insight into the characters and their actions.

Practice 1:   Literary Elements

Read the passage below then answer the questions that follow.

      I first heard of Antonia on what seemed to me an interminable journey across the great midland plain of North America. I was ten years old then; I had lost both my father and mother within a year, and my Virginia relatives were sending me out to my grandparents, who lived in Nebraska. I traveled in the care of a mountain boy, Jake Marpole, one of the "hands" on my father's old farm under the Blue Ridge, who was now going West to work for my grandfather. Jake's experience of the world was not much wider than mine. He had never been in a railway train until the morning when we set out together to try our fortunes in a new world.

–My Antonia, Willa Cather (1873 –1947)

1.   From whose point of view is the story told?

   A.   Jake Marpole   C.   a 10 year old orphan

   B.   a railway conductor   D.   the grandfather's

2.   In what person is the story told?

   A.   first person   C.   third person limited

   B.   third person omniscient   D.   none of the above

3.   What is the setting of this paragraph?

   A.   a journey across the plains of North America

   B.   the Blue Ridge Mountains of Virginia

   C.   a school in the country

   D.   an airplane on its way west

4.   What topic is MOST likely to be discussed in the plot of the story that follows?

   A.   a mountain climbing adventure   C.   surfing in California

   B.   the identity of Antonia   D.   a journey to Virginia

5.   From the clues given in the passage, which of the following is MOST likely the time period in which this story takes place?

   A.   1400s –1500s   C.   late 1900s – early 2000s

   B.   late 1800s – early 1900s   D.   some time in the future

CHARACTER DEVELOPMENT

Characters are the people who populate a literary work. Characters are important because they help tell the story. To make writing rich and meaningful, an author must make his characters believable and well developed. An author uses **character development** to show readers things like the character's physical appearance and to reveal aspects of the character's personal history, attitudes, motivations, and fears. The more readers can understand and relate to the character, the more believable that character becomes. When readers identify with a character, they are more drawn in to the story.

There are several ways that an author can develop characters.

Physical Description	Descriptions of the character's appearance and style of dress give us clues to a character's values and situation.
Interaction with other characters	How a character speaks with and responds to people around him provides insight into the character's nature.
Interaction with the environment	How a character reacts to events is an indication of his personal history and his character.
Speech	The character's speech reveals things like what part of the country he is from and how much schooling he has had.
Thoughts and feelings	The character's private response to events gives us information about the character's true nature

Paying attention to these clues gives readers a growing picture of the character's purpose and significance in the story.

Practice 2:   Character Development

Read this excerpt from *Little Women* by Louisa May Alcott (1832–1888), and then answer the questions that follow.

Fifteen-year-old Jo was very tall, thin, and brown, and reminded one of a colt, for she never seemed to know what to do with her long limbs, which were very much in her way. She had a decided mouth, a comical nose, and sharp, gray eyes, which appeared to see everything, and were by turns fierce, funny, or thoughtful. Her long, thick hair was her one beauty, but it was usually bundled into a net, to be out of her way. Round shoulders had Jo, big hands and feet, a fly-away look to her clothes, and the uncomfortable appearance of a girl who was rapidly shooting up into a woman and didn't like it.

1. How old is Jo?

    A. 12

    C. 15

    B. 20

    D. The description does not tell us.

2. Which word BEST describes Jo's physical appearance?

    A. awkward   B. graceful   C. elegant   D. immature

3. Which word BEST describes Jo emotionally?

    A. insecure   B. thoughtless   C. indecisive   D. rebellious

4. How would you expect Jo to behave based on her description in the passage above?

    A. She would always obey her parents.

    B. She would look for ways to bother her sisters.

    C. She would not always think before speaking.

    D. She would be afraid to try new things.

THEME

Theme is the underlying meaning or message in a piece of writing. Themes are usually universal; they are common truths that most people can relate to. A work of literature can have more than one theme. Some examples of universal themes are the battle between good and evil, aspects of human nature, the sanctity of life, and the inevitability of death. Some common themes in American literature are the American dream, cultural diversity, and tolerance. For instance, one of the themes in F. Scott Fitzgerald's *The Great Gatsby* is the disintegration of the American dream.

Cultural Diversity

Theme can be subtle and is usually not stated outright. The reader must uncover the theme by considering the elements of the story. To find the theme in a work of fiction:

- Look for clues in the **title**.
- Look for underlying meaning in the **symbols** the author uses.
- Consider the **wording** the author chooses.
- Think of one statement that sums up the author's **message**.

Read the passage below. Try to determine the theme before looking at the answer choices.

George Washington, first president of the United States, was known for his truthfulness. Legend has it that as a boy, George used his new hatchet to cut down one of his father's cherry trees. When his father saw the tree, he asked George if he had done it. Anticipating his father's anger, George was afraid to admit that he had. Nevertheless, the boy decided to tell the truth. He admitted, "Yes, Father. I cut down the cherry tree with my hatchet. I cannot tell a lie." George Washington's father was proud of George for telling the truth.

. What is the BEST statement of the theme?

    A. Young children should not be given hatchets.

    B. Don't cut down trees without asking the owner.

    C. It is always best to tell the truth.

    D. Actions have consequences.

Choices "A" and "B" are lessons George's father and George, respectively, would have learned from this incident. Many people would also call these statements common sense. Choice "D" is true but does not apply to this passage. Choice "C" best describes the overall message, or theme, of the passage.

Practice 3: Theme

Read the passage below. Then answer the questions that follow.

> They stood there in silence watching men and women come and go—solitary and in groups—groups tired and groups laughing—groups respectable and groups questionable—humanity—worn humanity—as it crossed that bridge.
>
> She recalled that first night she had talked with him—that first time a hot day had seemed to her anything more than mere hot day, that night on the Mississippi—where distant hills were to be seen. She remembered how she had looked around the world that night to see if it needed "saving."
>
> It seemed a long time ago since she had not been able to see that the world needed saving.
>
> –from *The Visioning* by Susan Glaspell (1876–1948)

1. What is the theme of this passage?

    A. People in groups don't take life seriously enough.

    B. There are beautiful views from the Mississippi River.

    C. Humanity needs saving.

    D. The world is a crowded, busy place.

2. Which phrase from the passage BEST helps clarify the author's theme?

    A. "humanity—worn humanity"

    B. "the first night she had talked with him"

    C. "that night on the Mississippi"

    D. "that first time a hot day had seemed to be anything more than a hot day"

3. Which of the following descriptions BEST reveals the significance of the bridge in this passage?

    A. A bridge can collapse, resulting in a disaster.

    B. A well-constructed bridge is the result of a smart engineer.

    C. A bridge can pass over water or a ravine.

    D. A bridge could symbolize a transition that the speaker hopes the people will make.

4. Which statement would the author of this passage MOST likely agree with?
   A. Humanity is in need of saving, though many people may not recognize this need.
   B. Humanity is beyond saving, and it is useless to hope for a change.
   C. Most people will achieve everything they want in life.
   D. There are a few people who make life difficult for everyone else.

LITERARY DEVICES

Authors use many other techniques to create meaningful fiction. Following are some common **literary devices** that authors use to enrich and give meaning to works of fiction.

MOOD

Authors also choose their words thoughtfully depending on the mood they want to convey in their writing. **Mood** is the feeling or atmosphere an author creates in his work.

Read the passage that follows. Underline the words and phrases that the author uses to create an eerie mood.

I looked upon the scene before me—upon the mere house, and the simple landscape features of the domain—upon the bleak walls—upon the vacant eye-like windows—upon a few rank sedges—and upon a few white trunks of decayed trees—with an utter depression of soul which I can compare to no earthly sensation more properly than to the after-dream of the reveler upon opium—the bitter lapse into every-day life—the hideous dropping off of the veil.

–"The Fall of the House of Usher" by Edgar Allan Poe

If you identified words like "bleak," "vacant eye-like windows," "rank," "decayed," "depression," "bitter," and "hideous" you are right. Poe uses these words to build an unsettling mood in his short story.

IMAGERY

Imagery is a form of figurative language that involves using words that appeal to the five senses. When an author uses imagery, he writes with the objective of putting a picture in the reader's mind. Using imagery is one of the ways authors can appeal to a reader's aesthetic values. **Aesthetics** are people's responses to and thoughts about art and beauty. An author may use vivid descriptions that prompt a reader to respond to the aesthetic aspects of his writing.

Read the passage that follows. Then close your eyes and try to picture the image.

The Palace Hotel at Fort Romper was painted a light blue, a shade that is on the legs of a kind of heron, causing the bird to declare its position against any background. The Palace Hotel, then, was always screaming and howling in a way that made the dazzling winter landscape of Nebraska seem only a gray swampish hush.

–*The Blue Hotel* by Stephen Crane (1871–1900)

Crane's description of the color of blue and the words "dazzling" and "gray swampish hue" help paint a colorful picture of this scene in the reader's mind.

SYMBOLISM

Symbolism is the author's use of representations to convey meaning. A symbol is used to give an object, person, or idea deeper meaning beyond its literal meaning. A flag might represent patriotism. White could indicate peace or purity. A mountain might mean a challenge. In Nathaniel Hawthorne's *The Scarlet Letter*, the red "A" Hester Prynne wore on her dress was a symbol of the sin she had committed.

IRONY

Irony is a situation or comment which is the opposite of what a reader expects. **Verbal irony** involves saying one thing but meaning just the opposite. For instance, if a hurricane hit during the Super Bowl and an announcer said, "Well, it's a beautiful day for a game," he would be using verbal irony. Irony can also be situational. O. Henry used **situational irony** in his short story "The Gift of the Magi." Desperate for money to buy Christmas gifts, Della sells her hair to buy a watch chain for her husband, who in turn sells his watch to buy her hair combs.

> **Example:** In John Steinbeck's *Of Mice and Men*, George kills his friend Lennie because he loves him. George believes he is being merciful by sparing Lennie a brutal death.

. What literary device did the author use with this murder?

   A. imagery
   B. irony
   C. setting
   D. plot

The answer is B. It is ironic that a character would kill a good friend whom he does not want dead. Answers A, C, and D are all literary devices, but none of them is illustrated here.

ALLUSION

Allusion is a reference to a well-known piece of art, story, person, or event. Authors use allusion to quickly convey an idea or an emotion. Mark Twain used allusion in *The Adventures of Tom Sawyer*. In one scene, Aunt Polly thinks about how difficult Tom is to manage. She blames herself, saying, "I ain't doing my duty by that boy, and that's the Lord's truth, goodness knows. Spare the rod and spile the child, as the Good Book says. I'm a laying up sin and suffering for us both, I know." The saying, "spare the rod and spoil the child," is from the Book of Proverbs in the Bible. Aunt Polly uses it to show that she knows that her unwillingness to punish Tom perpetuates his poor behavior.

Besides the devices discussed here, authors of fiction often employ additional **figurative language** such as **metaphor** (direct comparison), **personification** (object or animal with human qualities), and **hyperbole** (exaggeration), all of which are described in more detail in the next chapter.

Practice 4: Literary Devices

Read the passage. Then answer the questions that follow.

A cloudy day: do you know what that is in a town of iron-works? The sky sank down before dawn, muddy, flat, immovable. The air is thick, clammy with the breath of crowded human beings. It stifles me. I open the window, and, looking out, can scarcely see through the rain the grocer's shop opposite, where a crowd of drunken Irishmen are puffing Lynchburg tobacco in their pipes. I can detect the scent through all the foul smells ranging loose in the air.

The idiosyncrasy of this town is smoke. It rolls sullenly in slow folds from the great chimneys of the iron-foundries, and settles down in black, slimy pools on the muddy streets. Smoke on the wharves, smoke on the dingy boats, on the yellow river,—clinging in a coating of greasy soot to the house-front, the two faded poplars, the faces of the passers-by. The long train of mules, dragging masses of pig-iron through the narrow street, have a foul vapor hanging to their reeking sides. Here, inside, is a little broken figure of an angel pointing upward from the mantel-shelf; but even its wings are covered with smoke, clotted and black. Smoke everywhere! A dirty canary chirps desolately in a cage beside me. Its dream of green fields and sunshine is a very old dream,—almost worn out, I think.

–Rebecca Harding Davis (1831–1910), "Life in the Iron-Mills"

1. Why do you think the author sets her description on a cloudy day?

   A. to symbolize the despondency she describes in the town

   B. to symbolize the hope she feels for the next day

   C. to ask the reader for help in escaping the town

   D. to show the contrast between day and night in the town

2. Which sense does "foul smells" address?

   A. taste   B. touch   C. smell   D. sight

3. Throughout, the author describes the air as thick and stifling. What best describes what the stifling air symbolizes?

   A. the town, which is also stifling

   B. the crowds, which the narrator does not like

   C. the smoke from the pipes, which makes it hard to breathe

   D. the window, which will not open

4. What mood does the author set by using words like "muddy," "flat," "clammy," "foul," "raging."

   A. a cheerful impression   C. an abandoned impression

   B. a hopeful impression   D. a depressing impression

5. What image that the author presents is MOST ironic?
   A. the animals seem to be just as susceptible to the depressing surroundings as the human beings are
   B. smoke and air, normally deemed light or even weightless, are described as thick and heavy
   C. the men on the street are smoking even though the air is already dense with smoke
   D. an angel figurine, a symbol of light and redemption, is broken

NONFICTION

What do an email, an article in *The Atlanta Journal Constitution*, and the instructions that came with an iPod have in common? All are examples of **nonfiction** writing. We encounter nonfiction materials daily. Major literary genres in nonfiction include biographies and autobiographies, diaries and journals, letters, speeches, essays, and memoirs. Other types of nonfiction include articles, letters, and advertisements in periodicals (newspapers, magazines) as well as informational materials (such as technical documents).

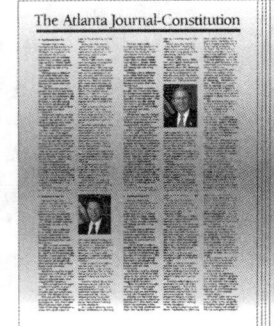

Readers can look for several literary elements to increase their understanding of nonfiction. When reading nonfiction it is important to know:

- **Who** wrote the text   What is the author's connection to the material she is writing about? Is she an expert in the field? Is it a personal experience?

- **Why** author wrote the text   Is the author's purpose to inform? To persuade? To explain? To describe?

- **When** the author wrote the text   What was happening at the time? Is the information still relevant?

LANGUAGE AND STYLE

An author does not just write the first words that come into his head. Authors use **language** and **style** purposefully, depending on their objectives for writing. Think about how you might choose different words and mannerisms when speaking with a friend as opposed to speaking with your grandmother. An author also chooses words carefully depending on the feelings he wants to evoke. An author's **rhetoric** (which means using language effectively and persuasively) refers to his choice of words and the crafting of those words into a meaningful and effective piece of writing. Authors use language for **rhetorical purposes** (to effect meaning or make a point) and **aesthetic purposes** (to create beauty and elicit emotional response).

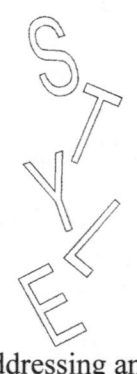

An author often chooses the words he uses and the way he uses them based on whom he is addressing and the point he wants to make. His **language** (the words he uses), **style** (the way he uses the words) and **syntax** (the grammatical structures he uses) depends on his audience.

Take for instance a politician writing two speeches to address two different groups regarding an auto manufacturing plant. He knows that the group of unionized auto workers has different interests and different frames of reference than the environmental group concerned about the chemical emissions of the auto plant. Therefore, not only will the topics of each speech differ, but so will the words the politician chooses and the style in which he presents his words. In the auto worker speech, he may use phrases like, "protect your pension" and "each of you is important in this union." In the environmental speech, he may use phrases like, "we will be decisive in our actions" and "we can't afford to destroy our natural resources."

An author purposefully selects which words he uses and how he uses them in order to elicit a response from his audience.

ANALYZING AN AUTHOR'S ARGUMENT

Sometimes authors write purely to give information. For example, an article in an encyclopedia is intended to present facts. **Facts** are indisputable evidence that can be proven. "Abraham Lincoln was the 16th president of the United States," is an example of a fact.

Sometimes authors write to persuade. In **persuasive writing**, an author attempts to convince the reader that his viewpoint is correct, or that the reader should take the course of action that the author recommends. Persuasive writing uses opinion. An **opinion** is a personal viewpoint on a topic that not everyone agrees on. "Abraham Lincoln was the best president the United States will ever have," is an example of an opinion.

Once an author states his opinion, he then must prove his opinion, or **claim**. He does this by presenting **evidence** that he believes will make his readers agree with him. **Evidence** is the **proof** an author uses to support the claim he has made. The author's topic and audience dictate the best kind of evidence to use. A person writing a letter to the *Atlanta Journal Constitution* about the conditions in a local animal shelter might include eyewitness accounts of what is happening there. A person writing an email praising a colleague's work on a report might point out the specific ways the employee helps the company be more productive.

> **Examples, strong** evidence: relevant examples, quotes from experts, studies and statistics

> **Examples, weak** evidence: examples that don't support the claim, vague claims, generalizations

Read the following claim and the two pieces of evidence that follow. Which piece of evidence best supports the claim?

Claim

Everyone should be tested for pre-diabetes at each annual checkup.

Evidence

1. Early intervention can help manage this disease before a patient experiences any symptoms. For some people with pre-diabetes, intervening early can return elevated blood glucose levels to the normal range and prevent it from developing into full-blown diabetes.

2. Treatment for pre-diabetes involves losing a moderate amount of weight through diet and exercise.

If you chose evidence point 1, you are right. This first point gives specific examples of how pre-diabetes screenings can have a positive impact on maintaining health. Point 2 does not support the claim. It is about early treatment rather than supporting the claim that everyone should be tested.

Logic

One of the most important components of persuasive writing is logic. **Logic** is the rational way of arriving at a conclusion. A strong argument supports an opinion using facts in a logical manner. A weak argument lacks the logic and proof a reader needs in order to be persuaded.

Inductive reasoning is the process of arriving at a conclusion based on a set of observations. Reasoning begins with observing specific details and leads to forming a general conclusion. Inductive reasoning is valuable because it allows us to form ideas about groups of things in real life. For example,

> **Observation**: My baby sister cries.
>
> **Observation**: My baby nephew cries.
>
> **Conclusion**: All babies cry.

Deductive reasoning is the process by which a person makes conclusions based on previously known facts. Deductive reasoning begins with general ideas and moves to specific examples. For example,

> **General idea**:   All children go to school.
>
> **Specific example**: John is a child.
>
> **Conclusion**:   John goes to school.

Generalizations are vague statements not supported by evidence. They are not helpful for supporting an argument.

> **Example:** "Symphonies are boring."

A **logical fallacy** is an error in reasoning. They are not helpful for supporting an argument.

> **Example:** "When the rooster crows, the sun rises. Therefore, the rooster causes the sun torise."

Recognizing the difference between logical and illogical arguments helps a reader evaluate the validity of an author's argument.

Practice 5: Analyzing an Author's Argument

Read the passage then answer the questions that follow.

Extended School Day

Our school district is considering extending the school day by an hour. The purpose of this change would be to provide a time for students to get help with their homework. This might be useful to some students. I think that the extra hour should be optional. Students who need extra help are probably just lazy anyway. Many students don't need an hour's worth, if any, help with their homework. This extra hour would take time away from other activities. 65% of our student body participates in after-school sports or clubs. An extra hour of school would take away time from these extra-curricular activities. In addition, many students work and cannot afford an hour's worth of lost pay each day. For some, an extra hour of homework help would be useful. For most, an extra hour of school would be both inconvenient and illogical.

1. What is the author's purpose in writing this piece?
   A. to inform
   B. to persuade
   C. to explain
   D. to describe a process

2. Which of the following sentences states an opinion?
   A. I think that the extra hour should be optional.
   B. 65% of our student body participates in after-school sports or clubs.
   C. Our school district is considering extending the school day by an hour.
   D. The purpose of this change would be to provide a time for students to get help with their homework.

3. Who is most likely the author's intended audience?
   A. her parents
   B. the school board
   C. a friend living in another state
   D. her gym teacher

4. Which of the following sentences is an example of a generalization?
   A. An extra hour of school would take away time from these extracurricular activities.
   B. I think that the extra hour should be optional.
   C. 65% of our student body participates in after-school sports or clubs.
   D. Students who need extra help are probably just lazy anyway.

RHETORICAL STRATEGIES

As with fiction, authors writing nonfiction also choose words carefully to make their writing powerful and memorable. **Rhetorical strategies** are the stylistic techniques authors use to make their writing stand out. Some examples of rhetorical strategies are:

Allusion   a reference to a well-known piece of art, story, person, or event

> **Example:** "She has a Mona Lisa smile."

Stereotype   a generalization that allows a reader to quickly identify a character with a group

> **Example:** "During the Cold War, a Russian was an enemy."

Simile   a comparison using "like" or "as"

> **Example:** "Her eyes were as big as saucers."

Metaphor   a comparison without using "like" or "as"

> **Example:** "Grandpa is a cunning old fox."

Hyperbole   a deliberate exaggeration

> **Example:** "I've heard that excuse a million times."

Litotes   a deliberate understatement used for emphasis

> **Example:** "That was a nice little snack," he said, loosening his belt a notch after leaving the banquet hall.

Rhetorical question   a question asked for effect rather than in expectation of a reply

> **Example:** "Can we afford to gamble with our children's futures?"

Practice 6:   Rhetorical Strategies

Read the sentences and identify the rhetorical strategy.

1. "It has rained every day for a week! Pretty soon we are going to have to build an ark!"
   A. stereotype   C. allusion
   B. metaphor   D. rhetorical question

2. "I'm so hungry I could eat a raw bear without salt."
   A. metaphor   B. hyperbole   C. allusion   D. litotes

3. "You look as pretty as a picture."
   A. simile   B. metaphor   C. hyperbole   D. stereotype

4. "Should children die because their parents can't afford healthcare?"
   A. hyperbole   C. rhetorical question
   B. allusion   D. simile

5. Old people spend every day playing bingo and snooping on their neighbors.
   A. litotes   B. allusion   C. metaphor   D. stereotype

6. As Tyrone cleans his messy room, he yells to his mom, "I've never had so much fun in my entire life."
   A. stereotype   C. hyperbole
   B. litotes   D. rhetorical question

7. Nilsa is the sunshine in my life.
   A. metaphor   B. simile   C. hyperbole   D. allusion

CHAPTER 2 SUMMARY

Fiction is imaginative writing that creates characters, people, places, and ideas. Important elements of fiction include the following:

- **Setting**: the time and place in which a story takes place
- **Plot**: the sequence of events in a work of literature
- **Time and sequence**: how a literary work is organized
- **Point of view**: the perspective from which a story is told
- **Character development**: the process of conveying information about characters
- **Theme**: the underlying message in a piece of writing
- **Language and style**: how an author's choice of words affects literature
- **Mood**: the feeling an author creates in a piece of literature
- **Imagery**: the use of words that appeal to the five senses
- **Symbolism**: the use of representations to convey meaning
- **Irony**: a situation or comment that is the opposite of what one expects
- **Allusion**: a reference to a well-known piece of art, story, person, or event

Nonfiction is writing that is true. Important elements of nonfiction include many of the above plus the following:

Argument: author's use of a claim, evidence, and logic to persuade an audience

Rhetorical strategies: stylistic techniques that make writing memorable

CHAPTER 2 REVIEW

Read the speech below. Then answer the questions that follow.

I have a dream that one day on the red hills of Georgia the sons of former slaves and the sons of former slave owners will be able to sit down together at the table of brotherhood.

I have a dream that one day even the state of Mississippi, a desert state sweltering with the heat of injustice and oppression, will be transformed into an oasis of freedom and justice.

I have a dream that my four little children will one day live in a nation where they will not be judged by the color of their skin but by the content of their character.

I have a dream today.

I have a dream that one day the state of Alabama, whose governor's lips are presently dripping with the words of interposition and nullification, will be transformed into a situation where little black boys and black girls will be able to join hands with little white boys and white girls and walk together as sisters and brothers.

–Martin Luther King, Jr. (1929–1968), "I Have a Dream"

1. What mood does King's repetition of the words "I have a dream" create?
   A. a feeling of hope and inspiration
   B. a feeling of despair and frustration
   C. a feeling of tension and discord
   D. a feeling of anger and violence

2. What is King's purpose in speaking?
   A. to describe past wrongs
   B. to inspire change
   C. to explain history
   D. to entertain a crowd

3. In the first paragraph, what does the phrase, "the table of brotherhood" symbolize?
   A. joining hands to work together
   B. coming together as equals
   C. a table made by blacks and whites
   D. having a dream

4. Which of the following is an example of imagery in the passage?
   A. the sons of former slaves
   B. the red hills of Georgia
   C. my four little children
   D. I have a dream.

5. What audience is King most likely addressing?
   A. blacks
   B. whites
   C. both blacks and whites who want to change racial relations
   D. the President of the United States

6. What best describes the theme of this passage?

    A. racial relations can and should be improved in America

    B. we should return to slavery

    C. blacks are better than whites

    D. some people have better dreams than others

7. What is the point of view expressed in this passage?

    A. third person omniscient

    B. third person limited

    C. first person

    D. second person

Read the passage below. Then answer the questions that follow.

"There's one thing I wanted to speak with you about," said Miss Ophelia. "Augustine promised Tom his liberty, and began the legal forms necessary to it. I hope you will use your influence to have it perfected."

"Indeed, I shall do no such thing!" said Marie, sharply. "Tom is one of the most valuable servants on the place,—it couldn't be afforded, any way. Besides, what does he want of liberty? He's a great deal better off as he is."

"But he does desire it, very earnestly, and his master promised it," said Miss Ophelia.

"I dare say he does want it," said Marie; "they all want it, just because they are a discontented set,—always wanting what they haven't got. Now, I'm principled against emancipating, in any case. Keep a negro under the care of a master, and he does well enough, and is respectable; but set them free, and they get lazy, and won't work, and take to drinking, and go all down to be mean, worthless fellows, I've seen it tried, hundreds of times. It's no favor to set them free."

"But Tom is so steady, industrious, and pious."

"O, you needn't tell me! I've see a hundred like him. He'll do very well, as long as he's taken care of,—that's all."

–Harriet Beecher Stowe (1811–1896), *Uncle Tom's Cabin*

8. What literary device does Marie use in the phrase, "set them free, and they get lazy"?

    A. symbolism   B. mood   C. imagery   D. stereotyping

9. What best describes the theme of this passage?

    A. It is important to be honest.

    B. the certainty of death

    C. racial inequality during slavery

    D. the American dream

10. How does Marie's style of speech contribute to the theme?

    A. Her words show that she is questioning the justice of slavery.

    B. Her words show that she believes that slavery is justified.

    C. Her words show that she is working undercover to free slaves.

    D. Her words show that she thinks liberty can be earned.

11. What best describes Marie's viewpoints?
    A.   She thinks that negroes need the guidance of white people.
    B.   She thinks that slavery should be against the law.
    C.   She thinks that all people are created equal.
    D.   She thinks that Tom should be freed.

12. How does the feeling of this passage from *Uncle Tom's Cabin* differ from Martin Luther King's speech in the previous passage?
    A.   King's speech offers a hopefulness that *Uncle Tom's Cabin* does not.
    B.   The feeling of King's speech is depressing.
    C.   King's speech creates a more unsettled feeling than *Uncle Tom's Cabin* does.
    D.   *Uncle Tom's Cabin* creates a joyous feeling.

13. What best describes the setting of this passage?
    A.   Sweden in 1960   C.   the American South during slavery
    B.   America in 2007   D.   New England during the colonial period

Read the passage below. Then answer the questions that follow.

Edna walked on down to the beach rather mechanically, not noticing anything special except that the sun was hot. She was not dwelling upon any particular train of thought. She had done all the thinking which was necessary after Robert went away, when she lay awake upon the sofa till morning.

She had said over and over to herself: "To-day it is Arobin; to-morrow it will be some one else. It makes no difference to me, it doesn't matter about Leonce Pontellier—but Raoul and Etienne!"She understood now clearly what she had meant long ago when she said to Adele Ratignolle that she would give up the unessential, but she would never sacrifice herself for her children.

Despondency had come upon her there in the wakeful night, and had never lifted. There was no one thing in the world that she desired. There was no human being whom she wanted near her except Robert; and she even realized that the day would come when he, too, and the thought of him would melt out of her existence, leaving her alone. The children appeared before her like antagonists who had overcome her; who had overpowered and sought to drag her into the soul's slavery for the rest of her days. But she knew a way to elude them. She was not thinking of these things when she walked down to the beach.

The water of the Gulf stretched out before her, gleaming with the million lights of the sun. The voice of the sea is seductive, never ceasing, whispering, clamoring, murmuring, inviting the soul to wander in abysses of solitude. All along the white beach, up and down, there was no living thing in sight. A bird with a broken wing was beating the air above, reeling, fluttering, circling disabled down, down to the water.

–From *The Awakening* by Kate Chopin (1850–1904)

14. What BEST describes the setting of this passage?
   A. a quiet beach
   B. a bustling city
   C. a river at night
   D. a swimming pool

15. What BEST describes the character of Edna in this passage?
   A. an excited bride planning her wedding
   B. a despondent woman who has lost her will to live
   C. a child with a difficult decision to make
   D. a woman worried about her sister

16. Which of the following sentences from the passage is an example of imagery?
   A. Despondency had come upon her there in the wakeful night, and had never lifted.
   B. She was not dwelling upon any particular train of thought.
   C. But she knew a way to elude them.
   D. The water of the Gulf stretched out before her, gleaming with the million lights of the sun.

17. From what point of view is this passage told?
   A. third person omniscient
   B. first person
   C. third person limited
   D. a child's

18. Which of the following BEST describes the way the author portrays the sea in the last paragraph?

   A. The sea is dangerous.
   B. The sea is a wonderful place to surf.
   C. The sea beckons people to the refuge it provides.
   D. Fishing is an exciting sea sport.

19. What emotion does NOT match the language the author uses to describe the sea?
   A. gentle   B. safe   C. inviting   D. treacherous

20. Which words does the author use in the last paragraph that contribute to the feeling the author wishes to evoke?
   A. "murmuring" and "clamoring"
   B. "voice" and "ceasing"
   C. "mazes" and "voice"
   D. "wander" and "sea"

Chapter 3
Literary Structure:American Poetry and Drama

This chapter covers the following Georgia standard(s) relating to **poetry**.

ELAALRL1	Identify and analyze elements of poetry from various periods of American literature.
ELAALRL4	Demonstrate awareness of the author's use of stylistic devices. Analyze the use of imagry and language as it contributes to theme.

This chapter covers the following Georgia standard relating to **drama.**

ELAALRL4	Identify, analyze, and apply knowledge of the themes, structures, and elements of dramatic American literature. Identify and analyze types of American dramatic literature.

In addition to fiction and nonfiction, discussed in the previous chapter, there are two other major types of literature: **poetry** and **drama**, which are reviewed in this chapter.

POETRY

Poetry is a form of literature that can be either spoken or written. Poems are generally short, and they often express deep emotion. Poetry may also be set to music and take the form of a song.

American poetry began during the Colonial Era. The poems that colonists wrote as an expression of art were naturally influenced by British poetry. As America's unique identity developed, so did its poetic forms. By the 1800s, British literature had less influence, and a distinct American style began to emerge. Walt Whitman, Ezra Pound, and T. S. Elliot are famous and influential poets in the history of American poetry.

Walt Whitman

A poet's **personal life** and the **times in which he writes** both contribute to and affect his poetry. A poet's experiences, like personal loss or a national tragedy, will manifest themselves in his writing. The period in time during which a poet writes can also influence his poetry. For instance, a poem about nature by Henry David Thoreau written during the Transcendentalist period, which celebrated nature, might be very different from a poem written about nature immediately after Hurricane Katrina.

Poets choose their **words** and **structure** their poems with particular care, as poems are generally the shortest form of literature and are intended to express deep meaning and emotion. Poets use specific devices to create meaningful, sensation-rich poetry including **form**, **sound**, and **figurative language**.

TYPES OF POEMS

Narrative poems tell stories. Epics and ballads are narrative poems.

An **epic** poem tends to be very long. *Patterson*, by poet William Carlos Williams (1883–1963), is a five-volume poem, longer than many novels.

A **ballad** is a narrative poem that is meant to be sung. Ballads generally end tragically. Gwendolyn Brooks' poem "The Ballad of Late Annie" is an example of ballad poetry.

A **lyric poem** is a short poem in which the poet expresses thoughts and feelings. Lyric poetry does not tell a story; rather, it shows the poet's intense personal emotions. Lyric poetry tends to be melodic as originally this type of poem was set to music. "I Hear America Singing" by Walt Whitman is an example of a lyric poem.

A poet determines which type of poem he will write in part based upon the theme he wishes to address in his poetry. As in other forms of literature, **theme** is the message a writer intends to convey in his work. Themes in lyric poetry, given its emotional nature, might be awe at God's creations or sorrow at the inevitability of death. Themes in narrative poetry, because of its story-like nature, might be the effects of pride or the triumph of good over evil.

POETIC FORMS

There are several different forms a writer can use when creating a poem. Poems can follow a particular structure (fixed form) or no particular structure (free verse).

Fixed form poetry rhymes and has a traditional structure. A sonnet is an example of fixed form. A **sonnet** is a 14-line poem that follows a strict structure and rhyme scheme.

> **Example:** "Sonnet VI" by Alan Seeger (1888–1916)
>
> Give me the treble of thy horns and hoofs,
> The ponderous undertones of 'bus and tram,
> A garret and a glimpse across the roofs
> Of clouds blown eastward over Notre Dame,
> The glad-eyed streets and radiant gatherings
> Where I drank deep the bliss of being young,
> The strife and sweet potential flux of things
> I sought Youth's dream of happiness among!
> It walks here aureoled with the city-light,
> Forever through the myriad-featured mass
> Flaunting not far its fugitive embrace, —
> Heard sometimes in a song across the night,
> Caught in a perfume from the crowds that pass,
> And when love yields to love seen face to face.

Blank verse is another example of poetry in fixed form. Blank verse is a poem written in unrhymed iambic pentameter. **Iambic pentameter** is a pattern in poetry consisting of five iambic feet per line with a pattern of the unstressed syllable followed by one stressed syllable.

> **Example:** Here are the first few lines of "Death of Hired Man" by Robert Frost (1874–1963), a combination of lyric and dramatic poetry that uses blank verse.
>
> Mary sat musing on the lamp-flame at the table
>
> Waiting for Warren. When she heard his step,
>
> She ran on tip-toe down the darkened passage
>
> To meet him in the doorway with the news
>
> And put him on his guard. "Silas is back."

Free verse follows no particular structure, rhythm, or rhyme. The poet Walt Whitman (1819–1892) wrote extensively in free verse. This excerpt from "Song of Myself," a poem in his famous collection *Leaves of Grass*, shows the irregular structure his poetry tended to take.

All truths wait in all things
They neither hasten their own delivery nor resist it,
They do not need the obstetric forceps of the surgeon.

Read the poem below. Then answer the questions that follow.

November

Yet one smile more, departing, distant sun!
    One mellow smile through the soft vapoury air,
Ere, o'er the frozen earth, the loud winds run,
    Or snows are sifted o'er the meadows bare.
One smile on the brown hills and naked trees,
    And the dark rocks whose summer wreaths are cast,
And the blue gentian flower, that, in the breeze,
    Nods lonely, of her beauteous race the last.
Yet a few sunny days, in which the bee
    Shall murmur by the hedge that skirts the way,
The cricket chirp upon the russet lea,
    And man delight to linger in thy ray.
Yet one rich smile, and we will try to bear
The piercing winter frost, and winds, and darkened air.

–William Cullen Bryant (1794–1878)

1. This poem is written in what form?

    A. fixed form
    B. free form
    C. internal rhyme
    D. narrative style

The answer is "A." This poem is written in fixed form. Each line follows a set pattern of rhyme, with every other line rhyming (and the final two lines rhyming). This is a 14 line sonnet, which is an example of fixed verse poetry.

2. This poem can best be described what type of poem?
    A. epic   B. ballad   C. narrative   D. lyric

The answer is D. This poem is best described as an example of lyric poetry. It is not a narrative poem that tells a story, which eliminates C as a possible answer. Choices A and B are forms of narrative poetry so they can be eliminated as well.

RHYTHM AND RHYME

Rhythm is a musical quality in poetry produced by the repetition of stressed and unstressed syllables. This pattern of sounds is designed to create a sense of movement in the poetry. It generally consists of one heavily stressed syllable and one or more lightly stressed syllable.

Read the excerpt below aloud to a classmate. Listen for the patterns of stress on the syllables.

> It was many and many a year ago,
> In a kingdom by the sea,
> That a maiden there lived whom you may know
> By the name of Annabel Lee
> And this maiden she lived with no other thought
> Than to love and be loved by me.

> –From "Annabel Lee" by Edgar Allan Poe (1809–1849)

Did you hear how your voice went up and down as it went from one syllable to the next? That pattern of stressed and unstressed syllables is the rhythm of the poem.

Rhythm is important in poetry that is set to music. In fact, rhythm took precedence over words in some Native American songs. Alice Fletcher, who lived with various tribes of Native Americans in the late 1800s, recorded this portion of a song about planting corn:

> How like lines of buffalo upon the slope,
>
> Lie our little brown hills, so full now of hope.
>
> Refrain: Ah hey they,
>
> Ah hey hey they,
>
> Ah hey they ha!
>
> Ah hey they,
>
> Ah hey hey they,
>
> Ah hey they ha!

> –from *Indian Games and Dances with Native Songs*, Alice C. Fletcher (1838–1923)

Notice how the rhythm of the refrain creates a sense of movement. This song was performed in conjunction with a dance, accentuating the feeling of movement in the song.

Other sound devices that a poet might use are:

Alliteration: a sound device using the repetition of similar sounds at the beginning of words

> **Example:** the tongue twister "She sells seashells by the seashore"

Consonance: a sound device using the repetition of consonant sounds at the end of words

> **Example:** brick/clock and stuff /off

Assonance: a sound device using repetition or pattern of similar vowel sounds

> **Example:** In "Twinkle, twinkle little star," the short "i" sound is repeated in the first line.

RHYME

Rhyme is a sound device in which the ending sounds of two or more words are the same. Poetry does not need to rhyme. Rhyme can be used for emphasis or to make a poem feel lighthearted. Therefore, the poet's purpose in writing and her intended meaning can affect whether or not a poet chooses to use rhyme in a poem.

A poet who chooses to make her poem rhyme might use one of the following common types of rhyme:

End rhyme: rhyme in the end word or syllable of a line of poetry

> **Example:** Rock-a-bye-baby
>
> On the tree**top**
> When the wind blows,
> The cradle will **rock**.
> When the bough breaks,
> The cradle will **fall**
> And down will come baby
> Cradle and **all**

(The author of this well-known lullaby was reportedly a pilgrim who sailed on the *Mayflower*.)

Rhyme scheme is the pattern of rhyme in a poem and is indicated using letters of the alphabet. A different letter is assigned to each end rhyme.

Read the following poem aloud. Then look at the rhyme scene as indicated by the letters after each line.

> If I can stop one heart from breaking, (a)
>
> I shall not live in vain; (b)
>
> If I can ease one life the aching, (a)
>
> Or cool one pain, (b)
>
> Or help one fainting robin (c)
>
> Unto his nest again, (b)
>
> I shall not live in vain. (b)

–Poem VI by Emily Dickinson (1830–1886)

Slant rhyme: rhyme when the final consonants rhyme, but the vowel sounds do not, as in *brown* and *brawn* or *done* and *bone*. Slant rhyme is also known as **half rhyme** or **near rhyme**.

Example: Hope is the thing with feathers

> That perches in the **soul**,
>
> And sings the tune without the words,
>
> And never stops at **all**.

–Emily Dickinson

Internal rhyme: rhyme within a line of poetry

Example: Once upon a midnight **dreary**, while I pondered weak and **weary**.

–from "The Raven," Edgar Allan Poe

Read the passage below. Then answer the questions that follow.

> One golden summer day,
> Along the forest-way,
> Young Colin passed with blithesome steps alert.
>
>
> His locks with careless grace
> Rimmed round his handsome face
> And drifted outward on the airy surge.

–from "The Lost Heart" by Horatio Alger (1832–1899)

1. What type of rhyme does the author use in this poem?
   A. internal rhyme
   C. end rhyme
   B. slant rhyme
   D. no rhyme is used

The answer is C. The poet uses rhyme in the end words of the lines of poetry.

2. What is the rhyme scheme of this poem?
   A. aab bbc
   B. aab ccd
   C. aba aba
   D. abb ccd

The answer is B. In lines 1 and 2, "day" and "way" rhyme, so both are assigned the letter "a." In line 3, "alert" does not rhyme so it is assigned the next letter, "b." In lines 4 and 5, "face" and "grace" rhyme so they are assigned the next letter, which is "c." "Surge" in line 6 is assigned the letter "d" as it does not rhyme with any of the above.

LANGUAGE

An author's choice of and use of words affects the meaning of his poetry. **Diction** refers to the author's choice of words. Words have specific and sometimes multiple meanings. Therefore, an author must choose words carefully to create the response he wishes his reader to have. Poorly chosen words can ruin the meaning and effect of a poem. For example, when describing a treacherous river that had claimed the life of one's love, a writer would likely use words like angry, frothing, and snarling, rather than words like gentle, dancing, and merry.

Tone expresses the author's attitude toward her subject. Just as you take on a different tone of voice depending on who you are talking to and what you are talking about, authors also take different tones in their work. For instance, tone may be hopeful, condemning, approving, or angry.

As with other types of literature, **mood** in poetry is the feeling an author creates in her writing. An author uses description and well-chosen words to make the reader feel emotions like fear, uncertainty and relief.

An author may also use **syntax**, or grammatical structures, to create meaning. An author may intentionally make subject verb agreement or objects of statements vague in order to make a universal statement or create a response of confusion or uncertainty in the reader.

FIGURATIVE LANGUAGE

Like writers of other types of literature, poets use literary devices such as irony and mood to convey meaning and elicit a response from their readers. Figurative language is of particular importance in poetry, where words are often limited and must therefore be packed with meaning.

Figurative language is the use of images and words that are loaded with meaning, allowing the reader to experience the emotions and viewpoints of the author. Figurative language is imaginative. It goes beyond the literal meaning of words to produce a response in the reader.

Figurative language is a common device used in literature. You will recognize several of the following devices from Chapter 2.

Types of Figurative Language

Allusion: a reference to a well-known story, piece of art, person, or event

        Example: Jen is a real Scrooge when it comes to money.

Conceit: an extended metaphor that applies to an entire poem

        Example: Colonial poet Edward Taylor (1642–1729) used conceit in his poem "Houswifery" to compare the making of cloth to God's salvation of man.

Hyperbole: an exaggeration or overstatement

        Example: a mile-high stack of pancakes

Imagery   the use of words that appeal to the five senses

        Example: Cold fingers of air crept under the door.

Irony   figure of speech in which the ordinary meaning of the words is more or less the opposite of what the poet intends

        Example: Help had arrived quickly, but the firehouse had already burned down.

Personification   giving human qualities to things that are not human, such as animals or objects

        Example: The dark was menacing.

Metaphor   a comparison without using "like" or "as."

        Example: Her hair is silk.

Metonymy   substituting a word for another word that is closely associated with it

        Example: "The press" refers to the news media.

Paradox   a statement that seems contradictory but upon reflection makes sense

        Example: "Slow and steady wins the race."

Simile   a comparison using "like" or "as"

        Example: The clouds are like pulled cotton.

Symbolism	the author's use of representations to convey meaning
	Example: Arose can symbolize beauty.
Synecdoche	a part is used to represent a whole or a whole is used to represent a part
	Example: "All hands on deck!" Part of the sailor (hands) is used to represent the entire sailor.
Understatement	the opposite of hyperbole
	Example: "That was a nice little snack," he said, loosening his belt a notch after leaving the banquet hall.

An author's use of figurative language can contribute to theme. Consider the theme of the inevitability of death. An author may portray death as tragic and heartbreaking by choosing words and images that create a dark, depressing tone. Or, he may portray death as a natural stage of life by using words and images that create a calm and soothing tone.

Practice 1: Language

Read the two excerpts of poetry below. Then answer the questions that follow each.

> A city street that is busy and wide is ground by a thousand wheels,
> And a burden of traffic on its breast is all it ever feels:
> It is dully conscious of weight and speed and of work that never ends,
> But it cannot be human like Main Street, and recognise its friends.

–from "Main Street" by Joyce Kilmer

1. What type of figurative language does the author use in this poem?

    A. allusion   B. personification   C. hyperbole   D. simile

2. How does the writer's diction in his use of phrases like "ground by a thousand wheels," "burden," and "work that never ends" affect the meaning of the poem?

    A. The writer uses this language to show that the street is subjected to heavy use.
    B. The writer uses this language to show how the town is in decline.
    C. The writer uses this language to show how the street is now abandoned.
    D. The writer uses this language to show how the street was destroyed.

O TENDERLY the haughty day
Fills his blue urn with fire;
One morn is in the mighty heaven,
And one in our desire.
The cannon booms from town to town,
Our pulses beat not less,
The joy bells chime their tidings down,
Which children's voices bless.

–from "ODE" by R W Emerson

3. What type of figurative language does the author use in this poem?
   A. imagery   B. metaphor   C. simile   D. metonymy

4. What kind of mood does the author set in this poem with words like "mighty," "pulses beat," and "joy bells"?
   A. a fearful and suspicious tone   C. a quiet and solemn tone
   B. an angry and revengeful tone   D. a proud and exciting tone

Poetry, as a short and emotionally rich form of literature, provides an excellent way to see how an author crafts his work to reflect its theme. Poetic structure, form, rhythm, rhyme, and language all come together to create underlying meaning in poetry. By analyzing a writer's use of poetic devices, we can uncover the message in the poetry.

DRAMA

Drama is literature that is meant to be read aloud and acted out—in other words, a play. Two well-known American plays are *Death of a Salesman* by Arthur Miller and *The Glass Menagerie* by Tennessee Williams. When writing a play, an author (who may also be referred to as a **playwright**) must envision many elements beyond just the plot—things like a character's tone of voice and how his movements and gestures on stage affect the meaning of his words, as well as technical elements like costumes, props and lighting. All of these elements affect the feeling of a play and the meaning an audience will take away from it.

TYPES OF DRAMA

A **tragedy** is a serious play with a sorrowful ending. Tragedies might seek to comment on important religious, political, social, or personal issues. *The Iceman Cometh*, which looks at the hopelessness of a group of people in a bar and ends in death, is a tragedy by Eugene O'Neill.

A **comedy** is a play intended to amuse the audience. A comedy often addresses the same topics as a tragedy does, looking at the humorous side of the characters' actions as they solve a problem. While a comedy is not always funny, it is lighthearted in nature. Neil Simon's *Rumors*, in which comic complications develop as people try to cover up scandalous events, is an example of a comedy.

A **political drama** is a drama that contains political components. A political drama might describe a political event or advocate a certain political view. For example, in *The Crucible*, Arthur Miller used the Salem witch trials to make a political statement about the McCarthy hearings of the 1950s.

A **modern drama** is a drama that explores themes of alienation and disconnectedness. Modern drama seeks to make the audience feel like it is looking in on real life. Marita Bonner's *The Purple Flower* is a modern drama.

Theatre of the absurd is a drama that portrays human life as without meaning. Theatre of the absurd depicts the frivolity of human existence. This type of drama tends to be disjointed and lacking in logical elements and structures such as plot and setting. Edward Albee's play *Who's Afraid of Virginia Woolf?* is an example of theatre of the absurd.

DRAMATIC ELEMENTS

As with other types of literature, analyzing various elements of drama can enhance the reader's understanding of a play. Understanding how an author uses characters, structures and dramatic devices gives a reader greater insight into the play's meaning.

CHARACTERS

Characters are the people in a play. Plays generally have the following character roles:

Protagonist	the main character of a play
Antagonist	the character who causes problems for the protagonist
Foil	the character who is the subject of jokes and who often serves as a contrast for the protagonist
Confidant	a character who serves as a "listener" to either the protagonist or the antagonist, thereby revealing the characters' thoughts and emotions to the audience

How a character looks, speaks and acts can give us important clues about the character's true nature. An author can develop a dramatic character through use of:

Physical description	how the character looks
	Example: Is she tall? Well- dressed? Slovenly?
Dialogue	how the character talks
	Example: Does he speak in dialect? Have an impressive vocabulary?
Action	what the character does
	Example: Does she have a bad temper? Is she foolhardy?
Gesture	how the character's motions and expressions reveal who he is
	Example: Is he clumsy? Meticulous?

Characters can help unveil a play's theme. Characters' words, mannerisms, actions, and the consequences of their actions can expose and develop the author's theme.

STRUCTURE

Plays are often broken into acts. An **act** is a major division in a play. A play might have one act or several acts. Acts are then further divided into **scenes**. Sometimes, acts follow the structure of the play. A play is typically divided into five parts. A play's **structure** refers to how it is organized, and what part of the story (or **plot**) happens when. Read the examples to see the structural elements of a famous American play, Arthur Miller's *Death of a Salesman*.

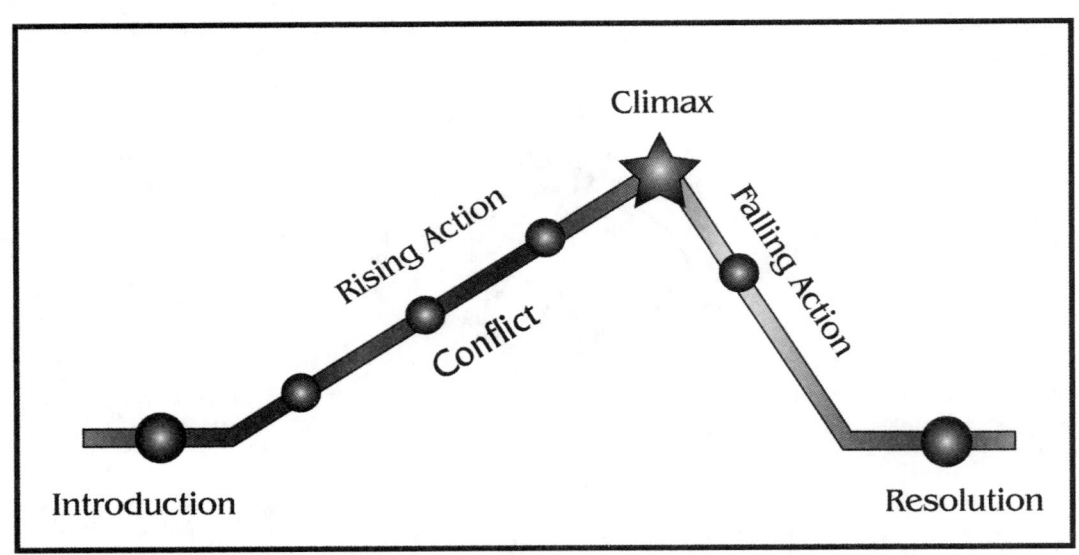

Typical structure of a play	
Exposition—the introduction to the story	This is the background information given at the beginning of a play so that the story makes sense. During the exposition, the audience learns about the characters and their roles. **Example:** During the exposition portion of Arthur Miller's *Death of a Salesman*, we learn that Willy Loman is an unsuccessful salesman who has a long history of denial, discord and failure within his family.
Rising action—introduces the conflict	During the rising action, obstacles begin to crop up that prevent the protagonist from resolving the problem. **Example:** During the rising action in Arthur Miller's *Death of a Salesman*, Willy Loman begins to have a harder and harder time doing his job, troubled as he is by his work failures and his understanding that he has made mistakes in what he has taught his sons.
Climax—the turning point	The climax of a play marks a change for the protagonist. In a comedy, his situation will begin to improve. In a tragedy, the opposite will happen. **Example:** At the climax of Arthur Miller's *Death of a Salesman*, Willy Loman is fired from his job.
Falling action—the conflict continues	During the falling action, the plot continues to unfold as the protagonist moves towards the resolution of the problem. **Example:** In Arthur Miller's *Death of a Salesman*, Willy Loman trades reality for memories, refusing help and sinking deeper into financial and mental problems.
Conclusion—the ending of the play	The conclusion of a play provides the resolution of the conflict and the end of the story. The ending of a comedy is often called a **denouement**—the protagonist is better off than he or she was at the story's outset. A tragedy ends with a **catastrophe**—the protagonist is worse off than he or she was at the beginning of the narrative. **Example:** At the conclusion of Arthur Miller's *Death of a Salesman*, Willy Loman commits suicide

The structure of a play, which reveals the plot of the play, can have a great impact upon the writer's theme. The significance a writer places upon some events and not others and cause and effect relationships in the course he has the action take can contribute to the theme of the work. Paying close attention to a play's plot often helps a reader understand the play's theme.

DRAMATIC DEVICES

Chapter 2 looked at how authors use literary devices such as imagery, symbolism and irony to create meaning in their writing. Playwrights use **dramatic devices** in the same way; to enrich the meaning of a play.

Stage directions are instructions for the actors which are written into the play. These directions tell actors when and where to move. They are generally written in italics and set off with parentheses ( ) or brackets [ ]. For example, a character's stage directions might read: [*Slouch in a chair with legs crossed, frowning.*]

The **fourth wall** is the imaginary wall at the front of a stage, supposedly removed to allow the audience to see the action of the play. The fourth wall is especially common in modern and contemporary plays such as Lorraine Hansberry's *A Raisin in the Sun.*

An **aside** is an actor's speech which is directed to the audience and is not supposed to be heard by the other actors. An aside often provides the audience with insight into the character's thoughts or feelings. An example might be a character turning to the audience and sharing a suspicion she has about another character.

Expressionism is a focus on presenting pain and suffering through exaggerated emotions on stage in order to elicit an emotional response from the viewers. Expressionist drama might use devices such as bright lights and loud sounds or voices. Eugene O'Neill's *The Hairy Ape* is an example of expressionist drama.

Minimalism is the opposite of expressionism. Minimalism uses an extreme reduction or simplification of form. Edward Albee's play *The American Dream* uses minimalism.

In **dramatic irony,** the audience knows more than the character and therefore understands the significance of a character's speech or actions in a way that a character does not. For example, Character A may be revealing secrets in an environment which he thinks is safe. However, the audience can see that Character B, who has been trying to find out those secrets, is hiding in a closet and hearing every word.

Practice 2: Drama

Answer the questions about dramatic devices

1. A playwright wants the audience members to feel as though they were sitting at a glass wall watching the action of the play. What dramatic device would the playwright be using?

    A. expressionism   B. fourth wall   C. dramatic irony   D. minimalism

2. A playwright wants an actor to deliver a line with a grimace, showing that he disapproves of the words he is saying. What dramatic device would the playwright use?

    A. dramatic irony   C. stage directions
    B. expressionism   D. minimalism

3. A playwright uses loud, unexpected sounds to elicit a response from the audience. His play is likely to be a/an _____ drama.
   A. expressionist   B. minimalist   C. ironic   D. directed

4. A character in a play, George, is happily planning his wedding to another character, Ellen. The audience knows that Ellen has married someone else, thinking that George does not love her. This is an example of _____.
   A. minimalism   B. expressionism   C. a tragedy   D. dramatic irony

Read the passage then answer the questions that follow.

> SCENE. *The drawing-room in the residence of MR. EDWARD ELSWORTH. Garden seen through doors. ROSE ELSWORTH occupied at a small table, stitching. KATE ELSWORTH stretched languidly upon a sofa, with a book in hand. MR. EDWARD ELSWORTH in an easy chair, with newspaper in his lap. Writing materials on table.*

KATE. Oh, dullness! dullness! I do wish Harry was at home, or Sir William would march some of his troops this way! What's the use of an army in the country, if one can't have a dance once in a while?

ROSE. What, indeed! All I desire is, sister, that they should be [Enter SERVANT with letters for MR. ELSWORTH.] left to the dance! That much they do very well.

KATE. I'm sure, Rose, I can't see what you find in these rebels to admire. As far as my observation has gone, they are only so many boors. There was Captain Arthur. Was there ever such a dunce? He had no manner whatever. He attempted once to walk a minuet with me, and I really thought he was a bear accidentally stumbled into coat and slippers.

–from Love in '76 by Oliver Bell Bunce (1828–1890)

5. This passage is from the introduction of the play. The introduction is also known as the _____ portion of a play.
   A. denouement   B. exposition   C. falling action   D. climax

6. According to the stage directions, what should the servant be carrying when he arrives on the stage?
   A. a tea pot   C. letters for Mr. Elsworth
   B. a rose   D. Captain Arthur

7. From Kate's description, what do we know about Captain Arthur?
   A. He is an accomplished dancer   C. He is actually bear, not a man.
   B. He is an awkward dancer.   D. He was rude to Kate.

8. Where is this conversation taking place?
   A. in a drawing room   C. on a ship
   B. in a garden   D. in a taxi

Playwrights use a variety of elements such as plot, characters, and stage directions to create meaning in their plays. By understanding dramatic devices and analyzing how an author makes use of them, we can gain insight into the author's underlying message.

CHAPTER 3 SUMMARY

Poetry

- **Poetry** is a short form of literature and is generally intended to express deep emotion. Poems can be **narrative**, such as **epics** and **ballads**, or **lyric**.

- **Fixed form** poetry, like **sonnets** and **blank verse**, follows a particular structure, while poetry written in **free verse** does not.

- **Rhythm** is the pattern of stressed and unstressed sounds in a poem. **Rhyme** involves lines in which two or more words sound alike. Common types of rhyme are **internal rhyme**, **end rhyme,** and **slant rhyme**. A poem's **rhyme scheme** is its pattern of end rhyme.

Language, the words an author uses and the way she uses them, is very important in poetry because it affects the reader's response to the poetry. **Figurative language** takes words beyond their literal meaning and is a common device in poetry.

Drama

- A **drama** is a play. The two main types of drama are **comedy** and **tragedy**. A drama is populated by characters such as the **protagonist** and the **antagonist**. The writer uses several methods to develop his characters such as their **appearance, dialogue, actions** and **gestures**.

- A drama typically follows several steps from beginning to end: the **exposition, rising action, climax, falling action** and **conclusion**.

- In addition to the devices used in other types of literature, playwrights also use **dramatic devices** such as **stage directions** and **the fourth wall**.

CHAPTER 3 REVIEW

Read the passages. Then answer the questions that follow.

> Let us go then, you and I,
> When the evening is spread out against the sky
> Like a patient etherized upon a table;
> Let us go, through certain half-deserted streets,
> The muttering retreats
> Of restless nights in one-night cheap hotels
> And sawdust restaurants with oyster-shells:
> Streets that follow like a tedious argument
> Of insidious intent
> To lead you to an overwhelming question ...
> Oh, do not ask, "What is it?"
> Let us go and make our visit.
>
> In the room the women come and go
> Talking of Michelangelo.
>
> The yellow fog that rubs its back upon the window-panes,
> The yellow smoke that rubs its muzzle on the window-panes,
> Licked its tongue into the corners of the evening,
> Lingered upon the pools that stand in drains,
> Let fall upon its back the soot that falls from chimneys,
> Slipped by the terrace, made a sudden leap,
> And seeing that it was a soft October night,
> Curled once about the house, and fell asleep.

–from "The Love Song of J. Alfred Prufrock," by T.S. Eliot

1. Which of the following lines from the poem is an example of simile?

    A. "Like a patient etherized upon a table"
    B. "Let us go and make our visit"
    C. "In the room women come and go"
    D. "Curled once about the house, and fell asleep"

2. The line, "The yellow fog that rubs its back upon the window-panes," is an example of which type of figurative language?

    A. symbolism   B. simile   C. metonymy   D. imagery

3. What structure does this poem follow?

    A. blank verse   B. fixed form   C. free verse   D. epic

4. What type of rhyme does the poet use in this poem?
   A. slant rhyme   B. end rhyme   C. consonance   D. assonance

5. This poem is presented in fragments—fragments of thoughts and fragments of sentences. What might such a presentation tell us about the author's theme?
   A. The author's message is that society as fragmented—isolated and alone.
   B. The author's message is that fog is like a cat.
   C. The author's message is that October nights can be foggy.
   D. The author's message is that surgery in the streets must stop.

6. How does the author's use of imagery, through phrases such as "half-deserted streets," "one-night cheap hotels," and "sawdust restaurants," show the reader how he feels about the city?
   A. The author sees signs of hope that the city will once again be great.
   B. The author prefers the city to the country.
   C. The author predicts that the city will soon be gone.
   D. The author feels that the city is decaying.

7. Why do you think the author might have chosen to make an allusion to Michelangelo?
   A. Michelangelo is a famous artist.
   B. Most readers would have heard of Michelangelo
   C. Michelangelo represents art and culture to many people.
   D. All of the above.

Souls and Raindrops

Light rain-drops fall and wrinkle the sea,
Then vanish, and die utterly.
One would not know that rain-drops fell
If the round sea-wrinkles did not tell.

So souls come down and wrinkle life
And vanish in the flesh-sea strife.
One might not know that souls had place
Were't not for the wrinkles in life's face.

–by Sidney Lanier

8. What two things is the poet comparing in this poem?
   A. the sea and rain   C. wrinkles and water
   B. souls and raindrops   D. faces and places

9. What is the rhyme scheme of this poem?
   A. aabb ccdd   B. abab cdcd   C. abba cddc   D. aaba caba

10. What emotion does the poet display in these lines?
    A. an ecstatic response to nature
    C. a confused response to nature
    B. a dismayed response to nature
    D. an angry response to nature

11. In line 5, "So souls come down to wrinkle life," the poet compares souls to raindrops. What type of figurative language does he use in this line?
    A. metaphor   B. simile   C. allusion   D. hyperbole

12. In the last line of the poem, which literary device does the poet use in the phrase, "the wrinkles in life's face"?
    A. slant rhyme   B. mood   C. rhythm   D. imagery

13. "Souls and Raindrops" is an example of a/an _____ poem.
    A. epic   B. narrative   C. lyric   D. sonnet

CHRIS—[Hurriedly.] Ay go up bow. All hands asleep 'cepting fallar on vatch. Ay gat heave line to dat fallar. [He picks up a coil of rope and hurries off toward the bow. ANNA walks back toward the extreme stern as if she wanted to remain as much isolated possible. She turns her back on the proceedings and stares out into the fog. THE VOICE is heard again shouting "Ahoy" and CHRIS answering "Dis way" Then there is a pause—the murmur of excited voices—then the scuffling of feet. CHRIS appears from around the cabin to port. He is supporting the limp form of a man dressed in dungarees, holding one of the man's arms around his neck. The deckhand, JOHNSON, a young, blond Swede, follows him, helping along another exhausted man similar fashion. ANNA turns to look at them. Chris stops for a second—volubly.] Anna! You come help, vill you? You find vhiskey in cabin. Dese fallars need drink for fix dem. Dey vas near dead.

ANNA—[Hurrying to him.] Sure—but who are they? What's the trouble?

CHRIS—Sailor fallars. Deir steamer gat wrecked. Dey been five days in open boat—four fallars—only one left able stand up. Come, Anna. [She precedes him into the cabin, holding the door open while he and JOHNSON carry in their burdens. The door is shut, then opened again as JOHNSON comes out. CHRIS'S voice shouts after him.] Go gat oder fallar, Yohnson.

JOHNSON—Yes, sir. [He goes. The door is closed again. MAT BURKE stumbles in around the port side of the cabin. He moves slowly, feeling his way uncertainly, keeping hold of the port bulwark with his right hand to steady himself. He is stripped to the waist, has on nothing but a pair of dirty dungaree pants. He is a powerful, broad-chested six-footer, his face handsome in a hard, rough, bold, defiant way. He is about thirty, in the full power of his heavy-muscled, immense strength. His dark eyes are bloodshot and wild from sleeplessness. The muscles of his arms and shoulders are lumped in knots and bunches, the veins of his forearms stand out like blue cords. He finds his way to the coil of hawser and sits down on it facing the cabin, his back bowed, head in his hands, in an attitude of spent weariness.]

–from *Anna Christie*, by Eugene O' Neill (1888–1953)

14. Which of the following is a character who does NOT speak in this excerpt of the play?
    A.   Chris   B.   Anna   C.   Mat   D.   Johnson

15. What is the setting of this part of the play?
    A.   a concert hall   C.   a house
    B.   a ship   D.   a grocery store

16. What are the words in brackets [ ] for?
    A.   optional lines for the actors to speak   C.   stage directions
    B.   the writer's notes   D.   comments from the writer's teacher

17. "All hands asleep" is an example of _____.
    A.   synecdoche   B.   dramatic irony   C.   exposition   D.   gesture

18. What does Chris's speech reveal about him?
    A.   He is an old man.   C.   He is in pain.
    B.   He is not a native English speaker.   D.   He has blond hair.

19. Which of the following is NOT a character trait of Mat Burke?
    A.   He is wearing dirty dungaree pants.   C.   He has dark eyes.
    B.   He is about 30.   D.   He has a wooden leg.

20. From the tone of and descriptions in this excerpt, what type of play is this likely to be?
    A.   a comedy   C.   an expressionist drama
    B.   a tragedy   D.   a minimalist drama

Chapter 4
Word Meanings

This chapter covers the following Georgia standard(s).

ELAALRL5	Understand and acquire new vocabulary and use it correctly in reading and writing.
ELAALRC3	Acquire new vocabulary in each content area and use it correctly.
ELAALRC4	Establish a context for information acquired by reading across subject areas.

Standard ELAALRL5 is part of Domain I: Reading and American Literature; Standard ELAALRC3 and ELAALRC4 are part of Domain II: Reading, Listening, Speaking, and Viewing across the Curriculum. On the EOCT in American literature and composition, questions addressing all of these standards will measure your ability to understand and apply vocabulary.

Having a rich vocabulary can be both a cause and an effect—you gain new words by reading, and knowing more words helps you read a variety of texts! In order to read literature, you need to understand the words that authors use; while reading literature, you learn new words constantly, and you learn different ways of using words for which you already knew at least one meaning. In this chapter, you will review ways of acquiring new vocabulary and understanding words in new ways.

IDENTIFYING WORD MEANINGS

One of the best ways to acquire new vocabulary is through reading, reading, and more reading. At any given time, there are only so many words in the English language, but authors throughout history have managed to put them together so many different ways in fiction, nonfiction, poetry, and drama that there is a nearly bottomless well of nuances to learn. Writers also add new words to the English language as they coin new terms or travel international and borrow from other languages. The globalization of finance, commerce, politics, and science also continue to bring new words into our language.

USING REFERENCE MATERIALS

When the context alone is not giving you enough clues about a word's meaning, it's time to turn to the **dictionary**. A good dictionary will list a word's multiple meanings, so it's important to continue paying attention to context when looking up a word.

A **thesaurus** is a dictionary of synonyms and antonyms and is especially useful when you are writing a paper and don't want to keep using the same word repeatedly. Because it provides so many synonyms, a thesaurus can also give you a better idea of what a particular word means.

Each field of study and industry has its own language, or lexicon. As you encounter old and new words in different subjects, it may be necessary to consult a **specialized** or **technical dictionary**. These dictionaries can cover a variety of subjects, such as law, literature, or computing. There are also dictionaries that don't pertain to a field of study but rather focus on a specific type of language, such as slang or regional dialect. Some authors include notes about unusual words at the bottom of pages or a glossary at the end of the book where specialized words are defined.

Practice 1: Using Reference Materials

Read the following questions. Then choose the reference book you should use to look up words you do not know.

1. Becky is doing research for a biology paper and come across the following passage in a botany book: "The articulated surface of the leaves helps deflect rain." She knows that "to articulate" means to speak or communicate, but she doubts that definition fits. Where should she look up the word *articulated* in this case?

   A. a general dictionary
   B. a thesaurus
   C. the book's glossary
   D. a medical dictionary

2. Kelsey is writing an essay and notices that he uses the word *primarily* several times. Where can he find other words to use in its place?

   A. an idiom dictionary
   B. an encyclopedia
   C. a general dictionary
   D. a thesaurus

Randi is reading short stories by Jack London and comes across this passage in "The 'Francis Spaight'" about the shipwreck of this vessel.

> Day dawned on the savage ocean, and in the cold gray light all that could be seen of the *Francis Spaight* emerging from the sea were the poop, the shattered mizzenmast, and a ragged line of bulwarks. It was midwinter in the North Atlantic, and the wretched men were half-dead from cold.

3. Where would Randi turn to find out the meaning of the words *poop, mizzenmast,* and *bulwark*?

   A. the encyclopedia, under "boat"
   B. the glossary of a book about ships
   C. the U.S. Navy Web site
   D. a book of quotations, under "sea"

MEANINGS IN CONTEXT

What happens when you come across a **word** or **phrase** you don't know? How about when you do know it, but it's used in some way you are not familiar with? The first thing you do—usually without even realizing it—is to figure out what it probably means in its **context**. Looking at what's around the word or phrase you don't know gives you **context clues** which help you figure out the new word's meaning.

> **Example:** I like the way the slacker characters maintain their slothful gormlessness in the face of urgent danger, and I like the way the British bourgeois values of Shaun's mum and dad assert themselves even in the face of catastrophe.
>
> <div align="right">from a review of the film <i>Shaun of the Dead</i> by Roger Ebert</div>

If you were reading this review, you might notice some words that you don't know. However, you probably get a general sense of what this sentence means because of all the known words *around* the unknown ones.

When Ky read this review, he understood its meaning, in a nutshell.

> The reviewer liked the way that the characters remained lazy while an emergency was happening, as well as how Shaun's parents were concerned about their lifestyle during a disaster.

Although he understood the general sense of what was being discussed, Ky needed to be sure his ideas were on target. He picked out the words he didn't know and then analyzed their context.

> **Unknown word:** *gormlessness*

> **Context:** the slacker characters maintain their slothful *gormlessness* in the face of urgent danger

Ky noticed that the words *slacker* and *slothful* are negative characteristics, and hypothesized that *gormlessness* is probably a negative word as well. Since *slacker* and *slothful* both denote slowness and laziness, he figured that *gormlessness* probably possesses similar connotations. The actual meaning of *gormlessness* is "stupidity," so Ky's use of context clues brought him very close!

You can also use your knowledge of the **parts of speech** to determine a word's meaning. For example, if a poet takes a noun you know and turns it into a verb you have never heard, you can still infer the meaning from the word you know, as shown below:

> She kept the light,
> The excitement sublime,
> Inside and sealed tight—
> Bottling it like fine wine
>
> –excerpt from poem by anonymous

noun	**becomes**	**verb**
bottle	by adding -ing	bottling

Since you know what a bottle is (container for liquid), it becomes a matter of turning an object into an action (bottling might be the action of pouring liquid into a bottle) and considering how the author uses the word (in this case symbolically, keeping feelings inside, as one keeps liquid in a bottle). The context clue of a simile ("like fine wine") helps you understand that the feeling is being kept safe and growing more precious, as fine wine.

WORDS WITH MORE THAN ONE MEANING

What if you know a word but the meaning you know does not seem to fit? Remember that there are words in American English that can have several meanings, so you may be encountering another meaning of a word than the one you already knew. As with learning new words, using context clues can help you learn further meanings of **multi-meaning words**.

> **Example:** It was with difficulty that I could bring myself to admit the identity of the wan being before me with the companion of my early boyhood.
>
> –excerpt from "The Fall of the House of Usher" by Edgar Allan Poe

Upon reading this sentence, Ashley wonders about the word *admit*. As she knows the word, it means "to confess," as in, "I admit that I was the one who left the door unlocked." While this is one meaning of *admit*, it doesn't make sense in this context. In fact, the primary meaning of *admit* is "to permit to enter." So, as you can see, it's important to know if a word has more than one meaning and to figure which one fits within the context.

CONNOTATION AND DENOTATION

In addition to multi-meaning words, there are many words that have not only a **denotation** (dictionary definition) but also a **connotation** (a suggested or implied meaning). For example, if you're at lunch and your friend says, "Don't be a pig," it doesn't mean you've turned into a domesticated farm animal raised for pork! Being called a pig *implies* that you may be eating in a sloppy way or eating huge portions—characteristics associated with pigs. Other connotations of pig in American English include someone who is messy ("Your room looks like a pig sty!") or slovenly, someone who is greedy, and a derogatory (negative) term for a police officer. When reading, try to be aware of all the possible meanings of the words used by authors.

Practice 2: Identifying Word Meanings in Context

Read the following excerpt, and answer the questions that follow.

> At Selkirk, the trading post near Pelly River, Daylight suggested that Kama lay over, rejoining him on the back trip from Dyea. A strayed Indian from Lake Le Barge was willing to take his place; but Kama was obdurate. He grunted with a slight intonation of resentment, and that was all. The dogs, however, Daylight changed, leaving his own exhausted team to rest up against his return, while he went on with six fresh dogs.
>
> –excerpt from *Burning Daylight* by Jack London

1. In the first sentence, which meaning of *rejoin* is the MOST appropriate in this context?

   A. to link together   C. to say in reply, especially in sharp response

   B. to unite after separation   D. to answer, as the defendant to the plaintiff's plea

2. In the second sentence, what does *obdurate* MOST likely mean?
    A. balanced   B. confused   C. stubborn   D. hesitant

3. In the third sentence, *intonation* means
    A. trace.   B. frown.   C. shout.   D. rhythm.

4. In the last sentence, the <u>denotation</u> of *against* is "opposite or in resistance to." The <u>connotation</u> in this context is
    A. as if it were.   C. under orders about.
    B. in anticipation of.   D. without any idea of.

OTHER STRATEGIES FOR FINDING MEANING

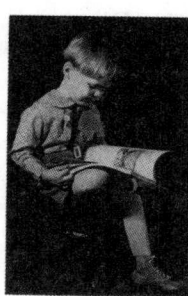

On top of using context clues, you can always look up the unfamiliar word in a **dictionary** or **ask someone** else what the word means. But even when you are by yourself or can't use a dictionary (as when you a re taking a test), you can use **word analysis strategies** to figure out word meanings.

Expert readers like the challenge of figuring out new words. You can use the same techniques they use to find word meanings. Here are some of those strategies:

USE PRIOR KNOWLEDGE

- Use your **prior knowledge**. Think about whether you have seen the unknown word before, and consider context in which it was used; then add that together to the context you see in the new text.

- Make sure that you **understand the rest of the text** surrounding the new word. Then think about what the word most likely means. Then, think about what the word most likely means.

Be sure to check the remainder of the passage you are reading to see if the unknown word appears again, giving you further clues to its meaning.

USE KNOWLEDGE OF ROOTS, SUFFIXES, PREFIXES, AND COGNATES

To figure out new words, use your knowledge of how words are constructed and what other words they may be related to. As you know, many English words come from other languages. Many have Latin or Greek origins, which are helpful to know, as they can assist you in figuring out new words that contain parts of those words.

An English word can have up to three parts:

prefix	a word element placed in front of a root which changes the meaning or makes a new word
root	a word; the word element that forms the base of appended words (words with a prefix and/or suffix)

prefix	a word element placed in front of a root which changes the meaning or makes a new word
suffix	a word element placed at the end of a root which changes the meaning and its function (for example, from a verb to a noun, as in the verb *like* changing to the noun *likeness*)

Prefixes and suffixes are also called **affixes**. Take a look at the small sample of roots and affixes in the chart below. Each prefix, root, and suffix combination below forms a word. For more review and examples of roots and affixes, see **American Book Company's** *Basics Made Easy: Reading Review.*

Prefix	Root	Suffix	Prefix	Root	Suffix
ad (to, towards, near)	**vert** (also **vers**; to turn)	**ize** (also **ise**) (to become like)	**para** (contrary to)	**dox** (opinion)	**ical** (quality of, relating to)
con (with)	**junct** (joined, joint)	**tion** (action, process)	**post** (after, behind)	**pone** (from **ponere**, to put, to place)	**ment** (act of)
dis (apart, removed)	**respect** (to value, to honor)	**ful** (full of)	**re** (back, again)	**cant** (from **catare**, to sing, to chant)	**er** (person who does something)
ex (out of)	**hal** (from **halare**, to breathe)	**ant** (one that)	**semi** (half)	**annual** (from **annus**, year)	**ly** (in like manner)
inter (between)	**medi** (from **medius**, middle)	**ate** (to act as)	**sub** (under, below)	**conscious** (knowing, aware)	**ness** (quality of)
non (not)	**conform** (to conform)	**ity** (quality of)	**trans** (across)	**port** (from **portare**, to carry)	**able** (also **ible**, capable of being)

COGNATES

Do you know another language? Are you taking Spanish, French, German, or other languagae classes in school? Then **cognates** can help you learn meanings of new words. In linguistics, cognates are words that have a common origin. Often, this shows up as words that look and sound similar in two languages, such as the following examples:

English *milk*, German *Milch*, Russion *moloko*

English *night*, German *Nacht*, French *nuit*

Within English, an example of cognates is the words *shears*, *sharp*, and *scape*, which all descended from the Pro-Indo-European word *sker-,* which means "to cut." Another example is the words *gender*, *generate*, *genre*, and *genus*, all descended from the word *gena-,* "to give birth."

Be careful, though, as there are also pairs of words that may look or sound alike but have completely different meanings. These are called **false friends**. For example, while you are probably familiar with the word different meanings of *raise* ("to rise, build up, lift"), be careful when you see *raze*, which actually means quite the opposite ("to tear down or destroy"). Also, you can be *confident* that you will do well on a test, but you might decide to divulge your grade only to your closest *confidant* (or "a person trusted with private affairs").

DEALING WITH IDIOMS

Idioms are figurative expressions and phrases that have come to mean something very specific in a particular language, quite apart from the literal meaning of the words. Usually, the literal meaning turns out to be impossible, so if you don't know what the words are really supposed to mean, an idiom can be quite confusing! Here are some well known examples of American idioms:

Phrase/Expression	Literal meaning	Idiomatic meaning
It's raining cats and dogs.	Cats and dogs are falling from the sky.	Rain is coming down very hard.
backseat driver	someone who drives from the back seat	a passenger who constantly gives the driver advice

For more examples of idioms used in American English, look in some of the many books about idioms or visit American English idiom sites like www.idiomconnection.com.

LITERAL AND FIGURATIVE MEANINGS

In chapters 2 and 3, you read about how authors use figurative language in literature through techniques such as **allusion**, **hyperbole**, **imagery**, **metaphor**, **simile**, and **symbolism**. (Review the list of figurative language on page ___.) Your knowledge of how writers use figurative language can help you figure out word meaning in a variety of texts.

Practice 3: Other Strategies for Finding Meaning

Read the following excerpt, and answer the questions that follow.

In the old days, when a Sioux warrior found himself in the very jaws of destruction, he might offer a prayer to his father, the Sun, to prolong his life. If rescued from imminent danger, he must acknowledge the divine favor by making a Sun Dance, according to the vow embraced in his prayer, in which he declared that he did not fear torture or death, but asked life only for the sake of those who loved him. Thus the physical ordeal was the fulfillment of a vow, and a sort of atonement for what might otherwise appear to be reprehensible weakness in the face of death. It was in the nature of confession and thank-offering to the "Great Mystery," through the physical parent, the Sun, and did not embrace a prayer for future favors.

–excerpt from *The Soul of the Indian* by Ohiyesa, a.k.a. Charles Eastman (1858–1939)

1. In the first sentence, the phrase "in the very jaws of destruction" is an example of figurative language. What does it mean here?

    A.   The warrior seems to be lost.
    B.   The warrior is in the mouth of a large animal.
    C.   The warrior is on the warpath.
    D.   The warrior faces a very dangerous situation.

2. When a warrior calls the Sun his father, this is an example of
    A.   allegory.   B.   metaphor.   C.   irony.   D.   metonymy.

3. In the third sentence, the author refers to "reprehensible weakness." Based on context as well as knowledge of roots and affixes, what does the word *reprehensible* MOST likely mean?
    A.   unwise   B.   shameful   C.   blameless   D.   defeated

4. The closest synonym for the word *embrace* as it is used in the last sentence is
    A.   hug.   B.   squeeze.   C.   accept.   D.   include.

Activity 1: More Practice with Finding Meaning

Choose and read 2–3 short stories by Edgar Allan Poe, Jack London, or Flannery O'Connor, or find 2–3 articles in magazines like *TIME* or *Newsweek*. As you read, underline or highlight words that you don't know. Use **context**, **denotation/connotation**, **prior knowledge**, **roots and affixes**, **cognates**, and **figurative language** (including **idioms**) to figure out the meaning. If you believe you already know what a word means, write down your definition. When you are done considering all the underlined words, look each of them up in the dictionary. Be sure to think further about which dictionary meaning fits and which words may be used figuratively in the passage.

MEANINGS IN HISTORICAL CONTEXT

The meanings of some words change over time. English is a living language, so words often take on new meanings in different time periods. For example, the word "cool" simply meant "neither warm nor very cold" until about World War II, took on the connotation of "excellent" in the jazz era of 1940s, was adopted into a string of superlatives like *hep*, *groovy*, and *crazy* in the 1950s and '60s, and today continues to mean basically "good," while many similar slang expressions have fallen out of use. Of course, it still retains the denotation, "neither warm nor very cold" as well.

When reading literature from a given period, keep in mind that there may be words you may not recognize. Even words you know may not always mean exactly what they mean today. In addition, you may find words that just make no sense (because they were used specifically during a particular period), which you need to look up. Many books provide glossaries or footnotes to help with obscure words, as you have probably seen in literature textbooks. For example, in reading a text from the Civil War Era, you might encounter references to "graybacks" (Southern soldiers), "hornets" (bullets), "fresh fish" (new recruits), and "toeing the mark" (obeying orders).

USING KNOWLEDGE OF INFLUENCES ON AMERICAN LITERATURE

Influences on American literature vary widely, from the ancient inspiration of classical Greece and Rome, to precedents of great literature of the world, to contemporary events going on around the writers of any given literary period in America. Knowing about these influences and being able to recognize allusions (chapter 2) is an important key to fully understanding what you read.

THE INFLUENCE OF THE CLASSICS

Greek and Roman mythology and literature have had an enormous effect on literature since their time, as well as on the structure of our language as a whole. Earlier in the chapter, you read about how Greek and Latin roots and affixes often form building blocks to help you understand new vocabulary. In the same way, knowledge of mythology and classic literature can help you recognize **allusions**, **metaphors**, **themes**, and more in anything you read.

A good place to start is by refreshing your memory about the names of Greek and Roman gods and how references to them weave through American English today. Take a moment to look up the name of Greek and Roman gods and their roles. The table on the next page has just a few examples.

Greek Name	Roman Name	Role	Symbols
Aphrodite	Venus	goddess of love and beauty	myrtle, dove
Ares	Mars	god of war	spear
Eros	Cupid	god of love	bow
Hera	Juno	goddess of marriage; wife of Zeus	peacock
Hermes	Mercury	god of merchants; messenger of Zeus	winged boots
Poseidon	Neptune	god of the sea	trident
Zeus	Jupiter, Jove	god of the sky, ruler of Olympus	thunderbolt, eagle

For further review of mythology and the impact of Greek and Roman classics on American literature, visit the library and ask the librarian for books about this topic. A great start is *Bulfinch's Greek and Roman Mythology: The Age of Fable* by Thomas Bulfinch. You can also visit Web pages like www.religionfacts.com/greco-roman/glossary.htm and ancienthistory.about.com/popular.htm.

Words derived from the names of these deities have become part of our vocabulary. When we say something is *erotic*, we're referencing Eros, Greek god of love. When we talk about a song being *hypnotic*, we're referencing Hypnos, Greek god of sleep. And the *cereal* that might eat in the morning refers to Ceres, the Roman goddess of agriculture.

The classics had influence on the earliest of American writers. Even the Puritans, who did not admire the constant warring of these civilizations admired the "flourishing state of learning" that came from them. Later, American authors and poets wove allusions to the classics into their work. Following are examples of such borrowings, which are numerous in poetry and prose to this day.

Work	Author	References
"Thanatopsis" (1817)	William Cullen Bryant	title is from Greek *thanatos*, meaning "death" and the suffix –*opsis* meaning "sight"
"To Helen" (1831)	Edgar Allan Poe	contains allusions to Fate, Diana, and Venus
Moby-Dick (1851)	Herman Melville	alludes often to Greek myth in lines like this one: "and in the Greek mythologies, Great Jove himself being made incarnate in a snow-white bull"

THE INFLUENCE OF THE BIBLE

Many American authors include allusions to Biblical themes, stories, and principles as nearly universal points of reference. In American literature, this is a natural consequence of the Pilgrims that populated the first colonies looking to scripture for guidance in every walk of life. For more than 100 years after the landing at Plymouth Rock in 1620, life and writing in the New England colonies were dominated by a culture centered on the Bible.

Many early settlers saw America as "the new Eden." From the earliest Colonial Era pamphlets, American authors called on readers' knowledge of the Bible not only to assist with understanding ideas but also to forward imperatives about the rights of the colonies to exist. In addition, for many newcomers to the New World, the Bible was the ultimate example of great writing as well as of faith and conduct.

Regardless of religious persuasion, most people know generally about the Bible and the many parables and histories contained in it. From the beginning and through the present day, authors use this fact to help convey ideas.

Here are just a few examples of well-known Biblical allusions in American literary works.

Work	Author	References
Moby-Dick (1851)	Herman Melville	Ishmael, the name of the narrator, alludes to the exiled son of Abraham. There are numerous references throughout the book to Biblical events and characters.
The Waste Land (1922)	T. S. Eliot	The narrator in the first section is called "the son of man," and the poem as a whole is an extended metaphor referencing God's warnings about the earth returning to dust (Ezekiel, Ecclesiastes).
East of Eden (1952)	John Steinbeck	This story of two families, the Trasks and the Hamiltons, draws many parallels to the Genesis story of Cain and Abel.

THE INFLUENCE OF CONTEMPORARY EVENTS

As you read in chapter 1, the literature of any period is tied to the events of its time. Some authors may write about past history or about the future or even fantastic tales out of time, but even these are influenced by the literary inventions to date as well as the writing style of the period.

Early American literature was influenced, of course, by the events and politics of Europe, as immigrants to the New World populated our shores. This quickly evolved into writings that spoke about the advantages (land, opportunity, religious freedom) and disadvantages (shortages of food, challenges in carving out the wilderness, conflicts with Native Americans) of the colonies.

Later events that held considerable sway on the literature of the each period included the Civil War, emancipation of the slaves, both world wars, industrialization, the Great Depression, the Civil Rights Movement, new technology, and various shifts in ideology and popular culture. As you read any literature, keep in mind why and when it was written.

Practice 4: Meanings in Literary Context

Read this excerpt from T.S. Eliot's "The Love Song of J. Alfred Prufrock." Then answer the questions that follow.

One of Eliot's earliest poems, published in 1915, "The Love Song of J. Alfred Prufrock" is about the archetypal troubled modern man. Throughout the poem, Prufrock tries to express his suppressed feelings to a woman, but his overtures are overly complicated and lack true emotion. This is part of the poem.

And the afternoon, the evening, sleeps so peacefully!

Smoothed by long fingers,

Asleep ... tired ... or it malingers,

Stretched on the floor, here beside you and me.

Should I, after tea and cakes and ices,   **(5)**

Have the strength to force the moment to its crisis?

But though I have wept and fasted, wept and prayed,

Though I have seen my head (grown slightly bald) brought in upon a platter,

I am no prophet—and here's no great matter;

I have seen the moment of my greatness flicker,   **(10)**

And I have seen the eternal Footman hold my coat, and snicker,

And in short, I was afraid.

And would it have been worth it, after all,

After the cups, the marmalade, the tea,

Among the porcelain, among some talk of you and me,   **(15)**

Would it have been worth while,

To have bitten off the matter with a smile,

To have squeezed the universe into a ball

To roll it toward some overwhelming question,

To say: "I am Lazarus, come from the dead,   **(20)**

Come back to tell you all, I shall tell you all"—

If one, settling a pillow by her head,

  Should say: "That is not what I meant at all;

  That is not it, at all."

And would it have been worth it, after all,   **(25)**

Would it have been worth while,

After the sunsets and the dooryards and the sprinkled streets,

After the novels, after the teacups, after the skirts that trail along the floor—

And this, and so much more?—

1. Given its historical context, Prufrock's dilemma in this poem MOST likely expresses

   A. men's discontentedness with their role as breadwinners.
   B. an overwhelming fear of growing old alone and of eventual death.
   C. modern man's fear of rejection and lack of personal identity.
   D. a disillusionment with society's norm that a man has to make the first move.

2. Which answer BEST describes the reference Eliot makes in lines 7 through 9?
   A. He makes an allusion to the prophet John the Baptist, whose head was delivered to Salome.
   B. He talks about the harshness of his modern life, including poverty and constant depression.
   C. The references to fasting, praying, and a feast on a platter allude to Roman classics.
   D. By saying he is going bald, he refers to the psychological fear of mortality.

3. In the second stanza of this excerpt, an allusion is made to Lazarus, whom Jesus raised from the dead in the Bible's Book of John. The story has come to be associated with restoration. What is the MOST likely reason it is used here?
   A. Prufrock believes that he cannot know whether he has made the right choice in a partner until the end of his life.
   B. It shows that the narrator believes in an afterlife and feels he will be better able to express himself once the constraints of living have ended.
   C. Prufrock is considering whether professing his love is worth it, even if the woman he chooses may not return his love in the end.
   D. Eliot is further showing his encyclopedic knowledge of the classics by using yet another allusion.

4. In line 28, Eliot <u>most</u> likely uses the phrase "skirts that trail along the floor" to stand for
   A. a wedding gown (synecdoche).
   B. the pants Prufrock wears (irony).
   C. the woman he loves (symbolism).
   D. females in general (analogy).

5. What technique, used widely in this period, does Eliot employ?
   A. imagery that serves to uplift the spirit
   B. a validation of reason over emotion
   C. stream of consciousness
   D. use of vernacular

WORD MEANINGS ACROSS SUBJECT AREAS

In addition to acquiring new vocabulary as you read literature, you will also see new words in other subject areas. Wherever new vocabulary comes from, learning new words will be useful across all subject areas. Learning words from various subject areas is yet another context to keep in mind when you read.

Here are just a few examples of words that mean different things depending on where they are used. As you look over the list, first think about the definition of each word as you know it. Then see how it is used in specific subject areas.

Noun	Meaning across Subject Areas
circulation	*newspaper industry:* number of people who subscribe *biology:* blood flow
deposit	*economics:* money placed in an account, securing a payment *science:* natural accumulation, sediment
equality	*earth science:* bend in a river *social science*: like treatment for individuals regardless of race, gender, or age *math:* properties satisfied by the = symbol
meter	*poetry:* the measured arrangement of words *music:* division of notes into bars *physical science:* a metric measure of length (39.37 inches); an instrument for measuring time, distance, speed, or intensity

Practice 5: Word Meanings across Subject Areas

Read this excerpt from *Frank's Campaign or the Farm and the Camp* by Horatio Alger, Jr. (1832–1899), in which a character describes the Battle of Fredericksburg during the Civil War.

A deluge of shot and shell from our side of the river rained upon the city, setting some buildings on fire, and severely damaging others. It was a most exciting spectacle to us who watched from the bluffs, knowing that ere long we must make the perilous passage and confront the foe, the mysterious silence of whose batteries inspired alarm, as indicating a consciousness of power.

1. In the first sentence, *shell* means
    A. covering.   B. armor.   C. ammunition.   D. protection.

2. The BEST synonym for the word *passage* in the second sentence is
    A. episode.   B. route.   C. channel.   D. road.

3. What is the MOST appropriate meaning for the word *batteries* in the last line?
    A. electrical cells   C. imposing groups
    B. poundings   D. artillery

4. What subject area provides the context to help a reader determine the meanings of words used in this passage?

   A. weather
   B. military
   C. government
   D. physical science

CHAPTER 4 SUMMARY

You can build your vocabulary in many ways.

Read as much as you can.

Use appropriate **reference materials** to look up words.

Use **context clues** to figure out new words from what's around them.

In addition to new words, you can learn further meanings of **multi-meaning words** and get to know both **denotations** and **connotations** for words.

Learn **word analysis strategies** to figure out word meanings.

Use your **prior knowledge** about where you may have seen a new word before.

Make sure that you **understand the rest of the text**.

Use and increase your knowledge of **roots and affixes**, **cognates**, and **idioms**, as well as **literal and figurative** language.

Remember to consider the **historical context** of what you read. The meanings of some words change over time. In addition, each era and literary movement is influenced by what preceded it. Literature often contains **allusions** to past works, like **Greek** and **Roman** mythology literature, the **Bible**, and other **classics**, as well as influences from contemporary events and ideology.

You can acquire new vocabulary in a variety of **subject areas**. Keep in mind that every subject area uses some specific vocabulary and that the same word may have different meanings depending on where it is used.

CHAPTER 4 REVIEW

Read the passages, and then answer the questions that follow.

excerpt from *Red Badge of Courage* by Stephen Crane (1871–1900)

A battery had trundled into position in the rear and was thoughtfully shelling the distance. The regiment, unmolested as yet, awaited the moment when the gray shadows of the woods before them should be slashed by the lines of flame. There was much growling and swearing.

"Good Gawd," the youth grumbled, "we're always being chased around like rats! It makes me sick. Nobody seems to know where we go or why we go. We just get fired around from pillar to post and get licked here and get licked there, and nobody knows what it's done for. It makes a man feel like a damn' kitten in a bag. Now, I'd like to know what the eternal thunders we was marched into these woods for anyhow, unless it was to give the rebs[1] a regular pot shot at us. We came in here and got our legs all tangled up in these cussed briers, and then we begin to fight and the rebs had an easy time of it. Don't tell me it's just luck! I know better. It's this derned old—"

The friend seemed jaded, but he interrupted his comrade with a voice of calm confidence. "It'll turn out all right in th' end," he said.

"Oh, the devil it will! You always talk like a dog-hanged parson[2]. Don't tell me! I know—"

------

1 **rebs:** rebel (Confederate) soldiers

2 **parson:** a pastor or preacher

---

1. What does *jaded* mean in the sentence, "The friend seemed jaded, but he interrupted his comrade with a voice of calm confidence"?
   A. friendly   B. weary   C. energetic   D. hopeful

2. In the first sentence of the passage, *trundled* MOST nearly means
   A. stopped.   B. rolled.   C. ran.   D. flew.

3. Which word or phrase from the passage also means *defeated*?
   A. awaited   B. cussed   C. tangled   D. licked

4. The author uses the phrase "kitten in a bag" to emphasize the youth's feelings of
   A. helplessness.   B. power.   C. cuteness.   D. youthfulness.

5. In the last sentence of the passage, how is the expression *dog-hanged* MOST likely being used?
   A. It is literal, referring to the parson having been hanged.
   B. It is a figurative term meaning something negative.
   C. It probably is included just to show soldier-talk.
   D. It seems to be an allusion to the Bible.

6. The words defined at the bottom of the passage are an example of
   A. a dictionary.   B. an idiom.   C. a glossary.   D. a quotation.

Walden

By Henry David Thoreau

Near the end of March, 1845, I borrowed an axe and went down to the woods by Walden Pond, nearest to where I intended to build my house, and began to cut down some tall, arrowy white pines, still in their youth, for timber. It is difficult to begin without borrowing, but perhaps it is the most generous course thus to permit your fellow-men to have an interest in your enterprise. The owner of the axe, as he released his hold on it, said that it was the apple of his eye; but I returned it sharper than I received it. It was a pleasant hillside where I worked, covered with pine woods, through which I looked out on the pond, and a small open field in the woods where pines and hickories were springing up. The ice in the pond was not yet dissolved, though there were some open spaces, and it was all dark-colored and saturated with water. There were some slight flurries of snow during the days that I worked there; but for the most part when I came out on to the railroad, on my way home, its yellow sand heap stretched away gleaming in the hazy atmosphere, and the rails shone in the spring sun, and I heard the lark and pewee and other birds already come to commence another year with us. They were pleasant spring days, in which the winter of man's discontent was thawing as well as the earth, and the life that had lain torpid began to stretch itself. One day, when my axe had come off and I had cut a green hickory for a wedge, driving it with a stone, and had placed the whole to soak in a pond-hole in order to swell the wood, I saw a striped snake run into the water, and he lay on the bottom, apparently without inconvenience, as long as I stayed there, or more than a quarter of an hour; perhaps because he had not yet fairly come out of the torpid state. It appeared to me that for a like reason men remain in their present low and primitive condition; but if they should feel the influence of the spring of springs arousing them, they would of necessity rise to a higher and more ethereal life. I had previously seen the snakes in frosty mornings in my path with portions of their bodies still numb and inflexible, waiting for the sun to thaw them. On the 1st of April it rained and melted the ice, and in the early part of the day, which was very foggy, I heard a stray goose groping about over the pond and cackling as if lost, or like the spirit of the fog.

7. The word *arrowy* in the first sentence refers to
   A. the height of the pine trees.   C. the age of the pine trees.
   B. the shape of the pine trees.   D. the color of the pine trees.

Read the sentence below and answer questions 8–9.

> It appeared to me that for a like reason men remain in their present low and primitive condition; but if they should feel the influence of the spring of springs arousing them, they would of necessity rise to a higher and more ethereal life.

8. In the above sentence, the word *low* means
   A. angry.   B. unhealthy.   C. short stature.   D. uninspired.

9. The word *ethereal* in the above sentence means
   A. spiritual.   B. superficial.   C. vulgar.   D. important.

Read the following sentence and answer questions 10–12:

> One day, when my axe had come off and I had cut a green hickory for a wedge, driving it with a stone, and had placed the whole to soak in a pond-hole in order to swell the wood, I saw a striped snake run into the water, and he lay on the bottom, apparently without inconvenience, as long as I stayed there, or more than a quarter of an hour; perhaps because he had not yet fairly come out of the torpid state.

10. In the context of the passage, what does the word *torpid* mean?
   A. energetic   B. predatory   C. dormant   D. aquatic

11. Thoreau says that "the owner of the axe, as he released his hold on it, said that it was the apple of his eye." From this statement, you know that
   A. the owner did not like his ax
   B. the owner cherished his ax
   C. the owner wanted a new ax
   D. the owner wanted Thoreau to keep the ax

12. What kind of statement is represented in question 11?
   A. idiomatic language   C. an allusion
   B. literal language   D. symbolism

Read the last part of the excerpt and answer questions 13–15.

> It appeared to me that for a like reason men remain in their present low and primitive condition; but if they should feel the influence of the spring of springs arousing them, they would of necessity rise to a higher and more ethereal life. I had previously seen the snakes in frosty mornings in my path with portions of their bodies still numb and inflexible, waiting for the sun to thaw them. On the 1st of April it rained and melted the ice, and in the early part of the day, which was very foggy, I heard a stray goose groping about over the pond and cackling as if lost, or like the spirit of the fog.

13. The word *arousing* typically means *waking*, as from sleep, or *exciting*, as in "an arousing drum solo." Considering the passage as whole, how does Thoreau use is figuratively here?
    A. He means getting more energy to take on more physical tasks.
    B. He is commenting about how lack of fresh water puts people in a stupor.
    C. He is referring to coming out of the daze of taking life for granted.
    D. He means that people should seek religion to rise above everyday life.

14. Leslie looked up the word *ethereal* in a dictionary. Which of the following definitions would BEST fit how the word is used in the passage?
    A. light, airy, or tenuous
    B. delicate or refined
    C. of or pertaining to the upper regions of space
    D. pertaining to, containing, or resembling ethyl ether

15. What is the BEST synonym for the word *groping* in the last sentence?
    A. feeling   B. searching   C. grasping   D. fumbling

Chapter 5
Understanding Mass Media

This chapter covers the following Georgia standards.

ELAALRL4	The student analyzes how an author's use of language, style, and underlying meaning affects presentations.
ELA11LSV2	The student analyzes effective techniques used in written and oral communication in various media genres.
	The student delivers effective presentations.

Standard ELAALRL4 is part of Domain I, and ELA11LSV2 is part of Domain II. Both standards aim to evaluate your understanding and use of presentation skills.

In Chapters 2 and 3 you read about ways to analyze literature to get the most out of it. You identified how things like an author's writing style, choice of words and tone affected her work. In this chapter, you will apply that knowledge as well as new ideas when you analyze other forms of writing and speech, including those presented by the media. The **media** is any form of communication—be it fact, opinion, entertainment, or something else—presented in any format—writing, graphics, or sound. It includes TV news, movies, music, the Internet, radio programs, newspapers, magazines, advertisements, and political debates. Media can be used to inform, to persuade, and to entertain an audience.

Many of us today think about media as the news media, or we may lump together all news and entertainment. That brings us close to the definition of **mass media**: a term used to describe media designed to reach a very large audience; the term was coined in the 1920s when nationwide radio networks and major newspapers and magazines began to reach millions of people. It's true that the media has a lot of control over what information we as consumers get. News channels pick the stories they report and the perspectives from which they report them. Media groups tell radio stations which songs to play and how often to play them. Advertisers pay to have their products placed in the movies we see. But we as consumers have control too. We can read and listen **critically** and not just accept everything we hear. We can find out who is giving a message and for what purpose. For example, health news we see on television might be coming from a research scientist who just completed a study on a new drug. Or, it might be coming from a doctor who is paid to endorse a weight loss plan. We can also get information from a variety of sources to make sure we are taking in a balanced picture.

Whenever you read or hear a message that requires you to make a judgment, whether it is which politician to believe or which shampoo to buy, there are several questions to consider that can help you make an informed decision. Some of the most important considerations to begin with are the **purpose of the message** and the beliefs and qualifications of the **person or organization presenting the message**. Reading and listening to the media with a critical eye and ear can help you make sense of the material.

ELEMENTS OF EFFECTIVE PRESENTATIONS

When you view or listen to a presentation, you probably come away with a reaction to it, whether that reaction is positive or negative. Have you ever walked out of a movie theater and said to your friend, "That was fantastic—let's see it again tomorrow"? or you may have said, "What a waste of two hours." When evaluating a media presentation, be it a movie, a speech, or an Internet news story, there are several factors to consider when deciding if the presentation was effective. These include the **author's purpose**, the appeal to the **audience**, the **content**, the **use of language**, and the impact of **aesthetic effects**.

AUTHOR'S PURPOSE

When assessing the material you read and hear, one of the most important questions to ask is why the author is writing, or why the speaker is speaking. An author or speaker may have one of several purposes. Generally, he probably wants to **inform**, to **persuade**, or to **entertain**. His purpose will dictate what techniques he will use to present the information. Figuring out the author's purpose is a good first step to understanding the message and how it relates to you.

TO INFORM

An informative presentation is intended to provide information about a topic. If you have ever watched *The History Channel* you might have come across shows that explore topics such as World War II weapons, secret societies, and how water is processed. Maybe you have attended a presentation at a home improvement store on how to install tile, build a fence, or landscape a yard. The purpose of such programs is to provide information. Informative presentations use techniques such as interviews with experts, diagrams, photographs, step-by-step demonstrations, and re-enactments to convey information.

TO PERSUADE

A persuasive piece is intended to get you to change your opinions or practices to align with the writer's or speaker's. Advertisements—whether on TV, radio, or in print—fall into this category. All are trying to make you believe that you need a product or that the advertiser's product is better than the competitor's. Speeches made during political debates also tend to be persuasive. A candidate is trying to persuade voters that he is the best person for the job. There are a variety of persuasive techniques that advertisers, speakers, and writers use:

Appeal to an authority	uses an expert in the field to create credibility **Example:** A doctor in a television commercial recommends a pain reliever.
Bandwagon	implies that if you don't join this movement, you will be left behind **Example:** An SAT tutoring company says that you need its service to compete with everyone else who is already being tutored.
Emotional appeal	attempts to elicit an emotional response **Example:** A magazine ad shows starving children to solicit money to help feed them.
Rhetorical question	sets the listener up to think about an answer **Example:** A speaker addressing alternative energy sources asks, "Are forests worth saving?"
Repetition	repeats a jingle, phrase, or slogan to make a message memorable **Example:** Martin Luther King Jr. repeats "I have a dream" multiple times for emphasis in his speech of the same title.
Generalities	makes claims that are vague and unprovable **Example:** "This soap is the best product on the market and will make your skin look like a million bucks."

To entertain

Sometimes the main purpose of a piece is to entertain. Many movies, music, sitcoms, and novels fall into this category. Authors use a variety of techniques to entertain an audience. They may use language that is humorous or special effects that amaze the viewer. The makers of *The Lord of the Rings* movies relied heavily on special effects when they used computer generated imagery (CGI) to create marvelous landscapes and fantastic creatures.

Practice 1:   Purpose of the Message

Read the paragraphs below. Then identify whether the purpose is to entertain, to inform, or to persuade.

On assembling at quarters for inspection or general exercise, unless directed otherwise, in port, the men are first to go to the starboard guns on the spar-deck, the port guns on the main deck, the starboard guns on the next deck below, and so on. At sea they are first to go to the weather guns, or, if the ship be dead before the wind, to the same sides as in port.

–from "Calls for Assembling at Quarters," *Ordnance Instructions for the United States Navy*, 1866.

1. Purpose: A. entertain   B. inform   C. persuade

Society in every state is a blessing, but Government, even in its best state, is but a necessary evil; in its worst state an intolerable one: for when we suffer, or are exposed to the same miseries BY A GOVERNMENT, which we might expect in a country WITHOUT GOVERNMENT, our calamity is heightened by reflecting that we furnish the means by which we suffer. Government, like dress, is the badge of lost innocence…

–excerpt from "Common Sense" by Thomas Paine

2. Purpose: A. entertain   B. inform   C. persuade

One day I witnessed the departure of an albatross, saluted by the very best croaks of the penguins, no doubt as a friend whom they were to see no more. Those powerful birds can fly for two hundred leagues without resting for a moment, and with such rapidity that they sweep through vast spaces in a few hours. The departing albatross sat motionless upon a high rock, at the end of the bay of Christmas Harbour, looking at the waves as they dashed violently against the beach.

–except from *An Antarctic Mystery* by Jules Verne

3. Purpose: A. entertain   B. inform   C. persuade

A large seabird of the biological family Diomedeidae, the albatross lives in the Southern Ocean and the North Pacific. It is one of the largest flying birds, with some species having a wingspan greater than 10 feet. Using aerodynamics efficiently, the albatross can cover great distance with little effort, eating along the way by diving just below the surface for fish.

Albatross

4. Purpose: A. entertain   B. inform   C. persuade

CONSIDERING THE AUDIENCE

When creating a message, be it a speech or an advertisement, one of the first things an author considers is the intended **audience**: who will read or hear the material. An audience might be the American people (a **mass audience**), basketball teams (a **targeted mass audience**), or your graduating class (a very **specific audience**). With a mass audience, it's impossible for an author to know everything about its members, so any appeal has to be fairly broad. Addressing a targeted mass audience (meaning it's a group that has some things in common), an author can appeal to the common things that audience cares about. Finally, with a specific audience, it is potentially possible to learn about every member and appeal directly to each one (although the group may still be too large to do that realistically, it is possible).

The more an author knows about his audience, the better he can create material that will appeal to them. For example, imagine that this ad appeared in your school newspaper. How appealing would it be to you?

> Luxury home builder blow-out special!
>
> Own your own luxury home for just $3,000 per month!
>
> Low down payment!
>
> Act now—all deals must be signed by the end of this month.

Most high school students have no immediate interest in buying a luxury home, especially at $3,000 per month! The ad would probably get a lot more response in a newspaper read by wealthy adults. Knowing the audience affects other aspects of presentations as well, including the content, language, and techniques a presenter uses to convey information.

CONTENT

In a presentation, the **content** (what is included) can vary though the topic can stay the same. Often, a presenter will make changes to presentation content based on who the audience is. For example, a mayor in favor of a new factory coming to town might be discussing it with two different groups of people. With residents of the town, the mayor would talk about issues that townspeople would find important, such as the job opportunities the factory would create. With the company that is building the factory, he would discuss issues like tax incentives in choosing this town over another.

Practice 2: Considering the Audience

Answer the questions that follow.

1. Which audience would be most interested in a Medicare presentation?

    A.   a swim team   C.   a group of senior citizens

    B.   a group of Americans living in Paris   D.   a group of 11th graders

2. In an advertisement for a frozen pizza, which statement would likely convince a health-conscious mother to buy the pizza?

   A. This pizza is the healthiest frozen pizza you can feed your children.

   B. Our box design is the most attractive on the market.

   C. Our boxes are made from recycled materials.

   D. This pizza comes in two varieties.

3. Which of the following statements in a car advertisement would be MOST likely to interest a group of high school seniors?

   A. This car has the largest trunk capacity in its class.

   B. This car is the coolest car on the road.

   C. This car has room for up to three infant car seats.

   D. This car is strong enough to tow a boat.

4. Which audience is MOST likely to read the local paper in your town?

   A. elderly people who used to live in your town but retired to a different state

   B. children under age 6 who live in your town

   C. people who are thinking about moving to your town

   D. people who live or work in your town

USING LANGUAGE

Part of what makes media effective is the **language** used. One of the reasons that the books (*Under the Tuscan Sun, Bella Tuscany*) of Frances Mayes (b. 1940) are so popular is that she uses vivid **imagery** in her writing about Italy. Her colorful descriptions of the landscape, towns, and people she meets there allow readers to see the Italy that Mayes sees. Mayes's enthusiasm for her subject comes through in the language that she uses, which clearly conveys her belief that Italy is a fascinating place, rich in history, beauty, and kind neighbors.

Notice writer William Cullen Bryant's use of imagery in his descriptive passage on Volterra:

> One of the ravines of which I have spoken— the "balza," they call it at Volterra—has plowed a deep chasm on the north side of this mountain, and is every year rapidly approaching the city on its summit. I stood on its edge and looked down a bank of soft, red earth five hundred feet in height.

–excerpt from *Etruscan Volterra* by William Cullen Bryant (1794–1878)

Writers and speakers use language effectively when they tailor their style to their topic or audience. **Style** is the way a speaker uses language, including grammar and word choice. An author's use of language can have meaning beyond the words that are spoken, particularly when an author consciously chooses a particular tone.

A speaker's **tone** (how he feels about the subject) can affect the meaning of the words and the audience's reaction. For example, a writer may have his character say words in a pleading way ("Please give me the knife," she begged), an angry way ("Give me the knife NOW!" she shouted), or a calming way ("Put the knife down so no one will get hurt," she soothed).

A writer might use style, tone, and imagery to reveal **underlying meaning**. Underlying meaning is the message in a writer's work. In a speech, the message might be "distrust big business" or "the federal government needs more power." In an advertisement, the underlying meaning might be "you will be happier if you buy this product." Read the excerpt of President Franklin Delano Roosevelt's speech to see how his language reveals his underlying meaning.

> *The Navy Department of the United States has reported to me that on the morning of September fourth the United States Destroyer Greer, proceeding in full daylight toward Iceland, had reached a point southeast of Greenland. She was carrying American mail to Iceland. She was flying the American flag. Her identity as an American ship was unmistakable.*
>
> *She was then and there attacked by a submarine. Germany admits that it was a German submarine. The submarine deliberately fired a torpedo at the Greer, followed later by another torpedo attack. In spite of what Hitler's propaganda bureau has invented, and in spite of what any American obstructionist organization may prefer to believe, I tell you the blunt fact that the German submarine fired first upon this American destroyer without warning, and with deliberate design to sink her.*

–excerpt from President Franklin Delano Roosevelt's Fireside Chat to the Nation, September 11, 1941

Franklin Delano Roosevelt

In the first paragraph, FDR's use of a stark, factual style demonstrates that the ship was overt in its actions. He uses plain language to describe the lighting conditions, mission, and American identifiers on the ship. These details imply that the American ship had nothing to hide. He lays out the scenario, leaving no room to debate that the ship did anything to provoke an attack. FDR's style of delivery provides the underlying meaning of his message: an obviously innocent ship was deliberately attacked and there was no excuse other than intent to do so.

Sometimes language can be useful to give us a quick understanding of a character. "Y'all beat them Dawgs now," is a quote from a Southern sports enthusiast that an author might use in his novel. In the quote, the speaker's use of dialect helps us identify who is speaking. While using dialect can give us important clues about the speaker, it can also lead to stereotyping. Authors often use **stereotypes** (a commonly held belief about a group of people) to quickly convey information so it will be recognized by the audience. Stereotypes can be positive ("Jewish people are successful") or negative ("women are bad drivers"). Stereotypes are used in the media to send a quick message. A generalization made in the stereotype may or may

not be true, and not everyone will agree with or appreciate a stereotype. Some people might perceive the speaker in the example above to be not only Southern but also uneducated because he uses dialect ("Y'all") and incorrect grammar ("*them* Dawgs."). Remember, when you hear dialect and language used incorrectly, that an author may be doing it purposefully to let the audience identify the character quickly, or it may be in a derogatory way that perpetuates stereotypes.

Activity 1: Understanding Mass Media

Find an example in the media that demonstrates a presenter's use of imagery, style, tone, or stereotypes. Share your finding with the class.

AESTHETIC EFFECTS

Visual and **aural techniques** are used by authors and speakers to enhance the words they use. Such **aesthetic effects** are all elements besides the words themselves that presenters use to help tell a story and get a point across.

Visual techniques include layout, lighting, camera angle, use of color and background. Movie directors, for example, choose specific visual techniques to achieve desired effects. Maybe they want to surprise a viewer by having a camera zoom in on a person, then having a hand reach into the frame and grab the victim, as happened in *Casino Royale*. A stage director may cut all lights and use just a spotlight on a character on a theater stage. A neighbor may use a diagram at the homeowner's association meeting to show how the new addition to his house will look. All of these visual techniques support the presenter's purpose or message.

Aural techniques include volume, use of music and harmony, and fluctuations in tone and rhythm. Aural techniques are often used for emphasis. An advertisement might use a popular song to capture attention and be memorable. Sound effects might accompany a children's puppet show. Appropriately used audio techniques can add interest to a presentation while making it more memorable.

EVALUATING EFFECTIVE PRESENTATIONS

There are many elements that go into an effective presentation. The following checklist will help you evaluate why a particular presentation was or was not effective.

___**Was the presenter's purpose clear?**	If the author intended to inform, persuade, or entertain, did she? At a magic show, did the magician impress you with her slight of hand? Did the *60 Minutes* piece focus on the facts of the trial it covered?
___**Did the presenter consider the audience?**	Was the presentation tailored to the audience? Did the speaker understand who he was talking to, what was important to them and how they felt on an issue?
___**Was the content appropriate?**	Were the points that were covered be of interest to and understood by the audience? Did the speaker support her position with relevant examples?
___**Was the language appropriate and effective?**	Did the scientist speak in language his audience could understand? Did the speech treat serious matters seriously and lighthearted matters with humor? Did any stereotypes used contribute productively to the message?
___**Did the aesthetics support the presentation?**	Did visual and audio techniques the presenter used add positively to the presentation? Did it make sense to use them as the presenter did?

APPLYING YOUR KNOWLEDGE

There are times, such as when you are doing a research project, that you will encounter different viewpoints from a variety of sources about the same topic. Let's look at how to evaluate the presentations using the principles from this chapter.

Scenario

You are at a neighborhood meeting addressing how Atlanta's need for a sewer overhaul affects your neighborhood. The Chattahoochee River is being polluted because of inadequate sewage systems that have not kept up with population and construction growth in the city. Lawsuits filed in the past few years have required the city to make major changes to the capacity of the sewer lines. The city is planning a project in your neighborhood that involves digging, rerouting traffic, and construction noise over a six month period. Naturally, the neighborhood is quite concerned about this prospect, but all parties agree that something must be done to correct the problem.

This meeting includes presentations by:

- Juan, a spokesperson for the Atlanta sewer project
- Susan, a spokesperson for the Upper Chattahoochee Riverkeeper, an environmental organization that monitors water cleanliness and promotes protection of the river.
- Henry, the president of your neighborhood association

Here are excerpts from each speaker's presentation.

From Juan, the spokesperson for the Atlanta sewer project:

Folks, I know this is inconvenient. I know you are thinking, "Why in my backyard?" Well, I wish it didn't have to be that way. If it were up to me, we would do all of the work we are required to do by law in undeveloped lands where there are no people to inconvenience and no traffic to disrupt. But the law and the map say differently and, unfortunately, buried right up the street from your neighborhood is a major intersection of sewer pipes that needs to be replaced. If you'll look at this map, you can see where the problem area is in relation to your neighborhood. We can't change where the problem is, but we can fix the problem. Everyone in this neighborhood needs clean water and produces waste water, and the system in place that serves your neighborhood is inadequate.

From Susan, the spokesperson for the Upper Chattahoochee Riverkeeper:

Is clean water really that important? Do we really need it? What we take for granted every day when we grab a drink, take a shower or water the lawn is not a luxury—it's a necessity. Water is a precious natural resource and every living thing, from people to animals to trees, needs it. The sewer systems Atlanta relies on are old and insufficient. Every day, more than 5,000 gallons of untreated waste water empties into the Chattahoochee. This pollution affects us all. We in Atlanta, as the producers of this pollution, have a responsibility to maintain a clean source of water for ourselves and every living thing that relies on this water.

From Henry, the president of the neighborhood association:

We all knew that something like this time was coming, but this plan is ridiculous. I've lived in this neighborhood for 30 years, and I continue to be amazed by how many houses they can pack into a small space. Sooner or later those sewer systems were bound to fail. But looking at the proposed plans in the handouts that the sewer project manager provided, this project will be more than an inconvenience for our neighborhood. With the road closed for six months, and the traffic diversion you've suggested, my neighbor Bob here will literally have the street running through his front yard. Nearly all homeowners in this neighborhood will have a trench dug in their property. How will you address the loss of our property value as you destroy trees and driveways? What about all the noise and inconvenience? We deserve better than this treatment, and we won't cooperate unless we get it.

Now let's look at some of the techniques each presenter used.

Juan started by acknowledging the feelings of the audience. He pointed out the logical reasons that the work had to be done in that particular place. He used a visual aid to clarify this fact. He reminded everyone that the project would fix a problem that will soon affect the neighborhood.

Susan began with a rhetorical question. She used a statistic to back up her argument. She attempted to inspire accountability by pointing out the need to look beyond personal inconvenience and take action for the long term good of ourselves and others.

Henry shows that he understands the cause of the problem but is concerned and angry about how the project will be handled. He points to specific inconveniences the neighborhood will face and demands reassurance that the project will address these matters conscientiously, threatening resistance if they're not.

Practice 3: Evaluating Effective Presentations

Read the questions below. Then answer the questions that follow. All questions are in reference to the scenario above.

1. Which presenter would be MOST likely to agree with the following statement: "This project needs to be done but not in my backyard."
   A. Susan, the spokesperson for the Upper Chattahoochee Riverkeeper
   B. Henry, the president of the neighborhood association
   C. Juan, the spokesperson for the Atlanta sewer project
   D. none of the above

2. Which presenter would be MOST likely to agree with the following statement: "Any inconvenience is worthwhile to keep our rivers clean."
   A. Susan, the spokesperson for the Upper Chattahoochee Riverkeeper
   B. Henry, the president of the neighborhood association
   C. Juan, the spokesperson for the Atlanta sewer project
   D. none of the above

3. Which presenter uses an emotional appeal to make a point?
   A. Susan, the spokesman for the Upper Chattahoochee Riverkeeper
   B. Henry, the president of the neighborhood association
   C. Juan, the spokesman for the Atlanta sewer project
   D. none of the above

4. Which of the following visual aids would be the MOST helpful to Susan in her presentation as the spokesman for the Upper Chattahoochee Riverkeeper?
   A. a photograph of raw sewage pouring into a river
   B. a map of all of the houses in the neighborhood
   C. aerial photographs of Atlanta
   D. a model of sewer pipes

5. Which piece of information would be BEST at reassuring the homeowners in the neighborhood?

    A. This really is not that big of an inconvenience.
    B. The fish and frogs in the Chattahoochee will thank you.
    C. The needs of the city are more important than your individual needs.
    D. We will restore your property to the exact condition in which we found it.

6. What is the purpose of Susan's presentation, as spokesperson for the Upper Chattahoochee River-keeper?

    A. to persuade the homeowners that this project is critical for clean water
    B. to entertain the homeowners with amazing stories
    C. to inform the homeowners about the process of the project
    D. to allay the homeowner's fears about their yards being dug up

7. What is the underlying meaning of Henry's presentation, as president of the neighborhood association?

    A. Clean water is overrated.
    B. We know this needs to be done, but how will you will make it bearable?
    C. The sewers are fine as they are.
    D. We will bring a lawsuit against you if you step on our property.

8. Whose presentation would likely include statistics about Atlanta's current sewage capacity and the expected demands on the system in years to come?

    A. Susan's, the spokesperson for the Upper Chattahoochee Riverkeeper
    B. Henry's, the president of the neighborhood association
    C. Juan's, the spokesperson for the Atlanta sewer project
    D. none of the above

9. What is the tone of the presentation by Juan, the spokesperson for the Atlanta sewer project?

    A. an apologetic tone   C. a defensive tone
    B. a combative tone   D. an angry tone

Effective speeches, advertisements, magazine articles, and other mass media successfully incorporate and address several elements: purpose, audience, content, language, and visual and aural techniques. When reading or listening to presentations, you can analyze the information you are given in light of these elements. Then, you can assess the relevance, accuracy and purpose of the information and take action if necessary.

CREATING A PRESENTATION

You just read about how to evaluate effective presentations. Now, let's look at how to incorporate those elements into your own presentations. At some point, you will be asked to give an oral presentation. Speeches and debates are common assignments in high school. Considering the following points will help you prepare your own effective presentations.

KNOW YOUR PURPOSE

One of the first things you will want to identify when planning your speech is your purpose. As you read earlier, speeches can be made to entertain, to persuade, and to inform. The reasons for making a presentation are just like those for writing, which you'll read more about in the next chapter, "The Writing Process."

Once you have defined your purpose, it is time to consider the other elements that go into an effective presentation.

KNOW YOUR AUDIENCE

Having defined your purpose, your next objective is to define your **audience**. You probably use different vocabulary and mannerisms when addressing your friends than when addressing your coach. In the same way, you will use different techniques depending on who you are addressing in your speech. It is important to know who you are talking to and what is important to them. Once you know this information, you can then determine the most effective way to appeal to the audience. For example, imagine that you are the student council president and need to talk to both the PTA and the student body about changes to the school lunch program. The two groups will likely have different priorities. PTA members may ask questions regarding nutrition, while students may ask questions regarding food choice. Anticipating what's important to your audience will help you be prepared and effective in your speech.

Both your purpose and your audience will affect the **content** of your presentation. Let's say your topic is Hispanic American writers. Depending on the purpose of your presentation, your content might focus on an author's life, what influenced him, or a comparison of his two most famous works. If your audience is a group of your peers, the content might be different than if your audience is a group of published authors. Content is influenced by your purpose and your audience.

Practice 4:   Creating a Presentation

Read the following statements. Then decide which **audience** the speaker is addressing.

1. If elected president, I pledge to save social security.
    - A.   a group of preschoolers
    - B.   a group of senior citizens
    - C.   a PTA association
    - D.   a medical convention

2. If elected president, I pledge to allocate more federal money for college scholarships.
    - A.   a group of preschoolers
    - B.   a group of senior citizens
    - C.   a group of high school students
    - D.   the Vice President

Read the following statements. Then decide the *purpose* for which the speaker is speaking.

3. We need to put alternative fuels to work if we want this earth to last much longer.
    - A.   to inform
    - B.   to entertain
    - C.   to persuade
    - D.   to confuse

4. Here are the steps involved in making honey.
    - A.   to inform
    - B.   to entertain
    - C.   to persuade
    - D.   to confuse

ORGANIZING YOUR SPEECH

Once you have determined the purpose of your speech, the audience you will be addressing, and the content you will include, it is time to plan how you will organize your speech. Writing a speech is much like writing a paper. You will need an **introduction**, a **body**, and a **conclusion**.

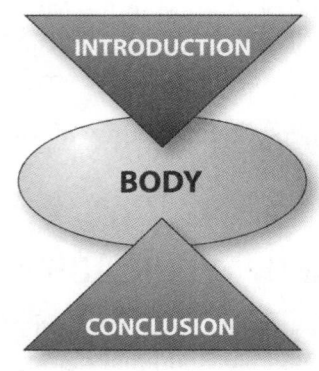

The **introduction** is the beginning of your speech. Here, you set the tone and grab the audience's attention. You might start out with a surprising statistic, a personal story, or a rhetorical question. Once you have the audience's attention, introduce your topic.

The **body** of your speech contains the point you want to make. This is where you will use detailed information, quotes, statistics and other material that supports your point.

The **conclusion** of your speech wraps up your point while telling your audience why your presentation was worth their time.

When preparing a presentation for class, your teacher will also likely require an outline or summary to be handed in, along with source information. Be sure to find out what style you should use to prepare your **works-cited page** or **bibliography**, on which you will list the resources you used to prepare your presentation.

USING LANGUAGE EFFECTIVELY

The words that you speak and the way that you speak them has great impact on your presentation. Consider the following ways to use language effectively as you prepare your presentation:

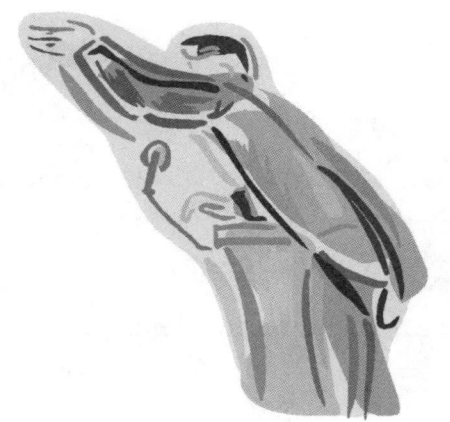

Use interesting language. Grab the audience's attention at the beginning of your presentation and keep it.

Use informal expressions for effect. Know your audience and speak in a way that will appeal to them.

Use Standard English for clarity. Standard English uses correct grammar, including subject-verb agreement, complete sentences, and no slang.

Use technical language for specificity. Keep in mind that your audience may need you to explain difficult technical concepts in simpler terms.

Practice 5: Organizing Your Speech and Using Effective Language

Read and answer the questions that follow.

1. Which language does not fit in effectively with the rest of the speech?

> Tropical fish come in a wide variety of colors. The color combinations and hues are really quite impressive. Check out these cool yellow ones with the squiggly purple lines. Parrot fish come in shades of blue, green, red, and yellow.

   A. Tropical fish come in a wide variety of colors.
   B. Parrot fish come in shades of blue, green, red, and yellow.
   C. The color combinations and hues are really quite impressive.
   D. Check out these cool yellow ones with the squiggly purple lines.

2.   Once you loosen the nut from the bolt, set the nut aside; you will use it in Step 17. Remove the bolt by pulling it at a perpendicular angle. Toss that little metal doodad you used earlier into the trash can. Use the socket wrench to tighten the bolt, using 2 full clockwise twists.

   A. Remove the bolt by pulling it at a perpendicular angle.
   B. Toss that little metal doodad you used earlier into the trash can.
   C. Once you loosen the nut from the bolt, set the nut aside; you will use it in Step 17.
   D. Use the socket wrench to tighten the bolt, using 2 full clockwise twists.

3. Which section of your presentation should contain proof of your point, such as statistics, specific details, and quotes from experts?
   A. the introduction   C. the conclusion
   B. the body   D. none of the above

4. Which of the following are reasons to practice giving your speech before you give your final presentation?
   A. You will be able to practice how loudly to speak.
   B. You will feel more confident.
   C. You can get constructive feedback from your test audience.
   D. All of the above

AUDIO-VISUAL EFFECTS

As you assess your presentation and consider what to include to make it effective, you may decide to include some audio or visual components. Audio-visual effects, such as music, PowerPoint, or video, can be an important part of your presentation. Depending on your topic, you might use **visual effects** such as pictures and **graphics**, and **musical effects** and **sound** as part of presentation.

Visual effects are images. A visual effect can be a movie clip, a photograph displayed on an overhead projector, or a poster of a famous author hanging on the wall. **Graphics** like charts and graphs can help illustrate your point by showing things like change over time and the differences in two items being compared. Visual effects can help capture (or recapture!) an audience's attention. Make sure that any visual equipment you plan to use will be available where you will be giving the presentation.

Music can be an effective way to capture your audience's attention. You might have music accompany graphics or you might use music on its own. You might use an audio recording to provide an example of what you are talking about. When using **sound**, consider and test for appropriate volume. As with visual images, make sure that the sound equipment you plan to use is available where you will be giving the presentation.

Activity 2: Audio-Visual Effects

Working with a partner, choose one of the following presentations. Develop a list of at least three audio or visual elements that would be effective in the presentation. Explain your answer. Share your answer with the class.

> a presentation on your school's sports program to a group of new students
>
> a letter to your local police department about the town's new curfew
>
> a commercial for a pest control company
>
> a horror movie

CHAPTER 5 SUMMARY

The **media** is any form of communication presented in written, spoken or printed form. You can analyze what makes a media presentation effective by looking at the **author's purpose**, how the **audience** is considered, the **content** of the presentation, the **language** (like **imagery**, **style**, **tone**, **underlying meaning** and **stereotypes**) the presenter uses, and the use of any **aesthetic elements**, like **video** and **audio aids**.

When you give oral presentations, you will want to use those same effective techniques. You will want to determine your **purpose** and think about the best information to use to prove your point. You will want to consider the approach that will be most effective with your **audience**. Your **content** will depend on your topic, purpose and audience. You will want to use a logical **organization** strategy for your speech, beginning with a strong **introduction**, a detailed **body**, and a convincing **conclusion**. The **language** you choose is important when creating an effective speech, as is whether or not you will use any **audio** or **visual aids** and how you will use them.

CHAPTER 5 REVIEW

Read the excerpts from the speeches. Then answer the questions that follow.

As we walk, we must make the pledge that we shall march ahead. We cannot turn back. There are those who are asking the devotees of civil rights, "When will you be satisfied?" We can never be satisfied as long as the Negro is the victim of the unspeakable horrors of police brutality. We can never be satisfied, as long as our bodies, heavy with the fatigue of travel, cannot gain lodging in the motels of the highways and the hotels of the cities. We can never be satisfied as long as a Negro in Mississippi cannot vote and a Negro in New York believes he has nothing for which to vote. No, no, we are not satisfied, and we will not be satisfied until justice rolls down like waters and righteousness like a mighty stream.

–Martin Luther King Jr. "I Have a Dream" speech

1. Who is the audience?

   A. schoolchildren
   B. the president of the United States
   C. King's family
   D. all black Americans

2. What is King's purpose in speaking?

   A. to persuade   B. to entertain   C. to inform   D. to anger

3. Which of the following statements best describes how King feels on the topic?

   A. We must keep working toward change.
   B. We have accomplished our goal.
   C. It is time to give up.
   D. We must lower our expectations.

4. What does King want the audience to do?

   A. start a war
   B. work toward racial equality
   C. leave the country
   D. go back to slavery

5. Why do you think King repeats the phrase "we can never be satisfied"?

   A. He can't think of anything else to say.
   B. He likes how it sounds.
   C. He is making his points memorable.
   D. He is tired of talking.

Immediately following the first attack, I implemented our government's emergency response plans. Our military is powerful, and it's prepared. Our emergency teams are working in New York City and Washington, D.C., to help with local rescue efforts.

Our first priority is to get help to those who have been injured, and to take every precaution to protect our citizens at home and around the world from further attacks.

The functions of our government continue without interruption. Federal agencies in Washington which had to be evacuated today are reopening for essential personnel tonight, and will be open for business tomorrow. Our financial institutions remain strong, and the American economy will be open for business, as well.

–President George W. Bush, September 11, 2001

6. What is Bush's purpose in speaking?
   A. to entertain   B. to inform   C. to persuade   D. to warn

7. Who is Bush's audience?
   A. the American people   C. his children
   B. terrorists   D. his father

8. What is Bush trying to do in his speech?
   A. anger the audience   C. calm and reassure the audience
   B. accuse the audience   D. frighten the audience

9. How does Bush accomplish his purpose?
   A. He gives specific facts about how the tragedy is being addressed.
   B. He makes threats to those responsible.
   C. He explains how America will retaliate.
   D. He reads the names of the victims.

Team, I know it's hard to come to practice every day. After school, your friends are going out for pizza, heading for the beach, and playing games of Frisbee. But I'm asking you to come here every day, to sweat, to run, and to get tackled. It's hard, and I know it. But this team needs you to train hard each and every day so we can be a winning team.

10. Who is the speaker?
    A. the school principal   C. your mother
    B. a team member   D. the coach

11. Who is the audience?
    A. sports fans   C. the PTA
    B. a college recruiter   D. the team

12. How does the speaker try to get the audience to do what he wants?
    A. by blaming them   C. by empathizing with them
    B. the berating them   D. by belittling them

13. What is the speaker's underlying message?
    A. The practices are too strenuous.
    B. Practicing is easy.
    C. This team is lazy.
    D. You all need to come to practice every day so we can win.

The purpose of a presentation can be to inform, to persuade or to entertain. For each topic, choose the letter that best describes the purpose of the presentation.

14. How to evacuate the school safely in case of a flood.
    A. to inform   B. to persuade   C. to entertain

15. How to operate a fire extinguisher.
    A. to inform   B. to persuade   C. to entertain

16. Why the movie version of *The Color Purple* is better than the book.
    A. to inform   B. to persuade   C. to entertain

17. What I learned at the beach this summer.
    A. to inform   B. to persuade   C. to entertain

11th Grade

End of Course Test
AMERICAN LITERATURE
and COMPOSITION

Chapter 6
The Writing Process

This chapter covers the following Georgia standard(s) relating to **writing**.

ELA11W1	Produce writing that establishes an appropriate organizational structure, sets a context and engages the reader, maintains a coherent focus throughout, and signals a satisfying closure.
ELA11W2	Demonstrate competence in a variety of genres.
ELA11W4	Practice both timed and process writing and, when applicable, use the writing process to develop, revise, and evaluate writing.

This chapter also covers the following Georgia standard relating to **reading** and **American literature**.

ELAALRL4	Employ a variety of writing genres to demonstrate a comprehensive grasp of significant ideas in selected literary works. Compose essays, narratives, poems, or technical documents.

The writing standards covered in this chapter are primarily from Domain III: Writing, along with ELAALRL4 from Domain I. Questions about these standards will measure your ability to recognize coherent and focused writing.

In chapter 5, you read about how language is used in mass media. You focused on identifying the purpose of communication (be it written or spoken), considered the person or organization behind the message, and evaluated the content of the message. In this chapter, you will apply the ideas of **purpose**, **audience**, and **content** to different **genres** of writing. You will review what it means to write well and evaluate passages of writing for their clarity and effectiveness.

Because the EOCT in American Literature and Composition is entirely multiple choice, you will not have to do any actual writing. Instead, the EOCT will test your writing abilities in other ways. For example, you may have to identify the key **organizational** elements of a passage of informational writing, such as the **controlling idea** or the **topic sentences**.

Paragraphs should be organized so that your ideas progress in a logical fashion. Having a strong thesis helps your paper stay **focused**. Consider the length of your assignment when formulating your thesis, and be sure to choose a stance that is neither too broad nor too narrow.

You will have to consider the **coherence** of a paragraph: that is, whether the reader can easily follow the argument you are building or the topic you are explaining. In order to be coherent, your sentences must be a logical progression of ideas. In addition, consider the **unity** of your paragraphs. This means that the supporting details should relate to the topic sentence, which in turn should relate to the thesis or controlling idea. The evidence you gather from primary and secondary sources should develop and support your thesis or controlling idea. (for more on paragraph structure and coherence, see chapter 9, Paragraph Structure and Manuscript Formatting).

Here are some examples of the way the questions may be asked on the EOCT:

•Which sentence does NOT fit with the main idea of the report?

•Which sentence is the BEST thesis for this passage?

•Which sentence is out of sequence in the paragraph?

•Which is the BEST placement for the following sentence?

•What is the main idea of the passage?

You may also be asked to read passages and evaluate them for clarity, proper sentence structure, and grammar. You will be like an editor, identifying the good writing and weeding out the poor writing. In this chapter, we will discuss the elements of good writing, such as using precise language, action verbs, sensory details, and active rather than passive voice. These editing questions may be asked like this:

- Which, if any, would be the BEST way to revise Sentence 1?

- Which phrase is too informal for the passage?

- What is the correct way to write the following sentence?

You may be asking yourself: "How do I prepare for a writing test that doesn't require me to do any writing?"

The key to doing well is improving your ability to recognize all the aspects of good writing and identify the author's **audience** and **purpose**. A great way to improve your writing skills is to read constantly and widely, closely analyzing what you read. Expose yourself to a variety of writing, such as newspaper articles, personal essays, short stories, scientific reports, etc. Familiarizing yourself with different types and genres of writing will help you notice how the language changes accordingly.

Read as much literature as you can. Read actively, asking questions such as these: How does an author communicate the main idea? How is language used to convey a mood? What makes writing "awkward" or wordy, and what makes writing clear and precise?

Keep in mind that good writing is well focused, clear, organized, and free of grammatical mistakes. In chapter 8, you can review and practice troublesome grammar rules and conventions of writing, so that you are comfortable when they appear on the test. This chapter reviews the foundations of writing and helps prepare you for taking the EOCT.

PURPOSE

In chapter 5, you learned to identify whether an **author's purpose** was to inform, to persuade, or to entertain in presentations and speeches. Similarly, as a writer, you must decide what your purpose is **before** you begin.

Most of the time, you are writing because your teacher has given you an assignment, so you may be thinking, "My purpose is to get a good grade!" Your teacher typically wants to know that you've learned something, so often your purpose is to inform. However, at some point in school you were probably given the chance to write a funny piece about your life or a persuasive letter about an issue you care deeply about. There are many reasons why you write, and thinking about your purpose will help guide your organization, reasoning, and use of language. Below are just a few of the many motives for writing.

Purpose	Example
To inform	A report on current environmental concerns in Georgia
To entertain	A screenplay of a slapstick comedy
To persuade	A letter to your parents, asking for a car
To instruct	A step-by-step guide to building a cabinet
To motivate	A speech written for a graduation ceremony
To tell a story	A short story inspired by a camping trip
To describe	A description of the beautiful architecture in Rome, Italy

Think about some of the writing assignments you've had in the past. What was your purpose for each one?

Thinking about what your purpose is will lead you to consider what **genre** you will be writing in.

GENRES AND TYPES OF WRITING

A **genre** is a category of writing that is characterized by a particular content, form, and purpose. The main umbrella categories for genre are **fiction** (or literary), which encompasses smaller genres such as romance, science fiction, mystery, poetry and drama; and **nonfiction**, which includes genres such as biography, personal letters, memoirs, and research reports.

Different genres often use a specific type of writing, such as **expository**, **persuasive**, **narrative**, and **technical**.

• **Expository** writing is used in news articles, directions, and informational essays. The goal is to provide information, explain a topic, or give directions to the reader. The writer should not inject personal opinion or analysis into expository writing.

- **Persuasive** writing is intended to influence the reader's thoughts or convince the reader to take a certain action. If you write a letter to your school principal asking for healthier cafeteria food, you would be writing persuasively. When you analyze literature, you are also being persuasive, because you want to prove to your reader that your interpretation is sound. In order to be persuasive, you must:

  - State your position on a well-defined and debatable topic.

  - Present your ideas clearly and in a logical fashion.

  - Support your ideas with specific evidence (facts, expert opinions, research, etc.).

- Anticipate different **perspectives** and opposing viewpoints: discuss them and then refute them, if possible, or explain why your ideas are better.

- End with a summary of your strongest points, a compelling final argument, and/or a call for action.

- **Narrative** writing tells a story, complete with a plot, climax, and resolution. The goal in narrative writing is to relate a sequence of events or discuss an experience in a way that is interesting to the reader. Fiction writing uses a narrative style.

- **Technical** writing is typically found in the math, business, and science fields. The goal is to explain clearly a very specific piece of information to a targeted audience that is familiar with the subject matter and terminology of the field. Although technical writing is more frequently associated with math and science, it can also be used in the humanities in the following genres:

  - **Historical investigative reports** compile information about a specific historical topic of interest; for example, the history of the different Native American tribes of Georgia.

  - **Literary analyses** examine a work of literature and usually focus on a very specific aspect of the work. In order to understand the writing, you will have to be familiar with the terminology frequently used in literary studies.

  - **Reflective compositions** are the opposite of expository writing. Instead of simply presenting ideas and information, you are responding and reacting to them.

Because technical writing is often used in computer science, there is a highly specialized vocabulary that people in the field understand and use to communicate with each other quickly and effectively. For example, articles written within the computer science field would be confusing to the average reader. Accordingly, a technical article written for a newspaper would have to be modified to fit its wider audience, and the writer would need to explain any terms that the average reader might be unfamiliar with. Here's an example of writing that would be understandable to someone in the computer science field:

> Applications are being significantly impacted by deprecated classes and methods. Refactoring would improve code efficiency.

The average reader would be confused by "deprecated" and "refactoring," and the concise style offers no further explanation to the audience. Also, the word "impacted" is an example of how nouns are frequently turned into verbs in technical and business language, a practice that should be avoided in formal academic writing.

Here's how the writing would have to be changed to fit a general audience:

> In computer programming, languages are updated frequently. Programmers are expected and sometimes required to keep up with the latest changes to a language, and will often have to go back to applications they have already written and distributed to make updates.

Notice how there is more explanation, and the writer assumes that the average reader will be familiar with the words "language" and "application" as they apply to the field of computer science.

For more about learning vocabulary across subject areas, see chapter 4: Word Meanings.

AUDIENCE

After you've thought about *why* you're writing and what writing strategy you will use, think about *who* is going to read your work. Are you writing for your classmates, your teacher, your parents, someone in the community, students who are younger than you? Chapter 5 discussed the difference between mass and specific audiences, focusing on the author's desire to appeal to each by creating the appropriate content. A good writer learns to take audience into account, adapting the language and content as necessary to fit the situation appropriately. For example, a paper you write for class will have a much more formal tone than an e-mail you send to a friend.

Also, consider the type of **manuscript formatting** or **style guide** you will use. A personal letter will require a different format than a literary analysis will, and the latter typically requires citation as well. You may also find that your history teacher wants your paper to be formatted differently from an English paper. For a reminder of the different requirements you may encounter, see chapter 9, Paragraph and Manuscript Formatting.

TYPES OF ORGANIZATION

Writing that is **chronological** organizes information according to a process or sequence of events. This method is frequently used in narrative writing such as a fictional story or re-telling of a historical event.

Cause and effect analysis is used when you want to explain *why* something happened. It can also be used to predict what outcomes will arise from a set of circumstances. For example, many people use cause and effect analysis in the aftermath of a disaster or crime. They want to know what factors led to the event, and often the goal is to figure out how to prevent a similar occurrence from happening again in the future.

You can organize your writing by drawing **comparisons,** or explaining the **similarities and differences** of certain ideas or subjects. For example, you can compare: how two authors use imagery, the development of American and European literature, or the styles of two famous speeches. Drawing comparisons can help you organize your writing and make your main points easy to follow.

Sometimes, **posing and answering a question** can be an engaging way to structure your writing, especially if you want to write persuasively. For example, you might ask, "Why should we exercise?" and then answer the question in a series of paragraphs that include the most important reasons you find.

Practice 1: Organization

Read each question. Then choose the best answer.

1. Which of the following is the BEST question for a *brief* essay about the Wilfred Owen poem "Dulce et Decorum est?

    A. What is the significance of the poem's title?

    B. What was Owen's experience in World War I?

    C. Does Owen use imagery in the poem?

    D. In what ways is Owen's writing similar to that of the other War Poets of World War I?

2. A cause and effect organization would work BEST for which of the following topics?

    A. a narrative about your first day of high school

    B. a paper on global warming

    C. a movie review

    D. an essay about a person you admire

3. Chronological organization would NOT be ideal for which of the following topics?

    A. a paper about the process you went through in designing a science experiment

    B. an essay explaining how to use a computer program to make a collage of digital photos

    C. a synopsis of a book about the events leading up to Battle of Gettysburg

    D. a paper about Flannery O'Connor's frequent use of the grotesque in her novels

4. After you read Edgar Allan Poe's poems "The Raven" and "Annabel Lee," your teacher asks you to write an essay discussing character development and the overall mood in each poem. Which would be the BEST way to organize your essay?

A. chronological   C. comparison/contrast

B. narrative   D. posing and answering a question

Read the passage below and answer the questions that follow.

Benjamin Franklin

Benjamin Franklin was born in Milk Street, Boston, on January 6, 1706. His father, Josiah Franklin, was a tallow chandler who married twice, and of his seventeen children Benjamin was the youngest son. His schooling ended at ten, and at twelve he was bound apprentice to his brother James, a printer, who published the "New England Courant." To this journal he became a contributor, and later was for a time its nominal editor. But the brothers quarreled, and Benjamin ran away, going first to New York, and thence to Philadelphia, where he arrived in October, 1723. He soon obtained work as a printer, but after a few months he was induced by Governor Keith to go to London, where, finding Keith's promises empty, he again worked as a compositor till he was brought back to Philadelphia by a merchant named Denman, who gave him a position in his business. On Denman's death he returned to his former trade, and shortly set up a printing house of his own from which he published "The Pennsylvania Gazette," to which he contributed many essays, and which he made a medium for agitating a variety of local reforms. In 1732, he began to issue his famous "Poor Richard's Almanac" for the enrichment of which he borrowed or composed those pithy utterances of worldly wisdom which are the basis of a large part of his popular reputation. In 1758, the year in which he ceased writing for the Almanac, he printed in it "Father Abraham's Sermon," now regarded as the most famous piece of literature produced in Colonial America.

–From the Introduction to *The Autobiography of Benjamin Franklin*, edited by Charles W. Eliot

5. What is the purpose of this passage?

A. to describe Franklin's relationship with his family

B. to give the reader a brief overview of Franklin's life

C. to explain why Franklin wrote an autobiography

D. to inform the reader about what life was like in the 1700s

6. What organizational method did the author use?

A. comparison/contrast   C. chronological

B. cause and effect   D. posing and answering a question

For more information and practice on structure and organization, see Chapter 9: Paragraph Structure and Manuscript Formatting.

THE WRITING PROCESS

The written word varies significantly from the spoken word. In everyday conversation, it is not unusual if our speech is jumbled, unclear, meandering, or disconnected. Thankfully, we have other means of facilitating comprehension, such as gestures, tone of voice, and facial expressions. Unfortunately, you don't have the same opportunity when writing. Accordingly, writers must take the time to make sure their work is clear and focused.

In order to craft a good piece of writing, it is important to organize yourself. Begin by **planning** what you want to say. **Prewriting** or **brainstorming** will help you get all your ideas out on paper.

(For more information on planning strategies and tools for prewriting, see American Book Company's *Basics Made Easy: Writing Review*)

Begin by asking yourself a few questions:

- What is your purpose for writing?
- What do you want to say?
- What evidence are you going to use to support your main idea?
- What sources will you use?
- Who is your audience?

At this stage, you don't have to worry so much about picking the perfect word or writing the best topic sentence. This is the rough, creative stage.

Next, write a first **draft** that includes everything you jotted down in the planning stage. Focus on the overall organization of your paper at this stage. Will the reader be able to follow what you're saying, or do you jump around from point to point in a disconnected manner?

Every draft will need work, so now it's time to **revise** your paper. Read over your paper, checking for clarity, logical flow, and plenty of supporting evidence.

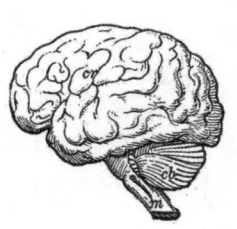

Always make sure to go back and **edit** your paper a few times, checking for grammatical and stylistic errors. Fix any awkward sentences, and clear up any vague statements. At both the editing and revising stages, it is helpful to take a break from your paper, if you can, in order to review it with fresh eyes. Reading the paper from the end to the beginning can also help you catch minor errors that you may have missed earlier. Sometimes your brain gets so used to seeing the same sentences that it fails to notice even the simplest mistakes, and reading from the end will help your writing seem more "fresh" to your brain.

Review of Writing Process Stages	
Prewriting:	Consider purpose, audience, genre, writing strategy, and type of organization.
Drafting:	Focus on formulating a clear thesis, topic sentences, and supporting details.
Revising:	Review for organization and coherence of ideas, effectiveness towards purpose and audience, sentence variety and parallelism, and level of formality.
Proofreading:	Check for errors in grammar, spelling, word choice, and punctuation.

STRUCTURE

THE THESIS STATEMENT

The **thesis statement** is a component of persuasive or analytical writing because it establishes your position on an arguable issue. Without a proper thesis, your paper may wander aimlessly, never settling on a coherent point. In informational (i.e., expository) writing, you will most likely establish a **controlling idea** instead, which tells the reader what aspect of your topic your paper will focus on and does not necessarily express an opinion or analytical statement.

FORMULATING AN ARGUMENT

When writing persuasively or analytically, your thesis statement and topic sentences need to be **arguable**. Your thesis is your main argument, and the rest of the paper works to support this argument.

An arguable statement:

- Attempts to persuade readers: whether it is to convince them or change their minds about a topic, inspire them to take action, or motivate them to explore an issue further on their own.

- Discusses an issue that does not have a clear solution, or asks a question that does not have one simple answer.

- Establishes a position or takes a side that not everyone will agree with.

BODY PARAGRAPHS AND SUPPORTING DETAILS

The **body paragraphs** are the "meat" of your work. Each paragraph should be composed of related sentences that make a single point. Together, they should develop your **controlling idea** or **thesis** and maintain **unity** by supporting the claim made in your topic sentence.

Each paragraph should have a **topic sentence** that provides a supporting idea for the thesis and indicates to the reader what the paragraph will discuss. A topic sentence is a general statement, with supporting evidence following in the body paragraph. Your topic sentences are the **subordinate** (or supporting) ideas to your controlling idea, which means that they should relate to each other and develop the **coherence** of your essay.

You will also need to incorporate **specific evidence and examples** from **primary** and **secondary sources** for your points. Evidence can come in the form of **anecdotes, facts, statistics, descriptions**, studies, or details from credible primary and secondary sources. Of course, be sure to appropriately cite your sources. The type of evidence you use will vary according to your topic, genre, and writing strategy.

 An **anecdote** is a short narrative, typically biographical, that writers insert into a larger piece of writing in order to illustrate a point. Because they are so brief, anecdotes deal with a single incident of relatively short duration. Anecdotes can be about you, someone you know personally, or famous people from past or present. Many magazine and newspaper articles begin with anecdotes to add a human element to a broader concern. For example, a newspaper article about Atlanta's traffic congestion might begin with a tale of how one resident commutes to work by using alternative transportation.

Statistics are collections of data that are gathered from a census, survey or lab experiment. Instead of gathering data from *every* member of a population, data is collected from a smaller sample in order to make observations and predictions about the whole population. Citing statistics is a good way to support your claims, as long as they come from a reliable source and are not taken out of context.

Be sure to use **description** in your writing in order to hold your reader's interest. Suppose you want to convince your principal to increase the number of minutes you have between classes. You could start out by saying, "Because our school is so large and there are so many people rushing to get to class, it is difficult to make it to class on time." Adding a description can help make your plea more convincing, as it draws your reader into your experience.

THE CONCLUSION

Regardless of what you write, you should always attain **closure**: don't leave your reader hanging! The **conclusion** should include a **detailed summary of the main points** and **restate the thesis** (but do not repeat it word for word). It should wrap up the essay in a meaningful and thoughtful way and remind readers, in a general sense, of what they have just read. The concluding paragraph can also discuss ways in which the topic can be probed further, providing "food for thought."

Depending on your purpose and audience, you can try a variety of strategies to conclude your writing, such as using a **quotation**, **question**, **vivid image**, or **call for action**: anything that brings the argument in your composition together.

For more about paragraph structure, see chapter 9, Paragraph Structure and Manuscript Formatting.

Activity: Purpose, Audience, and Structure

Look through essays in your English textbook and/or magazines, and find the purpose, audience, and structural elements (thesis, topic sentences, supporting details, closure) in each. Write down your findings and share them with the teacher or classmates.

Practice 2: Purpose, Audience, and Structure

Read the following passage, and answer the questions that follow.

> I do not claim that I can tell a story as it ought to be told. I only claim to know how a story ought to be told, for I have been almost daily in the company of the most expert story-tellers for many years.
>
> There are several kinds of stories, but only one difficult kind—the humorous. I will talk mainly about that one. The humorous story is American, the comic story is English, the witty story is French. The humorous story depends for its effect upon the manner of the telling; the comic story and the witty story upon the matter.
>
> The humorous story may be spun out to great length, and may wander around as much as it pleases, and arrive nowhere in particular; but the comic and witty stories must be brief and end with a point. The humorous story bubbles gently along, the others burst.
>
> The humorous story is strictly a work of art—high and delicate art—and only an artist can tell it; but no art is necessary in telling the comic and the witty story; anybody can do it. The art of telling a humorous story—understand, I mean by word of mouth, not print— was created in America, and has remained at home.
>
> The humorous story is told gravely; the teller does his best to conceal the fact that he even dimly suspects that there is anything funny about it; but the teller of the comic story tells you beforehand that it is one of the funniest things he has ever heard, then tells it with eager delight, and is the first person to laugh when he gets through. And sometimes, if he has had good success, he is so glad and happy that he will repeat the "nub" of it and glance around from face to face, collecting applause, and then repeat it again. It is a pathetic thing to see.

–excerpt from "How to Tell a Story," from *How to Tell a Story and Others* by Mark Twain

1. What is the controlling idea of this passage?

    A. why stories are humorous

    B. how to tell a story as well as Mark Twain

    C. how to tell a humorous story

    D. a humorous story is a work of art

2. Which of the following statements from the passage BEST supports the controlling idea?

    A. "The humorous story is American, the comic story is English, the witty story is French."

    B. "The humorous story is told gravely; the teller does his best to conceal the fact that he even dimly suspects that there is anything funny about it…"

    C. "…I have been almost daily in the company of the most expert story-tellers for many years."

    D. "…the teller of the comic story tells you beforehand that it is one of the funniest things he has ever heard…"

3. How does Twain establish his credibility to his audience?
   A. He compares English stories to American stories
   B. He explains that funny stories are a work of art.
   C. He says that he has been around talented story-tellers for years.
   D. He says that he knows how to tell a story properly.

4. Which of the following is NOT a purpose of Twain's?
   A. entertain   B. motivate   C. instruct   D. persuade

5. Which of the following types of supporting details does Twain use?
   A. descriptions   B. statistics   C. studies   D. anecdotes

6. Which statement below is NOT arguable?
   A. "There are several kinds of stories, but only one difficult kind—the humorous"
   B. "The humorous story is strictly a work of art"
   C. "I have been almost daily in the company of the most expert story-tellers for many years"
   D. "It is a pathetic thing to see"

7. Which of the following could be used as a topic sentence for paragraph 3?
   A. The humorous story is more sophisticated than the others.
   B. The humorous story is structured differently from the others.
   C. The humorous story can only be told in a brief fashion.
   D. The humorous story is the hardest story to tell successfully.

LANGUAGE AND STYLE

You have already read about analyzing an author's **language and style** in fiction and nonfiction in chapters 2 and 3, and using language effectively for mass media purposes in chapter 5. We will now focus on the use of language as it applies to essay writing. How do you make your message clear? How do you connect with your audience?

When writing, remember that *how* you say something is just as important as *what* you are saying.

What does it mean to have **style**? We often talk about the clothes we wear as a reflection of our personal style; that is, what we wear can make a statement about an aspect of our personality. In the same way, your writing is a means of self-expression. Your writing doesn't always have to express an opinion in order to be expressive; your identity can come through in your style. Remember that your choice of words will communicate a certain **tone** to the reader.

Here are two examples of writing by American authors. Think about the following questions as you read:

- How do their styles differ?
- How are their styles similar?
- What is the tone of each passage?
- Which language and style do you find especially memorable or striking? What makes them stand out for you?

Nathaniel Hawthorne

Heretofore, the mother, while loving her child with the intensity of a sole affection, had schooled herself to hope for little other return than the waywardness of an April breeze, which spends its time in airy sport, and has its gusts of inexplicable passion, and is petulant in its best of moods, and chills oftener than caresses you, when you take it to your bosom. . .

–*The Scarlet Letter*, by Nathaniel Hawthorne

Tom said to himself that it was not such a hollow world, after all. He had discovered a great law of human action, without knowing it—namely, that in order to make a man or a boy covet a thing, it is only necessary to make the thing difficult to attain.

–*The Adventures of Tom Sawyer*, by Mark Twain

DICTION

The word **diction** comes from the Latin word *dicere*, meaning "to speak, tell, say." Simply put, diction is word choice. When writing, it is important to use diction that is appropriate to your purpose, topic, and audience in order to communicate clearly, effectively, and accurately. Using diction that is too informal is a common problem because it is natural for us to want to write in a conversational tone. While using an informal tone can be appropriate in some writing situations, such as creative writing assignments or when e-mailing and text messaging your friends, formal diction is typically more appropriate for academic writing. Sometimes it can be hard to notice when you're even using informal diction because you're so used to communicating that way. Below are some examples of informal language, with their more formal counterparts.

Informal Language	Formal Language
He likes her a lot.	He is very fond of her.
I'm sort of over it.	I am not troubled by it anymore.
Guacamole looks kinda gross; it's all green and stuff.	I don't care for guacamole.

In addition to making sure your language is formal enough, you should also be careful to balance **specific** and **general** words. Avoid vague words, such as *nice, thing, stuff, great, bad, sad, good,* and *a lot*. Focus on providing the main idea, in general terms, to your reader, and then filling in with concrete details and examples.

For example, consider the following quote:

> No one can make you feel inferior without your consent.
> –Eleanor Roosevelt

Let's look at the word **consent**. If you consulted a thesaurus, you would find this list of similar words:

allowance, authorization, clearance, concurrence, granting, leave, license, sanction, sufferance

Now, try substituting these words in place of *consent* in the quotation. Notice how the words don't have exactly the same connotation, and a change in only one word can affect the tone of the whole sentence.

For more information and practice on using precise word choice, see chapter 8, Using Standard American English"

ACTIVE AND PASSIVE VOICE

In active voice, the subject is doing the **acting**:

> **Example:** The dog bit the man.

In passive voice, the subject is being **acted upon** by something:

> **Example:** The man was bitten by the dog.

Passive voice tends to make writing dull and wordy. The reader has to wade through piles of unnecessary words and "to be" verbs in order to uncover your main points. Usually, you can tell when a sentence is in passive voice when:

- You see a form of the auxiliary verb *be* followed by the past participle of the main verb (*was bitten*)
- You see the word *by* followed by the agent (the thing that is acting) of the verb (*by the dog*)

Here are some more examples:

Passive: My sister was passed in the race by a five-year-old.

Active: A five-year-old passed my sister in the race.

Passive: Bob's head was shaved by his mom.

Active: Bob's mom shaved his head.

To use active voice, you must use **action verbs**. For example: "I saw," "He ran," "She discovered." To eliminate wordiness, watch out for an overuse of "to be" verbs, such as **am**, **is**, **are**, **was**, and **were**. In other words, instead of saying:

It is shown in the story that hearts are easily broken.

Try   **In the story, the author shows that hearts break easily.**

Instead of saying: She is portrayed as the villain in the beginning.

Try: **In the beginning, the author portrays her as a villain.**

POINT OF VIEW

As you read in chapter 2, an author has different **points of view** to choose from when telling a story, such as first person, third person omniscient, and third person limited. In fiction, the perspective from which a story is told affects its interpretation. In a similar manner, the point of view that you use affects how readers receive your words. Many teachers prefer that their students avoid first person point of view when writing an essay for class, unless the essay is about a personal experience. In an analytical essay, such as the kind you write about literature, it is understood that your statements are *your* thoughts: after all, *you* are the one writing the essay. Therefore, it is unnecessary to use a phrase such as "I think." It is always a good idea to check with your teacher about which point of view he or she would prefer.

Practice 3:   Language and Style

For the following exercises, choose the answer that BEST revises the sentence for inclusion in an essay you're writing for class.

1. In Kate Chopin's "The Story of an Hour," Mrs. Mallard seems really freaked out about the news of her husband's death, but later you can tell that she is actually pumped about being a free woman.

 A. In Kate Chopin's "The Story of an Hour," Mrs. Mallard seems sad about the news of her husband's death, but later you can tell that she is actually excited about being a free woman.

 B. In Kate Chopin's "The Story of an Hour," Mrs. Mallard appears shocked at the news of her husband's death, but later the author reveals that she was actually expressing joy at her new-found freedom.

 C. In Kate Chopin's "The Story of an Hour," Mrs. Mallard is floored by the news of her husband's death, but later you know that she is happy about being free.

 D. In Kate Chopin's "The Story of an Hour," Mrs. Mallard is shocked at the news of her husband's death, but later it is revealed that she was actually cool with being a free woman.

2. When the senior class president squealed, "Let's have a long lunch for seniors and a short one for juniors," all the juniors flipped out.

   A. When the senior class president was like, "Let's have a long lunch for seniors and a short one for juniors," we flipped.

   B. We were kind of mad when the senior class president said, "Let's have a long lunch for seniors and a short one for juniors."

   C. The senior class president sparked uproar among the juniors when he said, "Let's have a long lunch for seniors and a short one for juniors."

   D. So, when the senior class president went, "Let's have a long lunch for seniors and a short one for juniors," the juniors were definitely upset.

3. The Greeks are like the pioneers of western civilization because they really thought individual freedom and opportunity was a good thing.

   A. The Greeks are considered the pioneers of western civilization because they valued individual freedom and opportunity.

   B. The Greeks are considered the pioneers of western civilization because individual freedom and opportunity were valued by them.

   C. The Greeks are considered the pioneers of western civilization because they thought that individual freedom and opportunity were important.

   D. The Greeks are like the pioneers of western civilization because they really thought individual freedom and opportunity was a good thing.

4. The boy was arrested for misappropriating clothing from the store, which is pretty dumb when you think about how there are cameras all over the place.

   A. The boy was arrested for taking clothing from the store, which is not smart when you think about how there are cameras all over the place.

   B. The boy, apparently lacking in intelligence, was arrested for stealing clothing from a store that had cameras installed in numerous places.

   C. The boy was arrested for stealing clothing from the store, which had cameras all over the place.

   D. The boy was arrested for misappropriating clothing from the store, which is pretty dumb since there are cameras and things everywhere.

5. We set out excitedly on our cross-country quest, but three hours later the transmission was shot and things were not good.

   A. We set out excitedly on our cross-country quest, but three hours later the transmission was shot and things were bad.

   B. We set out excitedly on our cross-country quest, but three hours later the transmission failed and things were really not going well.

   C. We set out excitedly on our cross-country quest, but after the transmission failed three hours later, our mood was somber.

   D. We set out and were excitedly starting on our cross-country quest, but after the transmission failed, we were disappointed.

RHETORICAL DEVICES

In chapter 2, "Literary Structure: Fiction and Nonfiction," you read about the rhetorical strategies, such as allusions, stereotypes, and metaphors, that writers of nonfiction use to make their writing stand out. As a writer, you can use these strategies yourself to emphasize your points. Below are additional **rhetorical devices** that make writing more memorable.

PARALLEL STRUCTURE

On the EOCT, you may be asked to revise a sentence so that it has **parallel structure**, or **parallelism**. A sentence has parallel structure when its nouns, verbs, phrases, modifiers, etc. are in a similar form. Look out for parallel structure when making a list of similar ideas. For example, if you say "I like running, biking, and swimming," you are making a list of the activities you enjoy.

Example: This weekend, I went running and shopped.

In this sentence, the verbs are not parallel, because they are not in the same form. The correct form is:

Example: This weekend, I went running and shopping.

Having parallel structure helps keep your writing clear and adds emphasis to your statements. For more on this, see chapter 8, "Using Standard American English."

REPETITION

Repetition is used to emphasize a point or to add dramatic effect. You will frequently find repetition being used in speeches, especially those made by politicians who are trying to influence and persuade a large number of people. For example, consider this passage from President John F. Kennedy's inaugural address:

John F. Kennedy

"So let us begin anew. . .remembering on both sides that civility is not a sign of weakness, and sincerity is always subject to proof. Let us never negotiate out of fear, but let us never fear to negotiate. Let both sides explore what problems unite us instead of belaboring those problems which divide us. Let both sides, for the first time, formulate serious and precise proposals for the inspection and control of arms."

Kennedy repeats "let us" and "let both sides," creating a feeling of unity and cooperation. His repetition focuses the attention on the statements that follow, increasing the chances that his words will linger in the ears of his audience.

ANALOGY

Like a metaphor or simile, an **analogy** is a comparison and finds points of similarity between two dissimilar things, often extending beyond a single sentence. Writers use analogies to make an unfamiliar idea more understandable to the reader. Analogies are another form of figurative language and thus make an author's writing more engaging to the reader. Consider the following example:

> Learning a new language is like being a small child all over again. You find yourself pointing at things, blurting out words, and hoping that someone will understand. Meanwhile, people around you seem to be speaking a mile a minute, laughing with each other, but you have no idea what they're saying. Frustrated that you can't express yourself or join in the conversation, you may have the urge to ball up your hands into fists and cry.

By using an analogy, the paragraph vividly compares the feeling of frustration when learning a language to that of being a small child. This gives you a chance to use your powers of description, a strategy discussed earlier in this chapter. It is more effective than simply saying: "Learning a new language is hard."

Practice 4:   Rhetorical Devices

Read the excerpt below and answer the questions that follow.

> **1)** Virtues are, in the popular estimate, rather the exception than the rule. **2)** There is the man and his virtues. **3)** Men do what is called a good action, as some piece of courage or charity, much as they would pay a fine in expiation of daily non-appearance on parade. **4)** Their works are done as an apology or extenuation of their living in the world,—as invalids and the insane pay a high board. **5)** Their virtues are penances. **6)** I do not wish to expiate, but to live. **7)** My life is for itself and not for a spectacle. **8)** I much prefer that it should be of a lower strain, so it be genuine and equal, than that it should be glittering and unsteady. **9)** I wish it to be sound and sweet, and not to need diet and bleeding. **10)** I ask primary evidence that you are a man, and refuse this appeal from the man to his actions. **11)** I know that for myself it makes no difference whether I do or forbear those actions which are reckoned excellent. **12)** I cannot consent to pay for a privilege where I have intrinsic right. **13)** Few and mean as my gifts may be, I actually am, and do not need for my own assurance or the assurance of my fellows any secondary testimony.

–Excerpt from *Essays, First Series*, by Ralph Waldo Emerson

1. Which of these sentences has an example of parallelism?
    A. sentence 2   B. sentence 5   C. sentence 6   D. sentence 13

2. Which sentence uses an analogy?
    A. sentence 3   B. sentence 7   C. sentence 10   D. sentence 13

3. Sentence 5 is an example of what figurative language?
    A. allusion   B. metaphor   C. metonymy   D. hyperbole

4. What comparison is made in sentence 9?
    A. convincing others to do good is like bleeding
    B. struggling to be a good person is like constant dieting
    C. doing good deeds and is like eating well
    D. leading a good life is like being in good physical health

5. Which of the following does NOT express Emerson's ideas about himself and his life?
    A. he wants to live for himself and does not want to attract attention
    B. he thinks that truly virtuous people are humble and not flashy
    C. he thinks that he is more talented than the average person
    D. he thinks that good deeds should not be done as an act of penance

---

CHAPTER 6 SUMMARY

On the EOCT in American literature and composition, you will be asked to analyze the **organization** of a writing sample and answer questions relating to the **audience**, **purpose**, and **structure** of a passage. Practice identifying the **controlling idea**, **thesis statements**, **topic sentences**, and supporting **details** of the passages you read. Are there any details that don't belong because they don't relate to the topic sentence? Do all the paragraphs relate back to the thesis? Can you follow what the author is trying to say? Notice how writing **style** and **diction** can change depending on the author's purpose and the subject matter. Also, notice how each author has a unique writing style. What effect does an author's use of language have on the passage? Be on the lookout for **rhetorical devices** that add impact to a passage, and beware of **passive voice** and **wordiness** that distract from what the author is trying to say.

CHAPTER 6 REVIEW

Read the passages below and answer the questions that follow.

> **1)** A great scientist, coldly analyzing the chemical processes essential to the creation of each new human being, scoffs at any possibility of immortality. **2)** With the microscope at his eye, he magnifies nature's mysteries; he sums up the investigations of the Hertwig brothers; he discourses learnedly of the nucleolus of the Cytula—or progeny cell. **3)** He declares that science is able to watch the creation of a human being, as it watches the progress of a chick in the egg. **4)** He asserts that each new creature is merely the result of a chemical process blending qualities of the mother and father. **5)** Having a "final beginning," man must have a final end. **6)** Man—a mixture of two sets of qualities—has no more chance of immortality than has beer, which is a mixture of malt and hops.

–Excerpt, *Editorials from the Hearst Newspapers* by Arthur Brisbane

1. Which sentence BEST expresses the controlling idea of this paragraph?
   A. sentence 1
   B. sentence 2
   C. sentence 4
   D. sentence 5

2. This passage is an example of
   A. narrative writing.
   B. persuasive writing.
   C. expository writing.
   D. technical writing.

3. Which sentence uses an analogy?
   A. sentence 2
   B. sentence 4
   C. sentence 5
   D. sentence 6

4. Sentence 2 is an example of what rhetorical device?
   A. analogy
   B. repetition
   C. parallelism
   D. metaphor

5. What type of evidence does the author use to support his controlling idea?
   A. description
   B. statistics
   C. facts
   D. primary sources

Read the following passage of student writing and answer the questions that follow.

> **1)** The American Revolution is taught at nearly every grade level, and as a result, every American student is familiar with the Boston Tea Party, Paul Revere riding to warn the colonists, and the Stamp Act. **2)** According to the *Washington Post*, however, this important piece of American history is barely covered in British schools. **3)** Some British students don't even know that America started out as a colony of Britain! **4)** India is another country that the British no longer control. **5)** Britain has tons more history than we do, so it makes sense that they probably don't have time to cover every event in one school

year. **6)** Another reason is that, as a member of the European Union, Britain has stronger present-day ties to her neighbors on the Continent; thus, a focus on European history and government makes more sense. **7)** Today, it is more relevant for Britain to focus on its current relationship with Europe than past connections to America. **8)** However, there is still an interest in American culture in Britain.

6. Which of the following is NOT a weakness of the passage?
    A. a lack of supporting details   C. coherence
    B. irrelevant information   D. lack of closure

7. Which information does NOT belong in the paragraph?
    A. sentence 1   B. sentence 4   C. sentence 5   D. sentence 6

8. What would be the BEST way to revise sentence 1 for parallelism?
    A. keep the sentence as it is
    B. …every American student is familiar with the Boston Tea Party, Paul Revere's midnight ride, and the Stamp Act .
    C. …every American student is familiar with the Boston Tea Party, Paul Revere riding to warn the colonists, and the Stamp Act that angered colonists.
    D. …every American student is familiar with and knows about the Boston Tea Party, Paul Revere riding to warn the colonists, and the Stamp Act.

9. What would be the BEST way to revise sentence 6 to improve clarity?
    A. Also, as a member of the European Union, Britain has stronger present-day ties to her neighbors on the Continent; thus, by focusing on European history and government, it makes more sense.
    B. Another reason is that, as part of Europe, Britain has stronger present-day ties to her neighbors on the Continent; thus, a focus on European history and government makes more sense.
    C. Another reason is that as a member of the European Union, Britain has stronger present-day ties to her neighbors on the Continent; thus, it makes sense that they would focus on European history and government.
    D. Another reason is that, as a member of the European Union, Britain has stronger present-day ties to her neighbors on the Continent; thus, a focus on European history and government makes more sense.

10. Which word is too informal for the passage?
    A. tons   B. some   C. cover   D. thus

Read the following passage and answer the questions that follow.

1) The Pony Express was the first rapid transit and the first fast mail line across the continent from the Missouri River to the Pacific Coast. **2)** It was a system by means of which messages were carried swiftly on horseback across the plains and deserts and over the mountains of the far West. **3)** It brought the Atlantic coast and the Pacific slope ten days nearer to each other.

4) It had a brief existence of only sixteen months and was supplanted by the transcontinental telegraph. **5)** Yet it was of the greatest importance in binding the East and West together at a time when overland travel was slow and cumbersome, and when a great national crisis made the rapid communication of news between these sections an imperative necessity.

6) The Pony Express marked the highest development in overland travel prior to the coming of the Pacific railroad, which it preceded nine years. **7)** It, in fact, proved the feasibility of a transcontinental road and demonstrated that such a line could be built and operated continuously the year around—a feat that had always been regarded as impossible.

8) The operation of the Pony Express was a supreme achievement of physical endurance on the part of man and his ever faithful companion, the horse. **9)** The history of this organization should be a lasting monument to the physical sacrifice of man and beast in an effort to accomplish something worth while. **10)** Its history should be an enduring tribute to American courage and American organizing genius.

–excerpt from *The Story of the Pony Express*, by David A. Schwan

11. Which of the sentences below BEST expresses the controlling idea of the passage?
    A. sentence 1 B. sentence 2 C. sentence 3 D. sentence 4

12. Which sentence provides a fact to support the controlling idea?
    A. sentence 3 B. sentence 8 C. sentence 9 D. sentence 10

13. Which sentence is NOT a good concluding thought for the passage?
    A. sentence 7 B. sentence 8 C. sentence 9 D. sentence 10

14. Which organizational method is used in the passage?
    A. chronological   C. posing and answering a question
    B. comparison/contrast   D. cause and effect

Read the following passage and answer the questions that follow.

1) Emily Dickinson spent much of her life secluded from the world in Amherst, Massachusetts. **2)** Despite living a hermetic life, Dickinson greatly influenced American poetry. **3)** By the time she was in her late 20s, she rarely left her home or entertained visitors and instead corresponded chiefly through letters. **4)** In fact, Dickinson published only seven poems in her lifetime. **5)** About 1,000 poems were discovered after her death, by her sister, Lavinia, and gradually others grew to admire the genius of her work. **6)** Although she lived in the 19th century, Dickinson's influence can only be found in 20th century poetry because her work was very not well-known until after her death. **7)** Dickinson went to college briefly, but left after a semester. **8)** Many people believe that Dickinson retreated from the world due to unrequited love, although these speculations lack any proof.

15. Which, if any, would be the BEST way to revise sentence 5?
    A. Around 1,000 poems were discovered after her death, by her sister, Lavinia, and gradually others grew to admire the genius of her work.
    B. Dickinson's sister, Lavinia, discovered around 1,000 poems after her death, and gradually others grew to admire the genius of her work.
    C. Around 1,000 poems were discovered after her death by her sister Lavinia and gradually others grew to admire the genius of her work.
    D. Dickinson's sister, Lavinia, was discovering around 1,000 poems after her death, and gradually others grew to admire the genius of her work.

16. What is the BEST placement for sentence 6?
    A. after sentence 1
    B. before sentence 4
    C. after sentence 7
    D. after sentence 8

17. Which sentence is LEAST relevant to the passage?
    A. sentence 1
    B. sentence 3
    C. sentence 7
    D. sentence 8

18. The author of this passage would probably agree with which of the following statements?
    A. Dickinson wrote moving poetry, despite being so removed from others.
    B. Dickinson did not like being alone, but was afraid to venture outside.
    C. Despite Dickinson's considerable talent, her poetry is underappreciated today
    D. Dickinson lived in solitude due to a failed romantic relationship.

19. The author's purpose is
    A. to entertain
    B. to inform
    C. to motivate
    D. to describe

Read the following passage of student writing and answer the questions that follow.

1) Many authors write novels that are influenced by their life experiences. 2) The oft-heard saying "write what you know" is truly a helpful bit of advice. 3) It makes sense that a story based on your life would be better, because it would be easier to write something believable and authentic if you have actually experienced it. 4) Also, the more interested you are in your topic, the better your writing tends to be. 5) You will often find that the themes of an author's work are influenced by the issues, both good and bad, of his or her own life.

6) F. Scott Fitzgerald is one such author whose novels revolve around interests and experiences that mirrored his own. 7) *The Great Gatsby* is his most famous work, but he also wrote short stories for *The Saturday Evening Post* to make extra money. 8) Sometimes, his reputation as a drinker affected how seriously the literary world viewed his work. 9) Fitzgerald struggled with a drinking problem, spending his money as quickly as he earned it, and later he faced his wife's constant mental breakdowns. 10) His works covered themes such as aspiration, success, and loss. 11) He first tasted fame after *This Side of Paradise* was published, and he quickly adopted the extravagant lifestyle of a young celebrity. 12) Although he often made plenty of money, he was not very adept at saving it.

13) He struggled with a serious drinking problem, and his wife Zelda suffered mental breakdowns and spent the latter part of her life in and out of various sanitariums. **14)** Fitzgerald was employed by Metro-Goldwyn-Mayer as a screenwriter, and later he continued screenwriting work as a freelancer.

15) Fitzgerald died of a heart-attack in 1940 as he was writing a novel about Hollywood life. **16)** Although *The Great Gatsby* is now regarded as an important work of 20th century American literature, at the time of Fitzgerald's death, he was not held in high esteem. **17)** It wasn't until 1960 that Fitzgerald was firmly established as an enduring and influential American writer.

20. Which statement is the BEST thesis for this passage?
    A. F. Scott Fitzgerald's works cover the themes of aspiration, success, and loss.
    B. An author's own troubles and experiences are often reflected in his or her writing.
    C. It is a good idea to "write what you know."
    D. F. Scott Fitzgerald was not highly regarded as an author at the time of his death.

21. What type of nonfiction writing is this passage?
    A. expository   B. persuasive   C. narrative   D. technical

22. Which sentence is the LEAST relevant to the controlling idea of the passage?
    A. sentence 7   B. sentence 10   C. sentence 11   D. sentence 13

23. Which of the suggestions below would NOT improve this passage?
    A. The author needs to discuss Fitzgerald's relationship with his wife.
    B. The author needs to relate Fitzgerald's experiences to the experiences of his characters.
    C. The author needs to add more specific details.
    D. The author needs to mention other authors in the second paragraph.

24. Which sentence uses passive voice?
    A. sentence 7   B. sentence 9   C. sentence 14   D. sentence 15

25. How should the following sentence be revised to create parallel structure?

> Fitzgerald struggled with a drinking problem, spending his money as quickly as he earned it, and later he faced his wife's constant mental breakdowns.

    A. Fitzgerald struggled with a drinking problem, spending his money as quickly as he earned it, and later he faced his wife's growing mental breakdowns
    B. Fitzgerald struggled with a drinking problem, spent his money as quickly as he earned it, and grappled with his wife's constant mental breakdowns.
    C. Facing his wife's constant mental breakdowns, Fitzgerald struggled with a drinking problem and spent his money as quickly as he earned it.
    D. Spending his money as quickly as he earned it, facing his wife's constant mental breakdown, and struggling with a drinking problem were all issues for Fitzgerald.

Chapter 7
The Research Process

This chapter covers the following Georgia standard(s).

ELA11W3	The student uses research and technology to support writing.
ELA11C2	The student uses appropriate formatting and documentation
ELAALRL4	the student analyzes historical records in relation to a literary work.

Standards addressing the research process come from Domains I, III, and IV. Questions about them will focus on your understanding of the research process, especially as it relates to American literature and formatting and documentation.

Imagine the following scenario. You have been saving your money for years. You just passed your driving test, and now you are ready to buy your first car. But which kind should you get? Some of the things you might do are walk through a car lot, take a few cars for a test drive, talk to friends who are car owners, ask your dad's mechanic for advice, do some research on the Internet, or flip through magazines that review cars. All of these activities are forms of research. **Research** is an investigation into a topic. You began with a problem (which car to buy) and will look to a variety of sources that have the information you need to solve your problem.

You will follow a similar process when you are asked to write a research paper in school. A **research paper** can inform the reader about a topic, or it can attempt to convince the reader to feel a certain way or to take a certain action. When written about literature, research papers often focus on things that influence a literary work. For example, a research paper might examine how an author's family life, experiences, or the historical period in which a piece was written affect the author's work.

CHOOSING A TOPIC

The first step in writing a research paper is to decide on a topic. Your teacher may give you guidelines for a topic, or the topic may be up to you. Given the choice, the best topic is one you are interested in within any guidelines your teacher provides.

Once you have a topic, the next step is to formulate clear **research questions** to determine exactly what it is you will investigate in your paper. You can define the specific topic you will research by asking a series of questions in order to arrive at your research question. A **research question** is the specific topic you will research. Read the steps that David goes through in order to arrive at his research question.

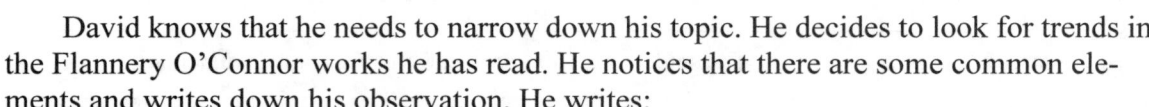

David is writing a research paper on Georgia author Flannery O'Connor.

1. **First**, David writes down his topic:

Topic: Flannery O'Connor

David knows that he needs to narrow down his topic. He decides to look for trends in the Flannery O'Connor works he has read. He notices that there are some common elements and writes down his observation. He writes:

2. **What I already know:** Setting and religion seem to be important in O'Connor's writing.

David wonders why these two elements are important to O'Connor. He writes:

3. **What I want to find out**: How did O'Connor's life affect her writing?

David thinks about what might have influenced O'Connor to view the world as she does. He writes:

4. **Research question**: How did Flannery O'Connor's world (her upbringing and where she lived) influence her writing?

Now David is ready to begin his research. He knows exactly what information he will be looking for. He may add additional research questions as he begins to read and sort through the information available on his topic.

Practice 1: Research Questions

Practice formulating your own research question. Choose one American writer from the list. Then fill in the chart below. For further practice, choose a second writer.

William Faulkner   Langston Hughes

Margaret Mitchell   Alice Walker

Topic _____

What I already know _____

What I want to find out _____

Research question _____

Research Sources

Once you decide on your topic and formulate your research question, the next step is to find the answers. There are many types of **research sources** that you can consult when looking for information. Depending on your topic, you might seek information from a library catalogue, a research librarian, an Internet search engine, or an interview.

You will need to read material from a variety of sources in order to get a full picture of your topic. In your research, you will probably come across both primary sources and secondary sources. A **primary source** is an original document that was created during the time you are investigating. Examples of primary sources are diary entries, a poem or story, and historical documents like the Declaration of Independence. A **secondary source** provides an interpretation of or commentary about a primary source. These sources are a step removed from the event. Examples of secondary sources are encyclopedia entries, magazine articles, or critical reviews.

You will need to read a variety of sources to get a complete picture of your topic. The following are some common types of sources you might encounter while researching.

An **encyclopedia** is a reference work that contains articles about a variety of topics. It is a good place to begin your research as it provides a broad overview of a topic.

An **almanac** is a book of data and facts about a variety of topics, organized in a format similar to an encyclopedia. An almanac is a good source to use if you want to find basic historical and statistical information about a city, state, or country.

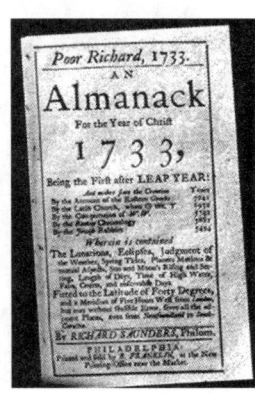

A **journal** is a publication that focuses on topics relevant to a specific industry or area of study. Journals contain articles written by experts in that particular field; therefore, the information in them tends to be specific and focused. Examples of journals for American literature include *Comparative Literature* and *Poets and Writers*.

News sources present current events and include daily newspapers such as the *Atlanta-Journal Constitution* and the *New York Times*, as well as weekly newsmagazines such as *Time* and *U.S. News and World Report*.

An **interview** is a conversation in which an interviewer asks an interviewee a series of questions in order to gather information. The interviewee is an expert or firsthand observer of an event and therefore has insight into the interview topic that others do not.

Field studies are conducted by scientists, but are the opposite of controlled lab experiments. Archaeologists, anthropologists, and other scientists conduct field work by making observations out in the world and publishing them in journals. For example, a linguist interested in southern English might conduct field work by recording the speech of various citizens of a small town in North Georgia.

Technical documents are commonly used in the fields of mathematics and science. They are written by experts in the field and contain a wealth of information, from instructions for a new computer application to the results of a complicated study.

A **microfiche** is a small piece of film containing a photograph from a page of a book or periodical, which is then magnified on a microfiche reader. While the use of microfiche helps libraries save space, its main advantage is that it preserves materials such as old newspaper and magazine articles that would otherwise deteriorate over time.

Willa Cather

The **Internet** is a very popular research tool. Using search engines such as Google or Yahoo!you can find information on thousands of Web pages. Think carefully about the best words to use when doing a search. For instance, a Google search using the keyword "Willa Cather" will return over 850,000 results! You will need to be specific with your search terms in order to find the information that you need.

Keep in mind that different sources can have different **perspectives** (points of view) about a topic. For example, an advertisement for fur coats will portray fur as a must-have luxury. An article by an animal rights group will portray a fur coat as a product that results from the cruel killing of defenseless animals. In the same way, you will want to be aware of differing perspectives when researching literary topics. Some **critics** (scholars who analyze and comment on literary works) will interpret an author's writing in one way, while others interpret it in another way. Keep different perspectives in mind and be aware of any **bias** (having a preference for a particular point of view) that a source may have.

In addition to being aware of perspectives, it is also important to consider the **credibility** of the sources you consult. Just because something appears in print does not automatically mean that the information is trustworthy. Questions to ask about material you read might include: How old is this information? Who wrote it or funded the research? Is the writer an expert? Does he have a bias that comes across in the writing?

Practice 2: Research Sources

Answer the questions that follow.

1. Which would be the BEST source to look in to find out in which years writer Ernest Hemingway lived?

    A. a novel   B. an interview   C. an encyclopedia   D. an e-mail

2. What is one question you might ask yourself to judge the credibility of information you find in a resource?

    A. "Does this person have a bias?"
    B. "Do I agree with this source?"
    C. "Did this information come from a primary source or a secondary source?"
    D. "Was this material written while I was alive?"

3. Your teacher asks you to use at least three primary sources in your research paper about an author. Which of the following would fulfill this requirement?

   A. a novel by the author, an interview with the author, and a letter written to the author

   B. a Web site about the author, an encyclopedia entry about the author, and a diary entry by the author

   C. an encyclopedia entry about the author, an email mentioning the author, and a speech by the author

   D. a survey about literature of the time, a journal article about the author's work, and a textbook mentioning the author

4. You are writing a research paper comparing *Beloved* by Toni Morrison to the film version starring Oprah Winfrey. Which words would be BEST to type into a search engine to find information on Morrison's novel?

   A. "Beloved"   C. "Morrison"

   B. "Beloved Toni Morrison"   D. "Oprah movie"

5. Which source would be the LEAST helpful for a research paper on American colonial architecture?

   A. an encyclopedia   C. a field study

   B. a journal   D. a technical document

6. You are interested in researching the history of American automobiles, and you want to find out which American car has proven to be the most reliable. Which source would probably have the MOST bias?

   A. a journal article from a historian

   B. an encyclopedia entry about the invention of the automobile

   C. an interview with a curator from the National Automobile Museum

   D. an article written by a representative of Ford Motor Company

USING SOURCES

Remember that your research paper should **reflect your ideas** about the research question you developed. It should not simply be a compilation of what you found in sources. So, at this point, it is a good idea to put down the research sources for a brief time and write a detailed outline or a first draft of the research paper you intend to write. Now, you're ready to use your primary and secondary sources as they should be used—to support the points you make in your paper.

ORGANIZING WHAT YOU FIND

 A good way to stay on top of all the bits of information you find is to keep a file of **note cards**. They are like recipe cards in a box, only this recipe will "cook up" a great research paper! As you read sources that relate to your research paper, make notes about important facts on the note cards, and then arrange them in the file box (usually alphabetically, though if writing about an author's life, for example, the organization could be chronological—use whatever method will help you easily find the information again).

Another way to track and organize your ideas is by using anecdotal scripting. In **anecdotal scripting**, a reader makes notes about a text. These notes might highlight important points, pose questions, summarize and paraphrase. Using anecdotal scripting will make it easier for you to find the information that you want to include in your research paper.

Another way to organize and record your research is to use an annotated bibliography. An **annotated bibliography** is a list of the sources you consulted and notes on each source. An annotated bibliography includes:

- **A summary of the work**: the main idea of the work
- **An evaluation of the author**: the author's qualifications
- **A description of the intended audience**: for whom this source is appropriate and useful
- **An evaluation of usefulness**: how this source helped you answer your research question

For example, James is writing a research paper on Southern writers. He found an online journal that covers both historic and contemporary writers from the South that he has been referring back to while doing his research. His annotated bibliography for this source might look like this:

> <u>Mississippi Quarterly</u>. 7 Mar. 2007. Mississippi State University. 21 Apr. 2007. <http://www.missq.msstate.edu/>.

INTEGRATING SOURCE INFORMATION INTO YOUR TEXT

Once you have gathered information, it is time to see how the information fits into your research paper. If information supports your point or provides explanation of your topic, you will want to include that information in your paper.

One of the ways to determine which information in a source is relevant to your point is by making **notes in the margins** of your draft research paper as you read through sources and organize your ideas. Using these notes, you can highlight areas in the text where you can use one or more of your sources to support a point you have made. You can then incorporate information you gathered during your research into the body of your paper by using direct quotes, paraphrases, and summaries. You will provide more information about each source you quote in the bibliography at the end of your paper.

Direct quotations are the exact words of the original author or speaker. Use quotation marks around the quoted words and attribute the words to the person who said or wrote them.

> **Example:** At the beginning of "Masque of the Red Death," Poe describes Prince Prospero as, "happy," "dauntless," and "sagacious."

When using longer excerpts of text (usually three lines or longer), do not use quotation marks. Instead, set off the quote from the rest of the text by beginning it on the next line and indenting it one inch from the left-hand margin.

> **Example:** Prospero shows unusual (and perhaps foolhardy) disregard for the danger from the dreaded disease:
>
> *It was towards the close of the fifth or sixth month of his seclusion, and while the pestilence raged most furiously abroad, that the Prince Prospero entertained his thousand friends at a masked ball of the most unusual magnificence.*

Paraphrasing (also called an **indirect quote**) is restating the words of another person in your own words. Paraphrasing does not use quotation marks, but it does give credit to the person who originally said it.

> **Example: Original material:** William Seward, Lincoln's Secretary of State, commented on the limitations of the Emancipation Proclamation. He said, "We show our sympathy with slavery by emancipating slaves where "we cannot reach them and holding them in bondage where we can set them free."
>
> **Paraphrase:** Lincoln's Secretary of State William Steward recognized that the Emancipation Proclamation created no actual change for slaves at the time.

Summarizing involves putting the original author's main idea into your own words. When you summarize you only include the author's main point. Summaries are much shorter than the original material and provide a broad overview of the original material.

> **Example:** The Declaration of Independence states the reasons that the colonists sought independence from England.

While using quotes is an important aspect of research papers, be careful not to overuse quoted material. Remember that quotes are used to support your thoughts and ideas and by citing the source.

Here is a list of the sources Madison used for a research paper about Phillis Wheatley's poetry and a description of how she incorporated them into her paper. The style used for formatting the sources below is MLA. You will learn more about how to document sources in the next section and in chapter 9.

Encyclopedia: At the beginning of the paper, Madison gives general background information about Wheatley. Madison used an online encyclopedia called Wikipedia. Because the information she used is very general and can be found in many sources, she does not need to cite the source in the text. Madison would record this source in her bibliography like this:

> "Phillis Wheatley," wikipedia.com. 25 Apr. 2007. Wikipedia. 26 Apr. 2007.
> <http://en.wikipedia.org/wiki/Phillis_Wheatley>.

Historical document: Madison uses a direct quote from Thomas Jefferson's *Notes on the State of Virginia*. Notice how in the text, Madison used the author's name, stated the source of the quote, and put the words in quotation marks. Madison would record this source in her bibliography like this:

> Jefferson, Thomas. *Notes on the State of Virginia*. 2 Nov. 2006., University of Virginia Library. 26
>   Apr. 2007 <http://etext.virginia.edu/etcbin/toccer-new2?id=JefVirg.sgm&images=images/modeng
>   &data=/texts/english/modeng/parsed&tag=pub-lic&part=all>.

Poem: Madison found a copy of one of Wheatley's poems on a Web site. Madison would record this source in her bibliography like this:

> Wheatley, Phillis. "On Being Brought from Africa to America." Jan. 1996. Project Guttenberg. 23 Apr.
>   2007 <http://www.gutenberg.org/dirs/etext96/whtly10.txt>.

Literary criticism: Madison read **literary criticism** (an interpretation and evaluation of literature) of Wheatley's work. She paraphrased Jone Johnson Lewis's analysis of Wheatley's poem, "On being brought from Africa to America." Madison would record this source in her bibliography like this:

> Lewis, Jone Johnson. "Phillis Wheatley." About.com. 2007. 26 Apr. 2007.
> <http://womenshistory.about.com/od/aframerwriters/a/wheatley_poems.htm>.

Madison successfully incorporated information from a variety of sources into her research paper. She used the information she found during her research to support her own ideas. In this section of her paper, Madison included sources by using direct quotes and paraphrasing. She made it clear whose ideas she was using and properly documented each source for inclusion in her bibliography.

Practice 3: Using Sources

Answer the questions that follow.

1. "Early to bed and early to rise makes a man healthy, wealthy, and wise," said Ben Franklin. This is an example of _____.

    A. a direct quote
    B. paraphrasing

    C. summarizing
    D. anecdotal scripting

2. Your teacher asks you to write two sentences that describe a short story you just read. Which technique should you use to do this assignment?

    A. a direct quote
    B. paraphrasing

    C. summarizing
    D. anecdotal scripting

3. During your research, you make a note on a source that raises an important point. Which process are you using?

    A. a direct quote
    B. paraphrasing

    C. summarizing
    D. anecdotal scripting

4. After reading a literary critic's analysis of Hemingway's use of bullfighting in his novel *Death in the Afternoon*, you restate her findings in your own words. Which technique are you using?

    A. a direct quote
    B. paraphrasing

    C. summarizing
    D. anecdotal scripting

5. Imagine that you are writing a research paper on Esther Forbes's *Johnny Tremain*. You have read the novel and know that the setting, the American Revolution, is an important aspect of the story. With a partner, evaluate how each of the following sources might be useful to a research paper. Share your answers with the class.

    Boston Tea Party

    - an encyclopedia

    - a passage from *Johnny Tremain*

    - a map from 1777 of military installations and British troop positions near Fort Ticonderoga in New York at the time of the Battle of Saratoga

    - an account of the Boston Tea Party in 1773 given by Georges Hewes, who participated in the event

DOCUMENTING SOURCES

When researching a topic for a paper, you might get information in the form of statistics, quotes, historical documents, surveys and studies. When using material that originated from someone else, always document the source of the information. Two ways to document a source are **parenthetical citations** and **footnotes**.

Parenthetical citations, or **in-text citations**, are used within a document to provide information about a source. All works mentioned in parenthetical citations should appear in the bibliography at the end of your paper. Parenthetical citations include the author's last name and the page number for the information cited. If the author's name is included in the text, only the page number should appear in the citation. In chapter 9, you will learn more about the format that parenthetical citations should follow.

Example: Emily Post admonished in her 1922 handbook of etiquette that one should never take more than one's share of food at the table (38).

A **footnote** is a notation at the bottom of a page which identifies a source used in the text. Within the text, a number is written in superscript format just after the part of the text the footnote is referencing. The corresponding number is then written at the bottom of the page. Specific information about the source follows this number. When a reader has this information, he can then go to the original source if he wants more information. Footnotes are an alternative to parenthetical citations. Your teacher will direct you as to which type of citations to use. All works mentioned in footnotes should appear in the bibliography. In chapter 9, you will learn more about the format that footnotes should follow.

Edith Wharton

Any sources referenced in your paper must be listed in your bibliography at the end of your paper. A **bibliography,** or **works cited** list, is a list of sources an author used when writing a research paper. The bibliography is a separate section at the end of a research paper. In a bibliography, an author provides specific information in the bibliography about each source. Bibliographies have a specific format. Bibliographies are presented in alphabetical order by author's last name. In chapter 9, you will learn more about the format for bibliographies.

Here is an example of a bibliographic entry:

Wharton, Edith. The House of Mirth. New York: Macmillan Press, 1987.

You will want to pay careful attention to these rules for documenting sources in order to avoid plagiarism. **Plagiarism** is using another person's ideas without giving that person proper credit. Any material that was created by someone else, be it a novel, a quote, an idea, or a photograph, needs to be documented.

Practice 4: Documenting Sources

Read the questions below. Then answer the questions that follow.

1. In your research paper, your teacher asks you to use citations that reference the source within the body of the text. These citations are called _____.

    A. bibliographies
    B. footnotes
    C. superscript
    D. parenthetical citations

2. Where is a bibliography found?
    A. in a different document than the rest of the research paper
    B. at the beginning of a research paper
    C. within the text of a research paper
    D. in a separate section at the end of a research paper

3. Why might a reader need to know specific information about a source you used in your research paper?
   A. so that she can consult the source herself if she needs to
   B. so that she can write to the author
   C. so that she can buy the book as a gift
   D. so that she can copy your paper

4. How can you avoid plagiarism when writing a research paper?
   A. by giving detailed information about each source
   B. by giving credit to the another person when you use their ideas
   C. by including all sources you used in your bibliography
   D. all of the above

FORMATTING AND PUBLISHING A RESEARCH PAPER

Once you have written your paper, it is time to format your paper. **Formatting** refers to the guidelines for how your written work appears on the page. A **style manual** is a guide for formatting citations and for preparing documents and papers. There are several different style manuals including the *Modern Language Association Handbook* (MLA), Turabian, and *The Chicago Manual of Style*. Your teacher will direct you as to which style manual you should use for your research paper. You will learn more about style manuals in chapter 9.

Some topics that are addressed in style manuals are of particular importance to research papers, such as **pagination**, **spacing**, and **margins**. The guidelines given in the topics below are based on MLA style. You will learn more about the specific rules for formatting various kinds of papers you might write in chapter 9.

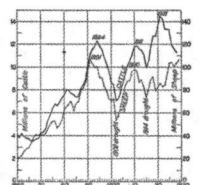

Whether your audience is your teacher or your fellow students, you will want to think of ways to make your paper memorable as well as informative. One way to accomplish this task is to add images. An **image** is a visual representation of something, such as a photograph, a chart, a drawing or a map. Have you heard the saying, "a picture is worth a thousand words?" Images such as charts, graphs, and pictures can be valuable additions to your research paper. An image can break up the text on the page while drawing the reader's eye to the image and its caption.

Timelines can help a reader see how events in an author's life impacted his writing. The Internet is a rich source for these kinds of images. Keep in mind that like text, you will need to document the source when using graphics.

Activity: Formatting and Publishing a Research Paper

Imagine that you are writing a research paper on the types of houses described in F. Scott Fitzgerald's *The Great Gatsby*. Use the Internet to find out when this novel was written and where it took place. Then, use the Internet to find at least three images that would be good accompaniments to a research paper on this topic. Be sure to document your sources. Share your images with your class using an email, a slide show, or printouts.

For more about documenting and formatting, also read chapter 9, Paragraph Structure and Manuscript Formatting.

CHAPTER 7 SUMMARY

A **research question** is the specific topic you will research in your research paper.

Sources are places to look for information. Examples of sources are books, speeches, surveys, magazines and the Internet.

Primary sources are original documents that were created during the time under study. **Secondary sources** provide an interpretation of or commentary on primary sources.

Sources are used to provide support for a point or information on a topic. When researching, you may use organizational strategies such as **note cards**, **anecdotal scripting** and **annotated bibliographies**. When using material from others in a paper you can use **direct quotations** (exact words of the original author or speaker), **paraphrasing** (restating the words of another person in your own words) or **summarizing** (putting the original author's main idea into your own words).

All sources must be **documented** using a specific format. Sources can be cited using **parenthetical citations** (a reference within a document that states the author's last name and page number) or by using **footnotes** (a notation at the bottom of a page which identifies a source used in the text). All sources cited in a research paper must be listed in the **bibliography**.

Style manuals provide specific **formatting** guidelines in regard to aspects such as margins, page numbers and spacing.

Images can give a reader deeper understanding of material in a research paper while providing visual interest.

CHAPTER 7 REVIEW

A. Answer the questions that follow.

1. Which of the following would make the MOST effective research question for a research paper about American literature?

    A. What are molecules?
    B. During which years was Willa Cather alive?
    C. How did Henry David Thoreau's friendships influence his writing?
    D. How many books did Flannery O'Connor write?

2. Which is the BEST source for finding out in what year an author was born?

    A. an encyclopedia
    B. a letter the author wrote to her mother
    C. an email from the author to her publisher
    D. a speech an author made during a book signing

3. Which of the following is an example of a secondary source?

    A. an interview   B. a textbook   C. a speech   D. a poem

4. You are researching the effects that Earnest Hemingway's health had on his writing. One source says that the author's depression caused Hemingway to stop writing; another says that his best works were written at the times he reported feeling the most depressed. What should you do to verify any information you might want to use in your paper?

    A. investigate the credibility of the sources
    B. check the accuracy of the information
    C. determine any bias the writers might have
    D. all of the above

5. You are using a quote from Alice Walker in your research paper. Her exact words are important. Which of the following types of quotation would you use?

    A. paraphrase   C. direct quote
    B. summary   D. anecdotal scripting

    Their Eyes Were Watching God by Zora Neale Hurston is the story of a woman who searches for love in four different relationships.

6. The sentence above is an example of _____.
    A. a direct quote   C. paraphrasing
    B. a summary   D. an annotated bibliography

7. Which of the following is NOT an important reason to document a source?

    A. Documenting gives credit to the original author or speaker.

    B. Documenting allows the reader to look up the original sources to get more information on the topic

    C. The original source gets paid each time his name is mentioned in a research paper.

    D. Documenting allows the writer to differentiate between his own ideas and those of another person.

8. When citing a source, information on it should appear _____.

    A. in a parenthetical citation or footnote and in the bibliography

    B. in both a parenthetical citation and a footnote

    C. in either the bibliography or a footnote

    D. in a footnote only

9. Which of the following is the BEST source for information on formatting a research paper?

    A. a dictionary   C. a journal entry

    B. your friends   D. a style manual

Imagine that you are writing a research paper on The Red Badge of Courage by Stephen Crane. Read the passage from The Red Badge of Courage and the historical source that accompanies it. Then answer the questions that follow.

> The men dropped here and there like bundles. The captain of the youth's company had been killed in an early part of the action. His body lay stretched out in the position of a tired man resting, but upon his face there was an astonished and sorrowful look, as if he thought some friend had done him an ill turn. The babbling man was grazed by a shot that made the blood stream widely down his face. He clapped both hands to his head. "Oh!" he said, and ran. Another grunted suddenly as if he had been struck by a club in the stomach. He sat down and gazed ruefully. In his eyes there was mute, indefinite reproach. Farther up the line a man, standing behind a tree, had had his knee joint splintered by a ball. Immediately he had dropped his rifle and gripped the tree with both arms. And there he remained, clinging desperately and crying for assistance that he might withdraw his hold upon the tree.

–The Red Badge of Courage, by Stephen Crane

10. What effect is Crane's language intended to have upon the reader?

    A. It is intended to amuse the reader.

    B. It is intended to show the reader the stark realities of war.

    C. It is intended to offend the reader.

    D. It is intended to change the reader's opinion.

11. Which of the following statements would Crane be MOST likely to agree with?

    A. War is glorious.

    B. War is a joke.

    C. War is horrifying.

    D. War is something everyone should experience.

12. Which of the following is an example of figurative language in this passage?

    A. "The babbling man was grazed by a shot ..."

    B. "The men dropped here and there like bundles."

    C. "'Oh!" he said, and ran."

    D. "He sat down..."

That on the first day of January, in the year of our Lord one thousand eight hundred and sixty-three, all persons held as slaves within any State or designated part of a State, the people whereof shall then be in rebellion against the United States, shall be then, thenceforward, and forever free; and the Executive Government of the United States, including the military and naval authority thereof, will recognize and maintain the freedom of such persons, and will do no act or acts to repress such persons, or any of them, in any efforts they may make for their actual freedom.

–(from *The Emancipation Proclamation*, issued by President Abraham Lincoln in September of 1862 and effective on January 1, 1863.)

13. What kind of source is *The Emancipation Proclamation*?

    A. a secondary source

    B. an encyclopedia

    C. a primary source

    D. a journal article

14. According to Lincoln, what will the military do by order of this proclamation?

    A. recognize and maintain the freedom of slaves

    B. burn the fields of slave owners

    C. imprison all Southerners

    D. provide jobs for all former slaves

15. What is the tone of this passage?

    A. humorous   B. excited   C. sorrowful   D. serious

16. How did Southern slave owners likely respond to the proclamation?

    A. They were angry.

    B. They were excited.

    C. They were relieved.

    D. They were surprised.

17. Why would this source be useful to your research paper?
    A. It tells why the Civil War came to an end.
    B. It helps explain the historic events of the time that are important to the story.
    C. It tells us about Lincoln's life.
    D. It gives us the opinion of a literary critic.

Chapter 8
Using Standard American English

This chapter covers the following Georgia standard(s).

ELA11C1	Demonstrates an understanding of proper English usage and control of grammar, sentence structure…diction, and syntax.
	Correctly uses clauses (e.g., main and subordinate), phrases (e.g., gerund, infinitive, and participial), and mechanics of punctuation (e.g., commas, semicolons, colons, ellipses, hyphens)
	Demonstrates an understanding of sentence construction (e.g., parallel structure, subordination, proper placement of modifiers) and proper English usage (e.g., consistency of verb tenses)
ELA11C2	Produces legible work that shows accurate spelling and correct use of the conventions of punctuation and capitalization

These standards encompass the content of Domain IV: Conventions. On the EOCT in American Literature and Composition, questions in this domain will measure your ability to apply the conventions of Standard American English, which are covered in this chapter. You will also be expected to demonstrate an understanding of different writing formats, which are covered in the next chapter.

When you take the EOCT, you will be asked to identify and correct grammatical errors. You may also be tested on different methods of sentence construction. Questions on the EOCT will address such topics as:

- Main and subordinate clauses
- Gerund, participial, and infinitive phrases
- Punctuation marks
- Verb tense consistency and agreement
- Proper placement of modifiers
- Precise word choice
- Spelling
- Parallel structure

This chapter will briefly review each of these topics and give you a chance to practice with exercises along the way.

CONVENTIONS HELP READERS UNDERSTAND WRITING

Using the conventions of Standard American English is essential for being understood. Whether you are writing or speaking, choosing appropriate words and phrases to express yourself goes a long way toward how people understand your meaning and whether or not they take you seriously. When you write, the way that you use language, grammatical construction, and punctuation determines whether a reader "gets it" or gives up because the errors are distracting and confusing.

Think about when you read. You may not always realize why, but you know when one text is easier to grasp than another. Read the examples below:

Writing containing errors that make it difficult to read and understand:

> *The little puppy finally setted free from his leash frolicking in the yard tryed again and again to catch the butterflies and bees among the flowers.*

The same line, with errors corrected:

> *The little puppy, finally set free from his leash, frolicked in the yard and tried repeatedly to catch the butterflies and bees that flew among the flowers.*

Now, who would not prefer to read (and get more meaning from) the second version? You need to use the conventions of Standard American English to make your writing clear, or readers will give up trying to figure out what you mean.

PUNCTUATION AND CAPITALIZATION

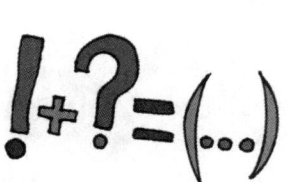

The appropriate use of punctuation is an important key to understanding. **Punctuation** signals how words, phrases, and sentences relate to one another and when a reader should pause.

END PUNCTUATION

End punctuation signals the end of a sentence. The mark used at the end of a sentence also indicates how that sentence should be read.

1. A **period** ends a declarative sentence (a simple statement of fact or argument).

    Example: I knew that he was going to run for office**.**

2. A **question mark** comes after a question. Questions are often signaled by inversion of the subject and verb (for example, *you do* becomes *do you* to form a question), or by starting with a question word such as *how*, *why*, *who*, *where*, or *when*.

    Example: How did you know that**?**

3. An **exclamation point** ends an imperative statement, like a command, or a sentence meant to convey excitement or urgency.

    Example: He can't keep a secret from me**!**

COMMAS

1. **Commas** help **separate the parts of a list** of three or more words or phrases.

    Example: Remember that we need to get crepe paper, glue, paint, and some nails before going to the float-building party tonight.

The choice of whether to use a **final comma before the conjunction** in a list is a matter of style, for which there are style guides (for example, American Book company uses the *Chicago Manual of Style*, which says the final comma should be used to prevent ambiguity). Ask your teacher what style you should be using.

2. They **show the relationship between related independent clauses** (complete sentences) when joined by a conjunction.

    Example: They wanted to take a vacation at the beach, but they didn't schedule far enough ahead for a good hotel near the shore.

3. They **set off nonrestrictive elements** (not essential to the meaning of a sentence) from the rest of the sentence. A *nonrestrictive element* is a phrase or clause that adds something but is not necessary to understanding a sentence, while a *restrictive element* is essential and not set off by commas.

    Example 1, nonrestrictive: We knew something was up when Larry, who has a sense of style, came to the club wearing plaid and stripes!

    Example 2, restrictive: Anyone who has a sense of style can see that most plaids and stripes don't mix.

4. A comma usually **follows an introductory word, phrase, or clause**.

    Exampled: Furthermore, the way that you enunciated made your speech easy to follow. After giving concrete examples, you finished with a strong conclusion. Given the well-prepared presentations you provided, you've earned an A in Speech.

5. Commas are used to **separate added comments or information** as well as transitional elements such as conjunctive adverbs.

    Example: We are, however, pleased you've joined us even though your new position, as we all know, is not quite as exciting as traveling the world with your previous employer.

6. They also set off **direct address**, **tag questions**, **interjections**, and **opposing elements**.

    Example 1, direct address: Sabrina, please come here.

    Example 2, tag question: You're not going to eat that, are you?

    Example 3, interjection: We grabbed our bikes and, wow, did we pedal fast!

    Example 4, opposing element: Rudy said to go right, not left, when you get to the corner.

7. They also are used to **set off direct quotations**. You would not use a comma after the quotation if it is a question or an imperative.

    Example 1: "When the going gets tough," Milo joked, "I usually take a nap."

    Example 2: She exclaimed, "I can't stand it!" and promptly turned and left.

8. Commas are used **between date and year** as well as **after the year**, and **between address, city, and state** as well as **after the state**.

    Example 1: She was born on July 14, 1886, and lived for nearly 100 years.

    Example 2: His address was 627 Charring Road, Hampstead, New Hampshire, for more years than I can remember. Then he moved to Boulder, Colorado, and we didn't hear from him much.

COLONS

1. A **colon** is often used to **introduce a list** (when the statement before the colon is an independent clause). It also can be used for **particular emphasis on what comes after the colon**, and it can be used **before a phrase or clause that restates or explains the first clause**.

    Example 1: She had everything she needed for the trip: a warm sleeping bag, a lightweight tent, a camp stove, mosquito repellent, and her trusty compass.

    Example 2: There was only one word for what he had become by selling secrets: traitor.

    Example 3: Sheila had her own opinion about the new sofa: She didn't like it.

Note that in Examples 1 and 2, there is **no initial capitalization** used in what follows the colon. Example 3 does use initial capitalization because what follows the colon is an **independent clause**; this is, however, a matter of style—some styles do not use initial capitalization after a colon at all—so ask your teacher which style you are supposed to use.

2. Colons have other specific uses. They are used **after a greeting in a formal letter**, to **set off hours from minutes** in writing the time, and to **separate chapters and verses of the Bible**. Finally, as you can see each time the word **Example:** is used, they also are used to **signal that something is coming that pertains to a designation**.

    Example 1: Dear Mr. Bennigan:

    Example 2: 2:45 pm

    Example 3: Please read Genesis 2:15.

SEMICOLONS

1. A **semicolon** can be used to **join two independent clauses** that are closely related. When a semicolon is used this way, no coordinating conjunction is needed. In other words, it acts like a comma plus *and* or *but* between sentences.

    Example: Manny couldn't study at the library; it was always closed by the time he got off work.

2. A semicolon can serve as a **stronger division than a comma**— becoming a "super comma"—when commas are already being used for other purposes. This includes linking an independent clause with a transitional phrase or conjunctive adverb, or in lists which already contain commas.

    Example: We brought the books, all 300 volumes, to the sale on time; yet, we weren't allowed to set up our table until someone had checked them all in!

QUOTATION MARKS

1. **Quotation marks** are used to signify a **direct quote**, indicating that whatever lies within the quotation marks was said or written exactly as it appears. Do not use quotation marks when making an indirect quote or paraphrasing (conjunctions like *that, if, who, what,* and *why* often introduce indirect quotes).

    Example of direct quote: Janet said, "I just don't get the plot of this novel."

2. Also use quotation marks to indicate the **title of a short work of literature** like a story, poem. speech, or article.

    Example: My favorite poem by Edgar Allen Poe is "The Raven."

3. It is standard to use double quotation marks ("like this"); single quotation marks ('like this') are used only for a quote within a quote or to indicate the title of a short work within a quote.

    Example: "We just read 'The Story of an Hour' by Kate Chopin," she told me.

4. **Periods and commas always stay within the end quotation marks.** The choice of whether other punctuation stays inside or goes outside the end quotation marks depends upon whether the mark is part of the quote or not.

    Example 1: As loudly as he could, he yelled, "Look out below!" (Here, the exclamation point is part of the quoted sentence, so it stays within the quotation marks.)

    Example 2: Did I hear you say, "You can have a cookie"? (Here, the question mark is part of the surrounding sentence, so it goes outside the quotation marks.)

ELLIPSES

1. Ellipsis (plural *ellipses*) means "omission" in Greek. An ellipsis appears as three dots (…) in Standard American English. Understandably, ellipses are used **when something is being omitted**, usually from quoted material. For instance, when you write a paper, you may want to cite something from a piece of literature but omit a lengthy description in the middle; you would use an ellipsis to show where you left something out.

> **Example:** "He was prodigiously pleased by her outspoken heartiness … The speech made him her friend; it couldn't well help it." (excerpted from *The American Claimant*, by Mark Twain)

2. Additionally, an ellipsis is sometimes used to **indicate a pause or an unfinished thought**.

> **Example:** Dracula never drinks…wine.

HYPHENS

1. A **hyphen** is used to join words, word parts, and numbers. It can also show the division of word syllables, as when words need to be broken across lines.

2. A hyphen **connects a prefix and a proper noun or proper adjective**. It also serves to **connect prefixes** that have not become one in our lexicon with words that follow them or which would become ambiguous or hard to read if they were joined (a current dictionary can help you learn which words have melded with certain prefixes).

> **Examples:** pre-Colombian, post-Impressionist, anti-hero / antifreeze, ecosystem / eco-awareness

3. A hyphen **joins two or more nouns that are used as one word**, such as great-grandfather, sister-in-law, or secretary-treasurer.

4. A hyphen **unites a compound adjective** (an adjective formed by two separate words) that comes before a noun.

> **Examples:** an even-tempered man, a well-deserved raise, an up-to-the-minute news report

5. A hyphen is used in writing out the **numbers twenty-one through ninety-nine**. **A fraction used as an adjective** needs a hyphen. A fraction used as a noun does not need a hyphen.

6. A hyphen shows a word has been broken into syllables and continued on the next line. The word must always be broken between syllables.

APOSTROPHES

1. An **apostrophe** shows **possession**. If the person or thing to which possession is attributed is singular, you will use an apostrophe followed by an "s"; if plural, then the apostrophe follows the "s." This does not apply to plurals which don't end in an "s."

    Examples: the book's pages, Mary's guitar, the Jones' dog, the children's game

2. An apostrophe indicates a **contraction**, a combination of two words that leave out certain letters. The places for the missing letters are marked with apostrophes (') as in *I'm* (I am), *wouldn't* (would not), and *you'll* (you will / you shall). There are lists of common contractions available in grammar books and on the Internet.

3. The apostrophe also shows **other omissions**, as in some long words, phrases, or numbers.
    Examples: government / gov't   rock and roll / rock 'n' roll
    six of the clock / six o'clock   1970s / '70s

4. Apostrophes can also be used to form **certain plurals**, where simply adding an "s" may be confusing. This includes plurals of letters
    Example: dot your i's and cross your t's.

Capital letters usually do not need an apostrophe.

    Example: I got all As last semester, so Mom bought me some new CDs.

This also includes symbols.

    Example: email addresses use @'s before their domain names.

CAPITALIZATION

1. An **initial capital** letter is used at the beginning of a sentence. This is called *sentence case*. Also capitalize the **first word of a direct quotation when it is a complete sentence**.

    Examples: We went to the library. The librarian asked, "How long will you need these books?"

2. In *title case*, capital letters are used on **all words in the title** of a work, except prepositions and articles (unless they come at the beginning of the title).
    Examples: *The Son of the Wolf*, by Jack London
    "Extracts from Adam's Diary," by Mark Twain

3. Always capitalize the **singular first-person pronoun**, *I*; always capitalize **proper nouns** (names of people, places, and things) and **adjectives formed by proper nouns**; always capitalize names of **days and months**; always capitalize **language and country names**, as well as **races and nationalities**.

Examples: That's what **I** said: The **J**ones twins are in the **J**apanese garden again. I wish their parents were back from **F**rance; they have not been home since **M**arch.

4. Capitalize **family relationship only when they refer to a specific person directly**, substituting for that person's name. Capitalize **titles** that come before a proper name.

    Examples: I think that **M**om could out-bake *other kids' moms* any day. Don't you think so, **S**is? If you don't believe me, as **P**rofessor Sawyer; she raves about her oatmeal cookies, which *my dad* really likes too.

If you or your teacher feel you need more practice with English grammar, usage, and conventions, please consult American Book Company's *Basics Made Easy: Grammar and Usage Review*.

Practice 1: Punctuation and Capitalization

Read the following sentences. In each set of sentences, choose the one that is correctly punctuated and capitalized.

1. A. Could someone tell me, why the windows are rolled down while its training outside?
    B. Could someone tell me why the windows are rolled down, while it's training outside.
    C. Could someone tell me why the windows are rolled down while its training outside!
    D. Could someone tell me why the windows are rolled down while it's training outside?

2. A. Bela will meet you at 621 Franklin Street, Tyler Georgia, on March 25, 1858 to discuss the deal.
    B. Bela will meet you, at 621 Franklin Street Tyler, Georgia, on March 25, 1858 to discuss the deal
    C. Bela will meet you at 621 Franklin Street, Tyler, Georgia, on March 25, 1858, to discuss the deal
    D. Bela will meet you at 621 Franklin Street, Tyler, Georgia on March 25, 1858 to discuss the deal

3. A. She must have gone to the store otherwise she would have taken the dog with her.
    B. She must have gone to the store; otherwise she would have taken the dog with her.
    C. She must have gone to the store; otherwise, she would have taken the dog with her.
    D. She must have gone to the store, otherwise, she would have taken the dog with her.

4. A. "Have you read "Paul's case" by Willa Cather?", the teacher asked.
    B. "Have you read "Paul's Case" by Willa Cather," the teacher asked.
    C. "Have you read 'Paul's Case' by Willa Cather?" the teacher asked.
    D. "Have you read 'Paul's case' by Willa Cather?" the teacher asked.

5. A. The 1950's began a period of realism in American literature paving the way for such authors as John Updike, Eudora Welty, and Ralph Ellison.

B. The 1950s began a period of realism in American literature, paving the way for such authors as John Updike, Eudora Welty, and Ralph Ellison.

C. The 1950's began a period of realism in American literature, paving the way for such authors as John Updike; Eudora Welty; and Ralph Ellison.

D. The 1950s began a period of realism, in American literature, paving the way for such authors as, John Updike, Eudora Welty, and Ralph Ellison.

VERB TENSE CONSISTENCY AND AGREEMENT

VERB TENSE CONSISTENCY

The tense of the verbs you use in your writing helps readers know when something took place and the relationship of actions of events to one another. Within a sentence, paragraph, story, or book, changes in verb tense help readers understand the time relationships among events. But unnecessary or inconsistent shifts in tense can be confusing.

First, let's briefly review the most commonly used tenses and participles.

1. **Present tense** is used to express an action or condition occurring now, always, or repeatedly.

   Examples: Ray Bradbury **writes** primarily science fiction and fantasy. I **am** a big fan and **read** his work regularly.

2. **Past tense** expresses a previous action or connection.

   Example: Mark Twain **wrote** *The Adventures of Huckleberry Finn*, which we **read** and **discussed** in class last year.

3. **Future tense** indicates action that will take place at a later time.

   Examples: I wonder what Stephen King's next novel **will be**. Whatever it is, someone probably **will make** it into a movie soon after its release.

4. **Present perfect tense** signals an event that began in the past and either ended in the past or continues to the present.

   Examples: Leila **has seen** several film adaptations of *Pride and Prejudice*. She **has decided** that none of them is as good as the book.

5. **Past perfect tense** indicates actions completed by a specific time in the past or before some other past action occurred.

   Example: By the beginning of the 20th century, Naturalism **had become** a popular literary movement.

VERB TENSE SHIFTS AND HOW TO FIX THEM

Example: In 1836, Ralph Waldo Emerson **has published** *Nature*, in which he **claims** it **was** possible to reach a spiritual state not through religion but by relating to the natural world.

There are several tense shifts in this sentence. First, with a past date provided, we know that these actions took place previously, so the main tense of this sentence should be past tense. *Has published* is present perfect and not appropriate for the action of publishing that clearly took place at a fixed time in the past; it should be simply *published*. *Claims* is present tense, which certainly can be used to express an idea that endures in literature, but it does not agree with *was*. We could change *was* to *is*; however, to attain true consistency in this sentence, the best choice is to change *claims* to *claimed*.

SUBJECT-VERB AGREEMENT

In addition to consistency in tense, there needs to be agreement between subject and verb in all cases. You have undoubtedly learned to conjugate most regular and irregular verbs at some time in school. However, there can be some tricky cases. In the following examples, the subject is bold and the verb is underlined.

Example 1, simple agreement: the **dog** <u>barks</u>, her **cousins** <u>listen</u>

Example 2, compound singular subjects: **Josh and Davey** <u>want</u> some ice cream *(but)* Neither **Mrs. Rampling** nor **I** <u>want</u> to go. (An interrupter like *or* or *nor* renders separates the subjects, unlike *and* which joins them, so they do not become plural.)

Example 3, subject separated from verb: A **bushel** of apples <u>is</u> keeping the doctor from our door.

Example 4, subject plus prepositional phrase: The **teacher**, along with all of the students, <u>does</u> not want to miss the pep rally tomorrow.

Example 5, collective nouns: The **jury** <u>deliberates</u> on the verdict *(acting as a group)*; sometimes the **jury** <u>disagree</u> and a verdict cannot be reached *(acting as individuals)*.

Example 6, indefinite pronouns: Of the two choices, **neither** *(choice)* <u>appeals</u> much to me. **Both** *(choices)* are rather unpleasant.

Example 7, subject following verb: Under the bed <u>are</u> **boxes** filled with memories.

Example 8, title used as subject: ***Children of the Frost*** <u>is</u> a collection of stories by Jack London.

Practice 2:   Verb Tense Consistency and Agreement

Read the following sentences. Fill in the blanks with the appropriate verb form and tense, chosen from the list below the question.

1.   Each of the rare stamps _____ a dollar or more.
    A.   cost   B.   costs   C.   costed   D.   can cost

2.   They _____ all of the strawberries before lunch;
    A.   eat   B.   ate   C.   have eaten   D.   had eaten
later they _____most of the blackberries, too.
    F   eat   G.   ate   H.   have eaten   J.   had eaten

3.   I like rock 'n' roll, but rhythm and blues really _____ my favorite music.
    A.   is   B.   was   C.   has been   D.   had been

4.   The mass production of books _____ after the invention of the Guttenberg Press.
    A.   begin   B.   begins   C.   began   D.   has begun

5.   "The Eyes of the Panther" _____ a successful story for Ambrose Bierce back in 1892.
    A.   is   B.   was   C.   are   D.   were

6.   Milford found that he _____ a protégé without knowing it; the young man apparently
    A.   take on   B.   took on   C.   has taken on   D.   had taken on
    _____ into his life and his work
    F.   sneaks   G.   sneaked   H.   has sneaked   J.   had sneaked
    while Milford _____ the other way.
    L.   looks   M.   looked   N.   was looking   O.   has been looking

THE IMPORTANCE OF WORDS

SPELLING

Naturally, spelling is important so that readers can understand the words you mean to use. The English language borrows heavily from other languages, so the rules of spelling vary greatly, mainly due to the different origins of the words. Good ways to improve spelling skills include studying the roots of English words, reading continually to increase vocabulary, and looking up new words in the dictionary. Following are some spelling rules that also are useful to learn. There are other rules that will help you with spelling, and if you or your teacher feel that you need more practice with spelling, consult American Book Company's *Basics Made Easy: Grammar and Usage Review* book.

Affixed words are words that have had a prefix (group of letters placed before a root word) or suffix (group of letters placed after a root word) added. Knowing how to use affixes helps you spell words that use them. Here are some common affixes and spelling rules to use with them.

Prefix	Meaning	Example	Suffix	Meaning	Example
de-	take away	derail	-dom	place or state	kingdom
bi-	two	bipolar	-ism	doctrine/belief	atheism
inter-	between	international	-acy	state or quality	accuracy
un-	not	unstoppable	-able, ible	capable of being	livable
dis-	apart, away	disorder	-ful	having a quality	bashful
il-, im-	not	immature	-ious, ous	of or with	delicious
pre-	before	preheat	-less	without	colorless

Rule 1.   Use *i* before *e*, except after *c*, or when a word is pronounced "ay" as in *reign*.

>   **Examples:** friend, receive, eight, perceive

Exceptions: Most of the time, Rule 1 provides the correct spelling of a word. Yet there are some exceptions in such words as *foreigner, forfeit, height, leisure, neither, science, scientific, seizes,* and *weird*.

Rule 2.   When prefixes are added to root words, the spelling of the root word does not change.

>   **Examples:** dis + satisfied = dissatisfied,   un + noticed = unnoticed

Rule 3.   When a suffix starting with a vowel is added to a word ending in a silent *-e*, such as *receive* and *smile*, the *-e* is dropped, making words such as *receiving* and *smiling*.

Exception 1: The *-e* is not dropped when it would change the meaning of the root word. (dye + ing = dyeing, not dying)

Exception 2: The *-e* is not dropped if the *-e* clarifies pronunciation. (flee + ing = fleeing, not fleing)

Exception 3: The *-e* is not dropped if the sound *c* or *g* must be kept soft. (courage + ous = courageous, not couragous)

Rule 4.   When a suffix starting with a consonant is added to a word ending in a silent *-e*, the *-e* is usually kept, such as in *largely* and *excitement*.

Rule 5.   When a suffix is added to root words ending in *-y*, change the *y* to an *i*, as in *silliness* and *dutiful*. Keep the *-y* if the suffix being added is *–ing* (flying), if the root word has a vowel before the *–y* (stayed), and in some one-syllable base words (shyer).

Rule 6. If a word ends in a consonant + vowel + consonant, and the suffix begins with a vowel, double the final consonant or the root word. This also applies if the word contains only one syllable or an accented ending syllable. Otherwise, do not double the last consonant in the root. (stop + er = stopper; begin + ing = beginning)

Rule 7. English words that have French, Greek, Latin, or Italian roots form the plural according to their language. Examples:

Singular	Plural	Singular	Plural
analysis	analyses	fungus	fungi
basis	bases	medium	media
beau	beaux	phenomenon	phenomena
crisis	crises	criterion	criteria
syllabus	syllabi	datum	data

Problems in understanding what's written also arise if a word is spelled correctly but is not the appropriate word for the context. Such errors occur with **homonyms**, words that sound alike but mean different things depending on their spelling. Below are a few commonly misused homonyms.

bare (lacking covering)	bear (large carnivore; verb meaning to withstand or hold)	
brake (stop abruptly)	break (a rest; verb meaning to smash)	
hear (to listen)	here (direction	
knew (past tense of know)	new (original, not old)	
roll (to turn over)	role (position or character)	
their (possessive pronoun)	there (direction)	they're (contraction of they are)
where (direction)	wear (what you do with clothing)	

Practice 3: Spelling

Select the word in each list that is not spelled correctly.

1.   A. health   B. moved   C. Southwest   D. autum

2.   A. floral   B. thirdy-eight   C. worker   D. money

3.   A. scant   B. connection   C. ajust   D. ignorant

4.   A. withold   B. repeat   C. grand   D. cancel

5.   A. mathmatics   B. wrist   C. charity   D. transportation

6.   A. frightened   B. happenning   C. going   D. swimming

In the following sentences, choose the appropriate homonym to fill in the blank.

7. I didn't _____ that Jessica was going away.
   A. know   B. no

8. He made a gesture that Robert couldn't _____.
   A. sea   B. see

9. Lucy wandered around the huge house for _____.
   A. days   B. daze

10. Haley asked me if I _____ make some tea.
    A. wood   B. would

11. There are _____ many
    A. to   B. too   C. two

    letters _____ to count!
    F. hear   G. here

12. Unfortunately, my father refused to cosign the _____,
    A. loan   B. lone

    so I can't _____ the house.
    F. buy   G. by

PRECISE WORD CHOICE

An important component of readers understanding and being able to visualize what is written is precise **word choice**. The way a writer chooses words for effect and description is called **diction**. It involves using words that best express a meaning. Such words are **specific** and **descriptive**; they **avoid distracting connotations**; and they are **not overused**. Similarly, phrases made up of precise word choices strive to be **accurate** (they don't resort to sweeping generalizations).

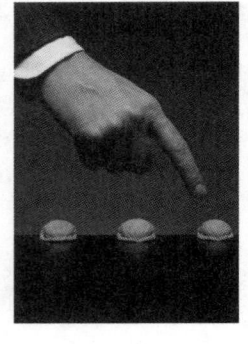

1. **Select specific words** that convey sight, sound, touch, taste, and emotion.

    Example: "The red rose grew more every day," is a pretty boring statement, not to mention being ambiguous: What grew, the stem or the flower? Does *more* mean bigger, rounder, or what? Take a look at how much information is offered with specific and descriptive words: "The rose's crimson blossom became plumper and more vibrant as it matured on its vine from sunup till sundown, slightly furling its petals each night."

2. It is also important to take into account all the **denotations** (dictionary definitions) and **connotations** (attributed meanings) of a word.

   Example: Calling someone *slender* is usually a compliment, as it means small or slight. But saying someone is *skinny* may not be (as one meaning of skinny is "thin in an unappealing way").

3. **Avoid clichés**; instead, find a fresh and vivid description to use. Instead of saying, "Your new kitten is as cute as a button!" find more meaningful words.

   Example: "Your kitten's huge eyes and adorable pink mouth make him look like a little cherub!"

4. Use **accurate descriptions** and steer clear of **sweeping generalizations** that show a viewpoint or description has not been well thought out.

   Example: Instead of saying, "Mysteries aren't worth reading" (an inaccurate statement, since they are enjoyed by many), a writer can be precise about what he or she means and say, "I have not enjoyed the mysteries I've read."

Practice 4:   Precise Word Choice

Read the following sets of sentences. In each set, choose the one that BEST uses precise word choice.

1. A.   Charlie could not sleep a wink during the night.
   B.   Charlie was awake all night, just tossing and turning.
   C.   Charlie had insomnia and slept no more than an hour all night.
   D.   Charlie tried to go to sleep but kept waking up and could not get back to sleep.

2. A.   The sunset was amazing.
   B.   The setting sun was a big red ball.
   C.   Setting slowly, the sunset was really breathtaking.
   D.   As it set, the sun threw a rainbow of colors across the sky.

3. A.   Tad went out with four girls in the last week.
   B.   Tad can go out with any girl he wants to.
   C.   No one says "no" to a date with Tad.
   D.   All the girls at school love Tad.

4. Which of the following could be considered a compliment to someone?
   A.   I told him he was a snake.   C.   I think he's a real fox.
   B.   What a weasel you are.   D.   She's such a worm.

5. What is the BEST way to revise this sentence to avoid using a cliché: "Monica fails to see that all that glitters is not gold"?
   A.   Monica thinks that everything is as it should be, so she never tries to make changes.
   B.   Monica prizes possessions and doesn't realize there are more important things.
   C.   Monica's eyesight is failing her.
   D.   Monica is dumb.

SENTENCE STRUCTURE

MAIN AND SUBORDINATE CLAUSES

The order in which words form sentences is called **syntax**, or sentence structure. A **clause** is an arrangement of words containing a subject and a predicate that can be a sentence or part of a sentence. A **main clause** is one which is **independent**, meaning that it can stand alone as a sentence. A **subordinate clause**, or **dependent clause**, depends on the main clause which it often modifies. **Subordinating conjunctions** (*as, before, since, though, until*, etc.) or **relative pronouns** (*who, which, that*) usually introduce dependent clauses. When the parts of a sentence are put together, they need to make sense—and that depends on using effective syntax.

Example 1: Because they drove all night, they arrived in San Antonio at dawn.

In this sentence, the main or independent clause is <u>they arrived in San Antonio at dawn</u>. This part of the sentence could stand alone. *They* is the subject, and *arrived* is the verb. <u>Because they drove all night</u> is the subordinating or dependent clause. The subordinating conjunction, *because*, introduces the subordinating clause.

Example 2: Anton has a puzzle that is very challenging.

In this sentence, <u>that is very challenging</u> is the subordinating clause. The relative pronoun, *that*, refers to the subject, *puzzle*, and *is* becomes the verb. <u>Anton has a puzzle</u> is the main clause.

GERUND, PARTICIPIAL, AND INFINITIVE PHRASES

A phrase is a group of words acting together as a unit. A **verbal phrase** does not serve as a verb in the sentence; instead, it functions as a noun, adjective, or adverb. There are three types of verbal phrases: infinitive, participial, and gerund. The verbal phrases are underlined in the examples below.

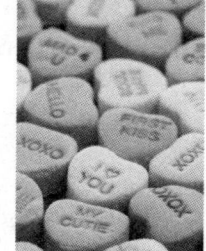

Infinitive phrases start with an infinitive which is followed by any objects and/or modifiers.

Example: Everyone wanted <u>to see clearly</u>.

Everyone is the subject, *wanted* is the verb, *to see* is the infinitive, and *clearly* is an adverb modifying the infinitive.

Participial phrases are made up of a past or a present participle plus any objects and/or modifiers. Participial phrases always function as adjectives within a sentence

Example: The woman <u>carefully arranging the flowers</u> is my wife.

Woman is the subject, *is* is the verb, *arranging* is the present participle, with *the flowers* being the direct object and *carefully* being a modifying adverb within the participial phrase.

Gerund phrases consist of a gerund and any objects and/or modifiers. It functions as a noun in a sentence.

Example: I dream of <u>traveling the world</u>.

I is the subject, *dream* is the verb, *traveling* is the gerund, and *the world* is its direct object.

The participial phrase and the gerund phrase can look deceivingly similar. After all, a gerund takes the same form as a present participle. Just remember that a **participial phrase serves as an adjective** in a sentence, and a **gerund phrase functions as a noun** (just as a gerund itself does).

Practice 5: Identifying Clauses and Phrases

Read the excerpt from *The Sketch Book of Geoffrey Crayon, Gent.*, by Washington Irving. Then, choose the answer that identifies each underlined clause or phrase.

Further reading and thinking, (1) <u>though they brought this vague inclination into more reasonable bounds</u>, only served to make it more decided. I visited various parts of my own country; and had I been merely a lover of fine scenery, (2) <u>I should have felt little desire to seek elsewhere its gratification</u>, for on no country had the charms of nature been more prodigally lavished. Her mighty lakes, her oceans of liquid <u>silver</u>; her mountains, with their bright aerial tints; her valleys, teeming with wild fertility; her tremendous cataracts, (3) <u>thundering in their solitudes</u>; her boundless plains, waving with spontaneous verdure; her broad, deep rivers, rolling in solemn silence to the ocean; her trackless forests, (4) <u>where vegetation puts forth all its magnificence</u>; her skies, kindling with the magic of summer clouds and glorious sunshine—no, (5) <u>never need an American look beyond his own country</u> for the sublime and beautiful of natural scenery… I had, besides all this, an earnest desire (6) <u>to see the great men of the earth</u>. We have, it is true, our great men in America: not a city but has an ample share of them. I have mingled among them in my time, and been almost withered by the shade into which they cast me; (7) <u>for there is nothing so baleful</u> to a small man as the shade of a great one, particularly the great man of a city. But I was anxious to see the great men of Europe; for I had read in the works of various philosophers, (8) <u>that all animals degenerated in America</u>, and man among the number. A great man of Europe, thought I, must therefore be as superior to a great man of America, as a peak of the Alps to a highland of the Hudson; and in this idea I was confirmed by (9) <u>observing the comparative importance and swelling magnitude</u> of many English travellers among us, who, I was assured, were very little people in their own country. (10) <u>I will visit this land</u> of wonders, thought I, and see the gigantic race from which I am degenerated.

1. A. main clause
    B. subordinate clause
    C. gerund phrase
    D. infinitive phrase

2. A. main clause
    B. subordinate clause
    C. gerund phrase
    D. infinitive phrase

3. A. main clause
    B. subordinate clause
    C. gerund phrase
    D. infinitive phrase

4. A. main clause
    B. subordinate clause
    C. gerund phrase
    D. infinitive phrase

5. A. main clause   C. gerund phrase
    B. subordinate clause   D. infinitive phrase
6. A. main clause   C. gerund phrase
    B. subordinate clause   D. infinitive phrase
7. A. main clause   C. gerund phrase
    B. subordinate clause   D. infinitive phrase
8. A. main clause   C. gerund phrase
    B. subordinate clause   D. infinitive phrase
9. A. main clause   C. gerund phrase
    B. subordinate clause   D. infinitive phrase
10. A. main clause   C. gerund phrase
    B. subordinate clause   D. infinitive phrase

PROPER PLACEMENT OF MODIFIERS

Understanding how clauses and phrases work also helps you avoid placing these parts of a sentence in the wrong places. Modifiers can be anything (word, phrase, subordinate clause) that adds information. If a modifier is in the wrong place, this can cause confusion.

A **misplaced modifier** is not in the best place to modify what it should.

> **Example:** The man was walking his dog wearing a fuzzy sweater.

Hmm. Who was wearing the sweater? The confusion here is caused by the participial phrase, *wearing a fuzzy sweater*, being too far from what it modifies (we'll assume the man is the one wearing the sweater). Here are two ways to fix this misplaced modifier.

> **Example:** The man wearing a fuzzy sweater was walking his dog.

A **dangling modifier** is a phrase or clause that comes at the beginning of sentence but does not modify the subject in the sentence.

> **Example:** While looking up at the clouds, a train roaring past interrupted my daydreaming.

Since the subject of the main clause is *train*, the prepositional phrase that precedes the clause should modify it; however, that would mean that train was looking at the clouds. Here are two ways to fix this sentence.

> **Example 1:** While I was looking up at the clouds, a train roaring past interrupted my daydreaming. (Adding a subject and verb to the prepositional phrase, it becomes a subordinate clause, and the two clauses now make sense together.)

> **Example 2:** While looking up at the clouds, I had my daydream interrupted by a train roaring past. (Changing the subject of the main clause means that now the prepositional phrase modifies the correct part of the sentence.)

PARALLEL STRUCTURE

To ensure effectively constructed sentences, pay attention to **parallelism**. For example, when describing two or more items in a series, keep their structure similar or the sentence will be unclear. Here are examples of parallel structure.

Used in	Non-Parallel	Parallel
Prepositional Phrases	The housekeeper looked inside the drawers, the bookcase, and under the recliner for the missing wallet	The housekeeper looked inside the drawers, on top of the bookcase, and under the recliner for the missing wallet
	The little boy ran under the chair, sprinted around the desk, and into the corner in order to catch the stray cat.	The little boy ran under the chair, sprinted around the desk, and crept into the corner in order to catch the stray cat.
Nouns	These gifted boys could name the types of trees, flowers, and some special kinds of birds in the forest.	These gifted boys could name the types of trees, flowers, and birds in the forest.
Pronouns	Take him, she, and them to the football game.	Take him, her, and them to the football game.
Verbs	Tiffany finished her homework and will do the dishes.	Tiffany finished her homework and did the dishes.
Phrases and Clauses	Three important reasons for the economic recovery in Mexico are the growth of tourism, the fact that we expanded free trade with NAFTA nations, and the increased value of the peso.	Three important reasons for the economic recovery in Mexico are the growth of tourism, the expanded free trade with NAFTA nations, and the increased value of the peso.
	At work, she may have time to eat her lunch if everyone gets their questions answered, she does not get another assignment, and if she comes in early.	At work, she may have time to eat her lunch if everyone gets their questions answered, if she does not get another assignment, and if she comes in early.

Practice 6: Modifiers and Parallelism

Read the following sentences. Choose the sentence that is correctly constructed (uses parallel structure and/or has correctly placed modifiers).

1. A.   The team that everyone thought would lose won the match.
   B.   The team that won the match everyone thought would lose.
   C.   Everyone thought the team that would lose won the match.
   D.   All of the sentences above are correctly constructed.

2. A.   The carpenter started renovating the house with careful measurements and arranging his tools.
   B.   The carpenter started renovating the house by measuring carefully and arranged his tools.
   C.   The carpenter started renovating the house by measuring carefully and arranging his tools.
   D.   All of the sentences above are correctly constructed.

3. A.   Carlos set nuts, attached ropes, climbed the cliff, and then helped his fellow climbers ascend.
   B.   Carlos set nuts, attaches ropes, climbs the cliff, and then helps his fellow climbers ascend.
   C.   Carlos set nuts, attaching ropes, climbing the cliff, and then helped his fellow climbers ascend.
   D.   All of the sentences above are correctly constructed.

4. A.   We ran through the gully, scrambled into the cave, and down the chute we descended.
   B.   We ran through the gully, scrambled into the cave, and descended down the chute.
   C.   We ran through the gully, we scrambled into the cave, and descended down the chute.
   D.   All of the sentences above are correctly constructed.

5. A.   When the dog started barking, the stranger left the neighborhood.
   B.   When the dog started barking at the stranger, he left the neighborhood.
   C.   The dog started barking at the stranger, so he left the neighborhood.
   D.   All of the sentences above are correctly constructed.

CHAPTER 8 SUMMARY

Conventions help readers understand writing by serving as "directions" toward meaning. Using the conventions of Standard American English is essential for being understood and taken seriously.

Punctuation signals how words, phrases, and sentences relate to one another; how sentences should be read; and when a reader should pause.

Verb tense helps readers understand the time relationships among events; unnecessary or inconsistent shifts in tense can be confusing. In addition, a **verb needs to agree with its subject** in all cases.

Correct **spelling** allows readers to understand the words you mean to use; spelling skills can be improved by studying the roots of English words, reading continually to increase vocabulary, and looking up new words in the dictionary.

Making **precise word choices** also supports understanding and involves using words that best express a meaning, ones that are **specific** and **descriptive, avoid distracting connotations**, and are **not overused**. Similarly, phrases made up of precise word choices are **accurate** and do not rely on sweeping generalizations.

Verbal phrases function as a nouns, adjectives, or adverbs. **Infinitive phrases** start with an infinitive which is followed by any objects and/or modifiers. **Participial phrases** are made up of a past or a present participle plus any objects and/or modifiers. Participial phrases always function as adjectives within a sentence. **Gerund phrases** consist of a gerund and any objects and/or modifiers, and they function as a noun in a sentence.

Modifiers, which add information to a word or phrase, must be in the right place to correctly modify what they should. A **misplaced modifier** is not in the best place to modify what it should; a **dangling modifier** is a phrase or clause that comes at the beginning of sentence but does not modify the subject in the sentence.

Parallelism refers to matching tense, form, and structure throughout a list or series of linked phrases/clauses. This helps clarify writing by keeping words, phrases, and clauses alike and easy to read when they are placed together.

CHAPTER 8 REVIEW

Read the sentences in numbers 1 through 5. In each set of sentences, choose the one that uses correct <u>punctuation and capitalization</u>.

1. A.   Let's go through the tunnel around the park and down Melcher Street to get home.
    B.   Let's go through the tunnel, around the park, and down Melcher Street to get home.
    C.   Lets go through the tunnel, around the park, and down Melcher Street to get home.
    D.   Lets go through the tunnel, around the park and down Melcher Street, to get home.

2. A.   My brother-in-law's business is for sale; are you interested?
    B.   My brother in law's business is for sale: are you interested?
    C.   My brother-in-law's business is for sale, are you interested?
    D.   My brother-in-laws' business is for sale; are you interested?

3. A.   Warren acted as though he was surprised but I wonder?
    B.   Warren acted as though he was surprised, but I wonder…
    C.   Warren acted as though, he was surprised, but I wonder…
    D.   Warren acted as though he was surprised; but I wonder?

4. A.   Henry David Thoreau read a great deal of pre-Revolution literature before writing "On the Duty of Civil Disobedience" and other essays.
    B.   Henry David Thoreau read a great deal of pre-Revolution literature before writing 'On the Duty of Civil Disobedience' and other essays.
    C.   Henry David Thoreau read a great deal of preRevolution literature before writing "On the Duty of Civil Disobedience" and other essays.
    D.   Henry David Thoreau read a great deal of pre-Revolution literature, before writing "On the Duty of Civil Disobedience" and other essays.

5. A.   When was the last time you read *Catcher In The Rye*?
    B.   When was the last time you read *Catcher In the Rye*?
    C.   When was the last time you read *Catcher in the Rye*?
    D.   When was the last time you read *Catcher in the rye*?

In numbers 6 through 10, choose the answers which appropriately fill in the blanks, paying attention to <u>subject-verb agreement and consistency of verb tenses</u>.

6.   We first _____ the boss that afternoon.
     A.   will meet   B.   met   C.   have met   D.   had met
     Later, I hoped we _____ a good impression.
     F.   will make   G.   made   H.   have made   J.   had made

7. Until this year, mathematics _____ my favorite subject.
   A. is   B. are   C. was   D. were

8. Though the movie _____ tested on the market,
   A. is   B. was   C. has been   D. had been

   We Were Ninjas _____ fare well with for
   F. did not   G. does not   H. do not   J. will not

   teens, who usually _____ similar action, adventure, and fantasy films.
   L. like   M. likes   N. liked   P. will like

9. The blood on the carpet gives away his guilt; his diary or his calendar _____ the rest of the story.
   A. tell   B. tells   C. told   D. have told

10. As Liam put on his coat, the phone _____ .
    A. is ringing   B. rings   C. rang   D. will ring

In numbers 11 through 16, select the word in each list that is not <u>spelled</u> correctly.

11.   A. beutiful   B. acrobat   C. perfect   D. balance
12.   A. misspell   B. acceptible   C. gauge   D. separate
13.   A. relevant   B. schedule   C. occasion   D. sematary
14.   A. acquit   B. wierd   C. exceed   D. possession
15.   A. comitted   B. jewelry   C. believe   D. independent
16.   A. equipment   B. foreign   C. catergory   D. knowledgeable

In the following sentences, choose the appropriate <u>homonym</u> to fill in the blank.

17. What are you going to _____ to the theater?
    A. wear   B. where

18. Some people thought the movie was really scary, but it has little _____ on me.
    A. affect   B. effect

19. What makes you think _____ coming to dinner?
    A. their   B. there   C. they're

20. To plant this bulb, _____ it in about six inches of soil, and then water it well.
    A. berry   B. bury

In each set of sentences in 21 through 24, choose the sentence that best uses <u>precise word choice</u>.

21. A.   The bridge desperately needs to be replaced because it is not safe anymore.
    B.   The bridge needs to be replaced desperately because it does not meet standards.
    C.   Desperately, the bridge needs to be replaced; it does not meet safety standards.
    D.   The bridge does not meet safety standards and needs to be replaced desperately.

22. A.   Availability of that volume is extremely scarce.
    B.   It is very difficult to find that book.
    C.   It's impossible to buy that book.
    D.   You can't get that book.

23. Which of the following could be considered a compliment to someone?
    A.   I learned how to play piano when I was just a kid.
    B.   I've known how to play piano since I can't remember when.
    C.   I started piano lessons when I was 8 and have been playing since.
    D.   Piano playing is something I seem to have been doing all of my life.

24. What is the best way to revise this sentence to avoid using a cliché: "It won't be easy, but Michael is the one who can pull it off"?
    A.   It won't be easy, but Michael has the skills to success.
    B.   It won't be easy, but Michael knows how it works.
    C.   It won't be easy, but Michael knows everything.
    D.   It won't be easy, but Michael is very strong.

Read the excerpt from *A Connecticut Yankee in King Arthur's Court*, by Mark Twain, and then choose the answer that identifies the <u>clauses and phrases</u>.

　　　(25) <u>If I could have foreseen what the thing was going to be like</u>, I should have said, No, if anybody wants (26) <u>to make his living</u> (27) <u>exhibiting a king</u> as a peasant, let him take the layout; I can do better with a menagerie, and last longer. And yet, during the first three days (28) <u>I never allowed him</u> to enter a hut or other dwelling. If he could pass muster anywhere during his early novitiate it would be in small inns and on the road; (29) <u>so to these places we confined ourselves</u>. Yes, he certainly did the best he could, but what of that? He didn't improve a bit that I could see.

　　　He was always frightening me, always (30) <u>breaking out with fresh astonishers</u>, in new and unexpected places.

25.　A.   main clause　　　　　　　　C.   gerund phrase
　　 B.   subordinate clause　　　　　D.   infinitive phrase

26.　A.   main clause　　　　　　　　C.   infinitive phrase
　　 B.   subordinate clause　　　　　D.   gerund phrase

27. A. main clause   C. infinitive phrase
     B. subordinate clause   D. participial phrase

28. A. main clause   C. gerund phrase
     B. subordinate clause   D. infinitive phrase

29. A. main clause   C. participial phrase
     B. subordinate clause   D. gerund phrase

30. A. main clause   C. infinitive phrase
     B. subordinate clause   D. gerund phrase

Read the following sentences; in each set, choose the sentence that uses <u>parallel structure and/or has correctly placed modifiers</u>.

31. A. Daniel told a frightening ghost story while we sat around the roaring campfire.
    B. While we sat around the roaring campfire, Daniel told a frightening ghost story.
    C. We sat around the roaring campfire while Daniel told a frightening ghost story.
    D. All of the sentences above are correctly constructed.

32. A. After his year-long training, Travis finished the marathon effortlessly.
    B. After his year-long training, Travis effortlessly finished the marathon.
    C. After his year-long training, effortlessly Travis finished the marathon.
    D. All of the sentences above are correctly constructed.

33. A. She should not, I advised Maria, spend money that she does not have.
    B. Maria should not spend money, I advised her, that she does not have.
    C. I advised Maria that she should not spend money that she does not have.
    D. All of the sentences above are correctly constructed.

34. A. Hold my hand as we walk across the stream and down the hill.
    B. As we walk across the stream and down the hill, hold my hand.
    C. Hold my hand as we walk across the stream and hike down the hill.
    D. All of the sentences above are correctly constructed.

35. A. Exhausted and starving, the trip back to the lodge worried me.
    B. The trip back to the lodge, exhausted and starving, worried me.
    C. Exhausted and starving, I was worried about the trip back to the lodge.
    D. All of the sentences above are correctly constructed.

Chapter 9
Paragraph Structure and Manuscript Formatting

This chapter covers the following Georgia standard(s).

ELA11C1	Demonstrates an understanding of proper paragraph structure.
ELA11C2	Produces writing that conforms to appropriate manuscript requirements.
	Reflects appropriate format requirements, including pagination, spacing, and margins, and integration of source material with appropriate citations (e.g., in-text citations, use of direct quotations, paraphrase, and summary, and weaving of source and support materials with writer's own words, etc.)
	Includes formal works cited or bibliography when applicable.

These standards are part of Domain IV: Conventions. On the EOCT in American literature and composition, questions in this domain will measure your ability to understand manuscript form, realizing that different forms of writing require different formats. Correct usage, grammar, and sentence structure (covered in the previous chapter, "Using Standard American English") must be employed when writing manuscripts, and this chapter will add the discipline of working with paragraphs. In addition, when you take the EOCT, you will be asked to read a passage and perhaps revise it for organization, purpose, citations, and format. This chapter will briefly review these topics and give you a chance to practice using them in the exercises provided.

Most of the writing you do right now probably consists of composing essays for classes and on tests. Because an essay needs to be written in paragraphs, a discussion about well-organized paragraphs begins this chapter, followed by formatting information that will help you successfully complete not only essays but also other kinds of writing that you do now or will do in the future.

PARAGRAPH STRUCTURE

A **paragraph** is a series of related sentences that make a single point about one subject.

A paragraph is brief, so **choose one subject**. Make a point (something you want readers to know) about that subject in the **topic sentence** which often begins a paragraph but may also be at the end or in the middle. Once you have stated your point, provide readers with information and evidence to explain your topic sentence; this **supporting detail** is what truly makes your point. Finally, tie it all together with a **conclusion** (a statement or decision about your point). If the topic sentence does not end the paragraph, a **concluding sentence** can bring the paragraph to a close, and if appropriate, lead into the next paragraph.

When you have written all of the sentences you plan to include in your paragraph, and you have eliminated any that do not belong, review and reorganize your paragraph so that it has **coherence**—a logical focus and flow of ideas.

Read the following paragraph and the discussion that follows.

excerpt from *The Autobiography of Benjamin Franklin*, by Benjamin Franklin (1706–1790)

My brother had, in 1720 or 1721, begun to print a newspaper. It was the second that appeared in America, and was called the *New England Courant*. The only one before it was the *Boston News-Letter*. I remember his being dissuaded by some of his friends from the undertaking, as not likely to succeed, one newspaper being, in their judgment, enough for America. At this time (1771) there are not less than five-and-twenty. He went on, however, with the undertaking, and after having worked in composing the types and printing off the sheets, I was employed to carry the papers thro' the streets to the customers.

First, try a sample question: **What is the topic sentence in this paragraph?**

A. My brother had, in 1720 or 1721, begun to print a newspaper.

B. It was the second that appeared in America, and was called the *New England Courant*.

C. At this time (1771) there are not less than five-and-twenty.

D. He went on, however, with the undertaking, and after having worked in composing the types and printing off the sheets, I was employed to carry the papers thro' the streets to the customers.

Reading the entire paragraph carefully, you see that it is about Ben Franklin's brother starting a newspaper and why it was important for America and for Ben. Since this is the case, A is the best answer, as this is the sentence that introduces the subject: it answers the questions *who*, *when*, and *what*. Sentence B makes an important point, but what it gives is further description about the newspaper, like its name and that it was only the second to be published in the country. Sentence C also adds explanatory information to show how wrong people were about America not needing more than one newspaper, and sentence D provides a cause–effect statement about Ben getting a job from his brother.

This is a good example of a coherent and well-organized paragraph.

- **Topic sentence:** The first sentence concisely tells us subject—his brother's newspaper.

- **Supporting detail:** The second and third sentences tell important details about the paper. This leads to an explanation, in the fourth and fifth sentences, about the paper's place in American history.

- In the **concluding sentence**, the author ties it all back to the topic sentence, reiterating that the paper was started and describing his involvement.

ORGANIZING PARAGRAPHS

There are many ways to organize a paragraph and to organize paragraphs within an essay. These include **chronological order**, **spatial order**, **order of importance**, **cause and effect**, and **comparison and contrast of ideas**. The structure that you use should be the most appropriate for the subject you are discussing and type of essay you are writing.

Chronological order	usually means beginning at a point in time and going forward, but the order can begin in the future with flashbacks or in the middle and going back and then forward again. It is especially useful when you are writing a **narrative**. In addition, this organization pattern can include discussions of **cause and effect**, which naturally implies the passage of time, when explaining why or how something happens or describing the effects of an idea or event.
Spatial order	can be used to describe a scene or a location. This can be effective for a variety of situations such as providing instructions and describing a setting.
Order of importance	is a common way to organize a paragraph as well as an essay, placing emphasis on certain ideas by placing them either at the beginning or at the end.
Comparing and contrasting ideas	is an ideal way to write assignments that require that you look at two objects or ideas or to choose one side of an issue or topic and convince the reader of the validity of your position.

Practice 1: Paragraph Structure

All of the sentences in each question make a paragraph, but they may not be in order. For each sentence, identify the topic sentence, supporting detail, and concluding sentence, as well as any unrelated information. Then, choose which organization type BEST describes the paragraph.

A "Look!" Richard gasped; at last, there was the symbol that matched the one on their ancient map. **B** Both held torches that formed a limited glow around them in the dank corridors. **C** Richard and Emily walked slowly through the catacombs, searching for the secret passage. **D** At every sound of something slithering in the darkness beyond their torchlight, Emily shuddered and squeezed Richard's arm.

1. The topic sentence is letter_____.

   Letter _____ is a supporting sentence.

   Letter _____ is a supporting sentence.

   The concluding sentence is letter_____.

2. This paragraph is organized in
   A. chronological order.
   B. spatial order.
   C. order of importance.
   D. comparison and contrast of ideas.

> **A** At least the basics of the garden must be in place—a yew hedge and a pond. **B** Elizabeth had decided that her house must have a perfect English garden. **C** The perennials and annuals of her choice could come last. **D** Elizabeth could have a small pavilion built to suit.

3. The topic sentence is letter_____.

   Letter _____ is a supporting sentence.

   Letter _____ is a supporting sentence.

   The concluding sentence is letter_____.

4. This paragraph is organized in
   A. chronological order.
   B. spatial order.
   C. order of importance.
   D. comparison and contrast of ideas.

> **A** Surprise and disappointment registered on the faces of the volunteers seated at three long tables facing Mack's desk and the district map behind it. **B** He hung up and looked from Maggie on his right, past Juan and Ginny, to Rick and Lee on his left: the votes were in…and he had lost. **C** Mack searched for something else to say while the staff looked wistfully at the vestiges of their work: the posters in the corner, the flyers stacked on the back tables, the colorful streamers hung from the ceiling. **D** The campaign signs had vibrant graphics and motivational messages. **E** It was clear by the look on Mack's face that the phone call had left him in shock.

5. The topic sentence is letter_____.

   Letter _____ is a supporting sentence.

   Letter _____ is a supporting sentence.

   The concluding sentence is letter_____.

   A sentence that should be removed because it contains unrelated information is _____.

6. This paragraph is organized in
   A. chronological order.
   B. spatial order.
   C. order of importance.
   D. comparison and contrast of ideas.

TRANSITIONS AND THE FLOW OF IDEAS

In addition to coherent order and organization, each paragraph, as well as you entire essay, needs a smooth flow of ideas. This is accomplished by using **transitional devices** within and between sentences and paragraphs and by **varying sentences** for clarity and emphasis. The following table provides examples of effective transitions and improving the flow of ideas.

Transitional Device	Example
to show time	now, at this time, at this point, immediately, simultaneously, concurrently, first (second, etc.), next, then, later, thereafter, after, afterward, subsequently, soon, finally, following this, formerly, previously
to show cause or effect	because, for, since, as a result of, for the reason that, evidently, due to
to show space	next to, along, within, near, on top of, to the right/left of, further
to show importance or emphasize	most importantly, absolutely, definitely, extremely, surprisingly, best, most, in fact, indeed, positively, naturally, always, forever, never, emphatically, unquestionably, without a doubt, certainly, undeniably
to compare	likewise, neither, both, similarly, where, also, correspondingly, equally
to contrast	whereas, although, conversely, meanwhile, after all, but, yet, however, on the other hand, on the contrary, in contrast
to add	and, again, in addition, besides, further, equally important, furthermore, too, next, what's more, moreover
to give an example	for example, for instance, to illustrate, in this case, in another case, take the case of, on this occasion, in this situation, to demonstrate
to summarize or conclude	so, to conclude, this shows that, in brief, on the whole, hence, therefore, accordingly, thus, as a result, consequently

Sentence Variety	Example
using introductory phrases	*While they watched the film,* they thought about ways in which it differed from the novel.
combining sentences	1 Every team needs to read one chapter for tomorrow. 2 Each team will present its chapter, and the whole class will discuss it. Every team needs to read one chapter for tomorrow because each will present its chapter, and the whole class will discuss it.
inserting sentences to clarify	**unclear:** The novels of James Fenimore Cooper depict the progress of the frontier settlement. Cooper chronicles these waves, portraying not only the gains but the losses. **clarified:** The novels of James Fenimore Cooper depict the progress of the frontier settlement. *From the wilderness inhabited by natives, through the arrival of frontiersmen, to the building of communities, each wave displaces earlier ones while bringing improvements in civilization.* Cooper chronicles these waves, portraying not only the gains but the losses.

Read the following passage, and then read the questions about it. A discussion after each question explains the answer.

> The first published book of poems by an American was also the first American book by a woman. Anne Bradstreet emigrated from England to America. She was 18 when she arrived in America with her family. She wrote conventional poems of the day about religion and the seasons, as well as clever poems about family life. The book was published in England. There were no printing presses yet in the American colonies.

1. In the first sentence, which transitional device would be the BEST addition in this context?

   A. **At this point,** the first published book of poems by an American was also the first American book by a woman.

   B. The first published book of poems by an American **then** was also the first American book by a woman.

   C. The first published book of poems by an American was **in fact** also the first American book by a woman.

   D. The first published book of poems by an American was **therefore** also the first American book by a woman.

The answer is **C**. It provides a note of emphasis for an interesting and significant fact. Answer A is incorrect because we have no reference for when "this point" is. Answer **B** makes it sound as though there are two consecutive events, though the passage talks about the publication of a single book. Finally, answer **D** implies a cause and effect where there is none.

2. What is the BEST way to combine the second and third sentences (reproduced here)?

   Anne Bradstreet emigrated from England to America. She was 18 when she arrived with her family.

   A. Anne Bradstreet emigrated from England to America, and she was 18 when she arrived in America with her family.

   B. Anne Bradstreet emigrated from England to America; she was 18 when she arrived in America with her family.

   C. Emigrating from England to America, Anne Bradstreet was 18 when she arrived with her family.

   D. When she was 18, Anne Bradstreet emigrated from England to America with her family.

Take a look at the rest of the passage and try combining additional sentences and inserting transitional devices.

Practice 2:   Transitions and the Flow of Ideas

This sample passage contains typical mistakes in transitional techniques. Read the three paragraphs, and then answer the questions pertaining to them.

A Brief Biography of Mark Twain

1 Mark Twain was born Samuel Langhorne Clemens in Missouri in 1835. **2** He began developing his humorous writing in the 1850s. **3** At 18, he headed to New York and Philadelphia and worked at newspapers there. **4** He returned home to Missouri and served as a steamboat captain for a time. **5** That's where his pen name comes from: *mark twain* is the warning term used on steamboats to indicate a river's depth is only two fathoms, the minimum at which a boat can navigate safely. **6** When the Civil War began, he and his friends joined up. **7** They were in a battle where Twain saw a man killed. **8** He decided he could not kill and deserted, going west with his brother, Orion.

9 He became editor of a Virginia City newspaper, and that's where he first used his pen name. **10** He went to San Francisco and continued writing, and he began lecturing about his many travels, now including a trip to Hawaii and the Mediterranean. **11** His tour of Europe and the Middle East inspired a series of travel letters compiled into the 1869 book, *Innocents Abroad*. **12** While abroad he met Charles Langdon and, in 1970, ended up marrying his sister Olivia. **13** He and Olivia had a son (who died shortly after birth) and three daughters, living most of their family life together in Hartford, Connecticut.

14 Twain lived a long life, surviving his wife and two of his daughters. **15** Their passing left him in a deep depression at the end of his life. **16** His last two works do not contain his usual wit. **17** He published many humorously observant and satirical accounts of his observations both in American and abroad. **18** His most famous works are the novels *The Adventures of Tom Sawyer* (1876) and *Adventures of Huckleberry Finn* (1884). **19** The author was extremely popular in his own lifetime as a novelist, essaying, and popular philosopher. **20** He has been called "the father of American literature," and *Adventures of Huckleberry Finn* is sometimes cited as the great American novel. **21** Mark Twain left a great legacy.

1. In the context, which is the BEST way to revise and combine sentences 6 and 7 (reproduced here)?

   When the Civil War began, he and his friends joined up. They were in a battle where Twain saw a man killed.

   A. He and his friends, when the Civil War began, joined up, and they were in a battle where Twain saw a man killed.

   B. When the Civil War began, Twain and his friends joined up and subsequently were in a battle where Twain saw a man killed.

   C. Twain and his friends joined up when the Civil War began, and Twain saw a man killed in a battle they were in.

   D. When the Civil War began, Twain and his friends, having joined up, were then in a battle where Twain saw a man killed.

2. Which would be the BEST transition device to add to the beginning of sentence 8?

   A. Finally,
   B. However,
   C. As a result,
   D. In summing up,

3. In the context, what is the BEST revision to make to the beginning sentence 10?

   A. Later he went to San Francisco, continued writing,
   B. Concurrently in San Francisco, he continued writing and
   C. So, he went to San Francisco, continuing to write and
   D. In any case, he went to San Francisco; he continued to write and

4. Which would be the BEST transition device to add to the beginning of sentence 13?

   A. At present,
   B. Therefore,
   C. Evidently,
   D. Eventually,

5. In the context, which is the BEST way to revise and combine sentences 15 and 16 (reproduced below)?

   Their passing left him in a deep depression at the end of his life. His last two works do not contain his usual wit.

   A. leave as is

   B. Their passing left him, at the end of his life, in a deep depression, and this made his last two works devoid of his usual wit.

   C. Their passing left him in a deep depression at the end of his life, and as a result his last two works do not contain his usual wit.

   D. His last two works, end of his life, were written without his usual wit, their passing having left him in a deep depression.

6. Which would be the BEST sentence to add after sentence 16 as a clarifying transitional device?

   A. Nevertheless, these books are part of his life's work
   B. However, this is an exception to his lifetime of work.
   C. For this reason, no one reads these books very much.
   D. Indeed, these works are unlike anything else he wrote.

7. Which would be the BEST transition device to add to the beginning of sentence 21?

    A.   Thus,   B.   In time,   C.   Moreover,   D.   Without a doubt,

UNDERSTANDING MANUSCRIPT REQUIREMENTS

Whether you are writing a paper for a class, developing a memo for work, or composing a letter, there are structures for how each manuscript should look on the page in addition to the conventions you use in the actual writing. Just as using appropriate words, correct sentence and paragraph structure, and logical organization helps a reader understand what you are saying, the formatting of your writing is critical to support that understanding.

Although you will not do any actually writing on the Georgia EOCT in American literature and composition, you may be asked questions about manuscript formatting as well as use of citations and bibliographies.

FORMATTING TEXT

There are basic guidelines to keep in mind about formatting. Specifics, however, will depend on the style manual you are instructed to use (see **page 215** in this chapter for a description of style manuals) and the individual instruction provided by your teacher for each assignment. Be sure that you understand the guidelines you should use for each assignment.

Essays you write for class begin with a **title** and **identification**. The title, your name, the date, and the class and teacher for which the paper is written can appear on a separate title page or at the top of the first page of the essay.

For any assignment longer than one page, use **pagination** to keep the pages in absolute order, even if they get separated or out of order. Styles for pagination vary. For instance, in MLA style, the page number appears with the last name of the author at the upper right corner of each page.

Example:

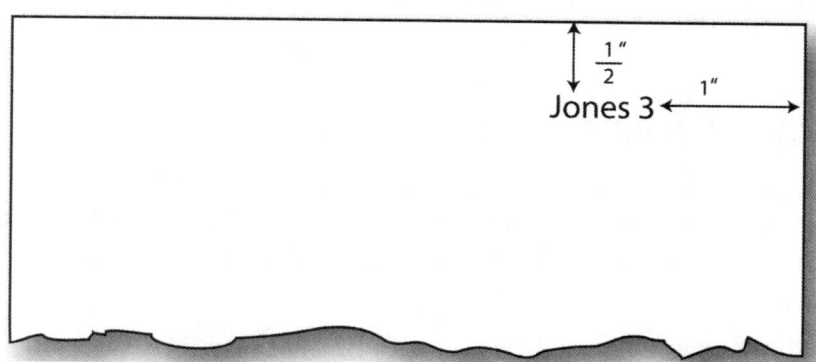

Tip: If you type your essays on a computer, the word processing program has ways to set up page numbers automatically. Refer to the manual that came with your software, explore the "page setup" menu, or access the "help" information while using the program for instructions about how to insert the pagination you need.

Leave **margins** of one inch on all sides of the paper, unless you are instructed otherwise. Margin spacing is typically preset at these measurements in word processing programs. Checks the settings to verify.

Double-space and **left-align** the text, and **indent the first line of each paragraph**. Left-aligning settings make your paper easier to read, and double-spacing leaves room for your teacher to make corrections and comments.

Example:

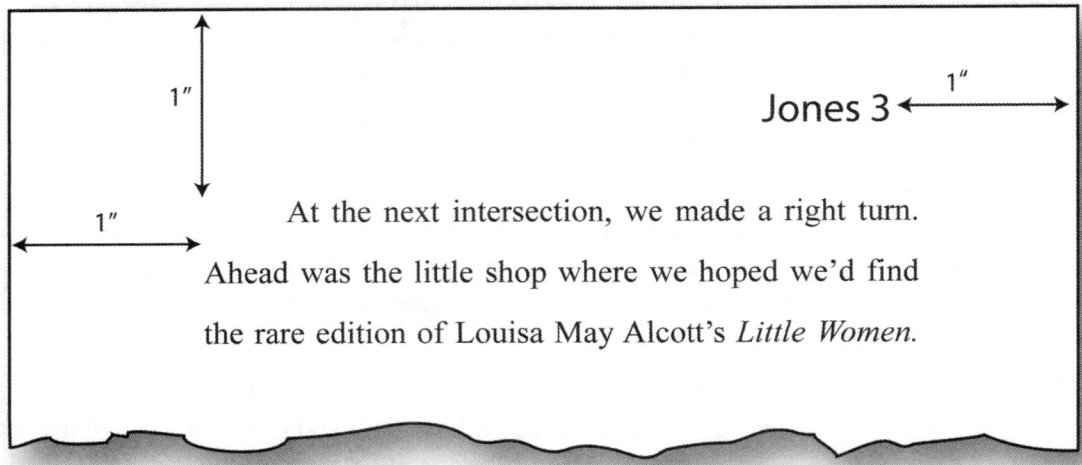

Use a readable and common **font** (type style), such as Times New Roman (most computer word processing programs are preset to this font). Trying a fancy font will not improve your grade, and it may hurt it if it makes your work less legible.

The style manual you are instructed to use also will details about how to format many other items, such as **long quotations**, **Web addresses**, and **headings** (if included). It is the best place to consult with all of your formatting questions.

CITING AND LISTING SOURCE MATERIAL

In chapter 7, The Research Process, you reviewed how to use research and technology to support your writing. This section provides an additional opportunity to review and practice integration of source material with appropriate citation and references within your correctly formatted manuscript.

Citation and bibliography style will depend on the style guide you are using. If you do not know what style you should use, ask your teacher. Here is a list of the common style guides and how they are used most often.

- **APA** (American Psychological Association): psychology and social sciences
- **MLA** (Modern Language Association): literature, arts, humanities
- **AMA** (American Medical Association): medicine, health, biological sciences
- **Turabian** (named after designer Kate Turabian): college writing in all subjects
- **Chicago**: used in modern books, magazines, newspapers, etc., for all subjects

When you look up any of these styles on the Internet, don't be surprised if you find minor variations in the rules. The only way to be sure that citations and source material lists are truly correct is to use the official guide for a specific style. If you are using a guide but cannot find the way to list a source that you want to use, use your best judgment based on how similar works are listed in the guide, and then ask your teacher to review your solution.

FORMATTING IN-TEXT CITATIONS

Remember that any material taken from another source must be given a citation, a reference to the author and original source. Depending on the style manual, in-text citations will look different, but they will correspond to full listings of the source material in a works-cited page or bibliography.

As you learned in chapter 7, there are three ways to use materials from sources: **direct quotation**, **paraphrasing**, and **summarizing**. Here is an example of a quote and what its works-cited entry would look like. MLA style is used for demonstration purposes.

Direct quotation example: During the Romantic Movement, authors looked to art, not science, for universal truth, believing that "Nature is the incarnation of thought. The world is the mind precipitated" (Emerson).

The corresponding entry in works cited, at the end of the essay, would read as follows:

> Emerson, Ralph Waldo. *Nature* 1844. *The Harvard Classics*. Ed. Eliot, Charles W. 26 Mar. 2007 <http://www.bartleby.com/5/114.html>.

When a page number helps further identify where to find the cited material, include that in the in-text citation. For example, if the poem quoted above was found in a book, the page number would be given after the author's name: (Emerson 27). If you reference more than one work by an author, use the title—or an abbreviation of a long title—in the citation rather than just the author's name: (*Nature* 27). If the text you write provides both the author's name and title of the work where the cited material is found, then all you need to provide in the page number.

Example: During the Romantic Movement, authors looked to art, not science, for universal truth. In his poem "Nature," Ralph Waldo Emerson wrote, "Nature is the incarnation of thought. The world is the mind precipitated" (27).

As always, check your style guide for details for the kind of citation you need.

FORMATTING WORKS CITED AND BIBLIOGRAPHIES

In addition to referencing source materials within your essay, you will also need a listing or the source materials themselves—this list is where a reader is referred by the in-text citations in your essay. Just as with in-text citations, the format to use for this list varies according to the style manual you use.

A **works-cited** page is a list of the sources that you have cited in your essay. Here is an example.

Works Cited
Alter, Jonathan. *The Defining Moment: FDR's Hundred Days and the Triumph of Hope*. New York: Simon & Schuster, 2006.
Biography – Stephen King: Fear, Fame and Fortune. Writ. Andy Thomas. Dir. Bill Harris. Nar. Peter Graves. Arts and Entertainment Network. 26 Sept. 2000.
Emerson, Ralph Waldo. "Nature" 1844. *The Harvard Classics*. Ed. Eliot, Charles W. 26 Mar. 2007 <http://www.bartleby.com/5/114.html>.

Notice that, in MLA style, the list appears in alphabetical order by author's last name. All lines of a listing, except the first line, are indented one-half inch. When more than one work by the same author is listed in works cited or in a bibliography, the author's name can be replaced by lines (---) after the first work listed.

Some style guides call for a **bibliography**, which is a list of all the sources you consulted in your research about a topic, whether or not you used and cited them. Sometimes your teacher may ask you to submit a complete bibliography, even though you also have a works-cited page. Here is a sample of the beginning of a bibliography in Turabian style (very similar to MLA style).

Bibliography
Bonnin, Gertrude Simmons (Zitkala-Sa). "A Warrior's Daughter." *Everybody's Magazine*, April 1902, 346-352.
Poe, Edgar Allen. "The Balloon-Hoax." *Edgar Allan Poe: Complete Tales & Poems*. New Jersey: castle Books, 2002.
London, Jack. *White Fang*. Serial Serialized in *The Outing Magazine*, May-Oct., 1906 [book online]; available from http://london.sonoma.edu/Writings/WhiteFang/ (accessed 6 Feb. 2007).
Wilkins, Mary E. "A Poetess." *A New England Nun and Other Stories*. New York: Harper & Brothers Publishers, 1891.

An assignment may also ask for an **annotated bibliography**, which is the same as the bibliography you have learned about, with one addition. Each source listed has a brief description of the work.

Bibliography
Bonnin, Gertrude Simmons (Zitkala-Sa). "A Warrior's Daughter." *Everybody's Magazine*, April 1902, 346-352.
A semi-autobiographical story about the author's Dakota Sioux upbringing, how the Dakota live, and how poorly native Americans were treated around the turn of the century.

Practice 3:   Manuscript Formatting

A Read the sample essay instructions, then answer the questions that follow.

> Your assignment for this week is an essay exploring an interesting facet of a favorite author. Remember to fully develop your essay, make a point, and use specific examples whenever possible. Express your opinion and bring in personal experience, but be sure to also include facts and pull from primary and secondary sources. Remember to revise your work for clarity and proofread for grammar, spelling, and punctuation. The length of the paper is 2 to 3 typed pages, double-spaced, in standard MLA format. Include your name, the class number (English 151), and the name of the assignment on your title page.

1. Where will the title of the essay appear?

   A. at the top right-hand corner of each page
   B. just above the introduction
   C. on the title page
   D. The teacher will need to be consulted for instructions.

2. As the essay is typed on a computer, how should the following settings be adjusted?

   Margins   Top _____   Bottom _____

   Left _____   Right _____

   A. ½" 1"   C. 1.5" 1"
      1" 1"   1"   1"

   B. 1" 1"   D. The teacher will need to be consulted for
      1" 1"   instructions.

   Line spacing

   F. single   H. 1.5 lines
   G. double   J. The teacher will need to be consulted for
                             instructions

3. Which style guide should be used to look up how to cite and list sources?

    A. *The Chicago Manual of Style*
    B. *Manual of the American Psychological Association*
    C. *MLA Handbook for Writers of Research Papers*
    D. *A Brief Citation Guide for Internet Sources in History and the Humanities*

B. Based on the directions on the previous page, Ramon drafts an essay about a favorite author of his, Anne Rice. Read the first paragraph of Ramon's draft below, and then answer the questions that follow.

> **1** Vampires, witches, demons…these characters populate most of the books written by Anne Rice. **2** I read *Interview with the Vampire* a couple years ago, and when the vampire said at the beginning that he wanted to the story of his life (Rice 3), I was hooked. **3** Rice wove together legend, history, and rich descriptions of New Orleans and Paris as a backdrop to characters that mourned as much as they terrorized. **4** I quickly read the rest of the Vampire Chronicles and several of her other novels. **5** Then I discovered that she also uses her descriptive and engaging writing to tell stories about true historical events, like the lives of 18th century castrati in *Cry to Heaven* and Louisiana's Free People of Color in *The Feast of All Saints*. **6** Now, she has published a new novel, *Christ the Lord Out of Egypt*, and said, "This book … is a sincere attempt to bring to life in fiction the world of Jesus of Nazareth." **7** That is what I appreciate most about Anne Rice: her ability to make history come alive.

4. In sentence 2, a citation is provided for what kind of reference?

    A. a direct quotation
    B. a paraphrase
    C. a summary
    D. an excerpt

5. Is the in-text citation used in sentence 2 correct?

    A. Yes, it is correct.
    B. No, it should also use the book title because several works by the same author are cited.
    C. No, it only needs the page number because the author and book title are mentioned.
    D. No, it does not need to be there.

6. Which other sentence in this paragraph should contain an in-text citation?

    A. sentence 3   B. sentence 4   C. sentence 5   D. sentence 6

7. Which of the following would be a correct and complete works-cited page for the paragraph you read?

    A.

Works Cited
Rice, Anne O'Brien. *Cry to Heaven*. New York: Ballantine, 1982.
---. *Feast of All Saints*. New York: Random House, 1979.
---. *Interview with the Vampire*. New York: Random House, 1976.

B.

Works Cited
Rice, Anne O'Brien.
---. *Interview with the Vampire*. New York: Random House, 1976.
---. *Feast of All Saints*. New York: Random House, 1979.
---. *Cry to Heaven*. New York: Ballantine, 1982.
Rice, Anne. "Rice on Writing, 2005." 10 Jan. 2007 AnneRice.com   <http://www.annerice.com/fa_writing_05.htm>.

C.

Works Cited
Rice, Anne O'Brien. *Christ the Lord Out of Egypt: A Novel*. New York: Knopf, 2005.
---. *Cry to Heaven*. New York: Ballantine, 1982.
---. *Feast of All Saints*. New York: Random House, 1979.
---. *Interview with the Vampire*. New York: Random House, 1976.
---. "Rice on Writing, 2005." 10 Jan. 2007 AnneRice.com   <http://www.annerice.com/fa_writing_05.htm>.

D.

Works Cited
Anne O'Brien Rice. 2005. *Christ the Lord Out of Egypt: A Novel*.
---. 1982. *Cry to Heaven*.
---. 1979.*Feast of All Saints*.
---. 1976.*Interview with the Vampire*.
---. "Rice on Writing, 2005." AnneRice.com.

CHAPTER 9 SUMMARY

When writing a **paragraph** (a series of related sentences), remember to **choose one subject**, make a point about that subject in the **topic sentence** provide information and evidence to explain the subject in the **supporting detail**, and tie it all together with a **conclusion** (a statement or decision about your point). Review and reorganize your paragraph so that it has **coherence** (a logical focus and flow of ideas).

To arrange the paragraphs of an essay together, choose an organizational structure such as **chronological order**, **spatial order**, **order of importance**, **cause and effect**, or **comparison and contrast of ideas** which is appropriate for the subject you are discussing and type of essay you are writing. Use **transitional devices** within and between sentences and paragraphs and **vary sentences** for clarity and emphasis.

Follow the manuscript formatting guidelines that you have been given by your teacher and/or that are in the style manual you have been instructed to use. Formatting details to observe include **title** and **identifying information**, **pagination**, **margins**, **spacing**, and **indentation**. Refer to the style manual you are using for details about how to include appropriate **in-text citations** for **quotations**, **paraphrases**, and **summaries**, as well as how to create a **works-cited page** or **bibliography**

CHAPTER 9 REVIEW

A. Read the following passages, and then answer the questions that follow.

A Vonnegut's fiction will continue to be read for its new and astounding ways to look at everyday things like love, family, work, war, and time. **B** Kurt Vonnegut died in April 2007 after a long writing career. **C** He was passionately vocal about politics. **D** Although many of his novels were written in the science fiction genre, they were widely read thanks to their pervasive themes about seeing absurdity in life and questioning authority. **E** He wrote 14 acclaimed novels and dozens of stories, essays, and screenplays.

1. The topic sentence is letter_____.

   Letter ____ is a supporting sentence.

   Letter ____ is a supporting sentence.

   The concluding sentence is letter____.

   A sentence that should be removed because it contains unrelated information is _____.

2. This paragraph is organized in
   - A. chronological order.
   - B. spatial order.
   - C. order of importance.
   - D. comparison and contrast of ideas.

   A Starting out in Missouri, Mark Twain rode the river—and was even a riverboat captain for a time—which figures prominently in many of his works. **B** Growing up in St. Paul, Minnesota, F. Scott Fitzgerald saw the lowland existence of the poor versus the bluff views of the rich, portrayed in *The Great Gatsby*. **C** From its northern source to its finish in the Gulf of Mexico, the Mighty Mississip' has inspired not only blues musicians but also a host of writers. **D** Finally, playwright Tennessee Williams set plays like *A Streetcar Named Desire* (New Orleans) in southern locations along the Mississippi. **E** Poet T.S. Eliot said his work, including the epic poem *The Waste Land*, was a result of living near the river in St. Louis.

3. The topic sentence is letter_____.

   Letter ____ is the first supporting sentence.

   Letter ____ is the second supporting sentence.

   Letter ____ is the third supporting sentence.

   The concluding sentence is letter____.

4. This paragraph is organized in
    A. chronological order.
    B. spatial order.
    C. order of importance.
    D. comparison and contrast of ideas.

B. Read the following passage. Answer the questions that follow.

> **1** Edith Wharton (born Edith Newbold Jones on January 24, 1862) arrived into a world of privilege. **2** Her parents, George and Lucretia Jones of New York City, were wealthy descendents of aristocrats. **3** As their daughter, Edith was taught by tutors at home, had her father's extensive library at her disposal, and was brought into society as a young lady of means. **4** When she was 23, she married Teddy Wharton. **5** They were married for 28 years. **6** But Edith discovered Teddy cheated on her, and then she began living a new, emotionally fulfilling life, in Paris. **7** Given her education, rich reading background, and new experiences gained in "real life," Edith began around 1900 to write prolifically. **8** In 1902 she designed and built an estate in Massachusetts called The Mount, where she wrote several of her novels, including her 1905 masterpiece *The House of Mirth*. **9** In it, and in many of her other novels, she uses subtle dramatic irony to depict upperclass New York society with humor, empathy, and satiric critique. **10** Edith divorced Teddy in 1912, and she traveled extensively and assisted with World War I refugees in Paris. **11** She won the Pulitzer Prize for her novel, *The Age of Innocence.* **12** She was in the middle of writing her last novel, *The Buccaneers*, when she died in 1938.

5. In the context, which is the BEST way to revise and combine sentences 5 and 6 (reproduced here)?

    > *They were married for 28 years. But Edith discovered Teddy cheated on her, and then she began living a new, emotionally fulfilling life, in Paris.*

    A. Though they were married for 28 years, Edith discovered that Teddy cheated on her, and she moved to Paris to live a new, emotionally fulfilling life.
    B. Edith discovered that Teddy, to who she was married for 28 years, cheated on her, and then began living a new, emotionally fulfilling life, in Paris.
    C. Edith began living a new, emotionally fulfilling life, in Paris, after discovering Teddy cheated on her, but they remained married for 28 years.
    D. After discovering that Teddy cheated on her, Edith moved to Paris; there, she lived a new, emotionally fulfilling life, but she and Teddy stayed married for 28 years.

6. Which would be the BEST transition device to add to the beginning of sentence 7?
    A. Most importantly, her education,
    B. Along with her education,
    C. As a result of her education,
    D. Despite her education,

7. In the context, what is the BEST revision to make to the beginning sentence 10?
   A. She divorced Teddy in 1912 before traveling
   B. After divorcing Teddy in 1912, Edith traveled
   C. While divorcing Teddy in 1912, Edith traveled
   D. After all, divorcing Teddy in 1912, Edith traveled

8. What organization does this paragraph use?
   A. chronological order.
   B. spatial order.
   C. order of importance.
   D. comparison and contrast of ideas.

C. Read the sample essay instructions, then answer the questions that follow.

> Write a well-developed essay about the poem you have chosen. Be sure to include explanation of its theme and figurative language. Your essay must include your name, email address, and a title, but no title page is needed. The essay should be double-spaced and should include a brief bibliography.

9. Where will the title of the essay appear?
   A. at the top right-hand corner of each page
   B. just above the introduction
   C. on the title page
   D. No title is needed.

10. What style guide should be used to look up how to cite and list sources?
    A. *MLA Handbook for Writers of Research Papers*
    B. *The Chicago Manual of Style*
    C. Kate Turabian's *A Manual for Writers of Term Papers, Theses, and Dissertations*
    D. The teacher will need to be consulted for instructions.

11. How should the lines be spaced in this essay?
    A. single
    B. double
    C. 1.5 lines
    D. The teacher will need to be consulted for instructions.

D. Based on the directions above, Lisa begins an essay about her chosen poem. Read the first paragraph draft below, and then answer the questions that follow.

> **1** An important poem to me is Robert Frost's *Fire and Ice*. **2** This poem seems to reflect the turmoil in today's world, speaking of an end coming due to our human emotions. **3** In the poem, Frost wonders how the world will end: "Some say the world will end in fire, / Some say in ice." **4** Some people have predicted that a real end to the world is near. **5** Though that may be farfetched, it may be that the world as we know it will change incredibly due to global conflicts. **6** All one needs to do is watch the evening news or read your local newspaper to get a glimpse. **7** Frost continues: "From what I've tasted of desire / I hold with those who favor fire." **8** In this line, fire symbolizes anger and passion, while the next line uses ice to stand for cold hatred and indifference. **9** Either way, Frost presents a sobering look at how our ideas and attitudes shape what goes on in the world.

12. In which sentences are citations needed?
    - A. sentences 1 and 3
    - B. sentences 3, 6, and 7
    - C. sentences 3 and 7
    - D. none of the above

13. No matter which style manual Lisa uses, which of the following lists of information about her chosen poem should Lisa use for her bibliography entry?
    - A. Robert Frost, "Fire and Ice," where the poem is found, page numbers where is appears
    - B. Robert Frost, "Fire and Ice," the year that the poem was written, where the poem is found
    - C. Robert Frost, *Fire and Ice*, where the poem is found, page numbers where is appears
    - D. Robert Frost, *Fire and Ice*, the year that the poem was written, where the poem is found

14. Based on this paragraph, how many works will appear in Lisa's bibliography?
    - A. none
    - B. one
    - C. two
    - D. three

GA EOCT in American Literature and Composition
Practice Test 1

The purpose of this practice test is to measure your progress in American literature and Composition. This practice test is based on the Georgia GPS standards for American Literature and Composition and adheres to the sample question format provided by the Georgia Department of Education.

General Directions:

1. Read all directions carefully.

2. Read each question or sample. Then choose the best answer.

3. Choose only one answer for each question. If you change an answer, be sure to erase your original answer completely.

Standards covered by each question are indicated next to the question. For standard ELAALRL1, a letter follows the standard number, indicating F = fiction, NF= nonfiction, P = poetry, or D = drama.

SECTION I

excerpt from Sarah Orne Jewett's "A White Heron"

Sylvia herself felt sleepy as she walked along. However, it was not much farther to the house, and the air was soft and sweet. She was not often in the woods so late as this, and it made her feel as if she were a part of the gray shadows and the moving leaves. She was just thinking how long it seemed since she first came to the farm a year ago and wondering if everything went on in the noisy town just the same as when she was there; the thought of the great red-faced boy who used to chase and frighten her made her hurry along the path to escape from the shadow of the trees. Suddenly this little woods-girl is horror-stricken to hear a clear whistle not very far away. Not a bird's whistle, which would have a sort of friendliness, but a boy's whistle, determined, and somewhat aggressive. Sylvia left the cow to whatever sad fate might await her, and stepped discreetly aside into the bushes, but she was just too late. The enemy had discovered her, and called out in a very cheerful and persuasive tone, "Halloa, little girl, how far is it to the road?" and trembling Sylvia answered almost inaudibly, "A good ways."

She dare not to look boldly at the tall young man, who carried a gun over his shoulder, but she came out of her bush and again followed the cow, while he walked alongside.

"I have been hunting for some birds," the stranger said kindly, "and I have lost my way, and need a friend very much. Don't be afraid," he added gallantly. "Speak up and tell me what your name is, and whether you think I can spend the night at your house, and go out hunting early in the morning."

Sylvia was more alarmed than before. Would not her grandmother consider her much to blame? But who could have foreseen such an accident as this? It did not seem to be her fault, and she hung her head as if the stem of it were broken, but managed to answer "Sylvy..."

1. **What conclusion regarding gender roles in Sylvia and the young man's culture can be drawn from this selection?** ELAALRL3 ELAALRC4

   A   It is a very free and open society for both genders, except when it is time to hunt.

   B   The culture values the communication between genders of every economic class.

   C   It is a culture based on urban values of strong female figures and silent males.

   D   It is a culture based on rural values of a strong male figure and submissive female.

2. **This story is told by a narrator. If it were written from Sylvia's point of view, which of the following would NOT be true?** ELAALRL1, F

   A   The description of the young man would be different.

   B   She probably would give more explanation of her thoughts.

   C   The tone and diction of the story would be more childlike.

   D   Readers would know what the young man is feeling.

3. **Based on Sylvia and the young man's interactions, what can be concluded about Sylvia, and how does this affect the plot?** ELAALRL1, F

   A   Sylvia is angry about the young man's successful hunting expedition, and she decides to take him to her grandmother for a scolding.

   B   Sylvia is shy but obedient, which causes her to answer the young man's questions even when she doesn't want to.

   C   Sylvia is afraid of her unruly cow, which causes her to be afraid of the unruly young man, too.

   D   Sylvia is frightened at the sight of the gun, and she is unable to speak.

4. **Nancy wants to write a paper discussing the various authors who influenced Sarah Orne Jewett's work. In which source should she begin her search?** ELA11W3

   A   a dictionary

   B   a newspaper

   C   an encyclopedia of literature

   D   another story by Sarah Orne Jewett

Read the sentence below.

> It did not seem to be her fault, and she hung her head as if the stem of it were broken…

5. **In this sentence, the author is comparing Sylvia's head to** ELAALRL1, F

   A   a flower.   C   an apple.

   B   a wine glass.   D   a tree.

6. **As it is used in Paragraph 3, the word *gallantly* MOST nearly means** ELA11RC3 ELAALRL5

   A   humorously.   C   nervously.

   B   crudely.   D   respectfully.

7. **Which word from the passage means *with restraint, cautiously*?** ELA11RC3

   A   determined   C   discreetly

   B   inaudibly   D   foreseen

8. **The name Sylvia is appropriate for the character because it comes from the Latin word *silva*, which means** ELAALRL5

   A   metal.

   B   wood, forest.

   C   loud.

   D   drowsy, sleepy.

GO ON

9. **"A White Heron" appears in**
   its entirety on a Web site
   about Sarah Orne Jewett. Which of the
   possible additions below would be
   LEAST helpful for students research-
   ing this particular story?

   ELA11W3
   ELA11LSV2

   A links to literary analyses of "A White Heron"

   B biographical information about Jewett

   C information on reoccurring themes in Jewett's work

   D links to the works of other female American authors

excerpt from Nathaniel Hawthorne's *The Scarlet Letter*

"I pray you, good Sir," said he, "who is this woman? and wherefore is she here set up to public shame?"

"You must needs be a stranger in this region, friend," answered the townsman, looking curiously at the questioner and his savage companion, "else you would surely have heard of Mistress Hester Prynne and her evil doings. She hath raised a great scandal, I promise you, in godly Master Dimmesdale's church."

"You say truly," replied the other; "I am a stranger, and have been a wanderer, sorely against my will. I have met with grievous mishaps by sea and land, and have been long held in bonds among the heathen-folk to the southward; and am now brought hither by this Indian to be redeemed out of my captivity. Will it please you, therefore, to tell me of Hester Prynne's—Have I her name rightly?—of this woman's offenses, and what has brought her to yonder scaffold?"

"Truly, friend; and methinks it must gladden your heart, after your troubles and sojourn in the wilderness," said the townsman, "to find yourself at length in a land where iniquity is searched out and punished in the sight of rulers and people, as here in our godly New England. Yonder woman, Sir, you must know, was the wife of a certain learned man, English by birth, but who had long ago dwelt in Amsterdam, whence some good time agone he was minded to cross over and cast in his lot with us of the Massachusetts. To this purpose he sent his wife before him, remaining himself to look after some necessary affairs. Marry, good Sir, in some two years, or less, that the woman has been a dweller here in Boston, no tidings have come of this learned gentleman, Master Prynne; and his young wife, look you, being left to her own misguidance."

"Ah!aha! I conceive you," said the stranger with a bitter smile. "So learned a man as you speak of should have learned this too in his books. And who, by your favor, Sir, may be the father of yonder babe—it is some three or four months old, I should judge—which Mistress Prynne is holding in her arms?"

"Of a truth, friend, that matter remaineth a riddle; and the Daniel who shall expound it is yet a-wanting," answered the townsman. "Madame Hester absolutely refuseth to speak, and the magistrates have laid their heads together in vain. Per adventure the guilty one stands looking on at this sad spectacle, unknown of man, and forgetting that God sees him."

"The learned man," observed the stranger with another smile, "should come himself to look into the mystery."

"It behooves him well if he be still in life," responded the townsman. "Now, good Sir, our Massachusetts magistracy, bethinking themselves that this woman is youthful and fair, and doubtless was strongly tempted to her fall, and that, moreover, as is most likely, her husband may be at the bottom of the sea, they have not been bold to put in force the extremity of our righteous law against her. The penalty thereof is death. But in their great mercy and tenderness of heart they have doomed Mistress Prynne to stand only a space of three hours on the platform of the pillory, and then and thereafter, for the remainder of her natural life to wear a mark of shame upon her bosom."

"A wise sentence," remarked the stranger, gravely, bowing his head. "Thus she will be a living sermon against sin, until the ignominious letter be engraved upon her tombstone. It irks me, nevertheless, that the partner of her iniquity should not at least, stand on the scaffold by her side. But he will be known—he will be known!—He will be known!"

10. Which of the following is one way that the author uses irony to make a point in this selection? ELAALRL1, F

A   The writer is using irony when the townsman explains that Hester has an educated husband who has not been heard from for almost two years. The writer is making the point that education is not a useful tool in keeping people out of trouble with the law.

B   The author is using irony when the stranger claims to have been a wanderer who has encountered mishaps on land and sea. The author is making the point that the stranger could very well be Hester's husband who has not been heard from in almost two years.

C   The author is using irony when the townsman explains that the courts have been lenient on Hester. The author is making the point that although these people are described as lenient, they have sentenced Hester to be an outcast for the rest of her life.

D   The writer is using irony when the stranger agrees that Hester has received a wise punishment, but he doesn't even know her. The writer is making the point that this stranger, because he has been to many places and seen many things, is a very good judge of character.

11. How do Hester's crime and punishment reflect the attitudes and beliefs of the time period and of the Puritans in her village? ELAALRL3

A   Hester has given birth to a baby and will not reveal who the father of the baby is. Openness and honesty are important to the townspeople, so Hester is being punished for refusing to tell the father's name. Wearing the scarlet letter "A" is her punishment.

B   Hester has been found guilty of various crimes, including kidnapping a baby. The Puritans cannot believe that a woman could commit such crimes, and so they try and punish her as if she were a man. Hester has been sentenced to serve time in prison and suffer public humiliation.

C   The townspeople are all Puritans, and they believe Hester has committed several sins. Primarily, she has abandoned her husband and taken their child with her. Although the village sentences her to spend time in prison and to wear the scarlet letter, most people feel her punishment is very lenient.

D   Hester has given birth to a baby who was clearly not her husband's child. This is so scandalous to the Puritans at this time that Hester could have been put to death for the crime. The people of her village do not consider her punishment of wearing the scarlet letter "A" and being an outcast to be harsh or unfair.

Buffalo Soldiers

After the Civil War, many blacks moved to the West to find a better life for themselves. Some became cowhands, ranchers, or shopkeepers. Some farmed the land in a harsh environment with few resources. Several African-American Army regiments served on the frontier and became skilled fighters.

These special soldiers lived among the Native Americans, but others worked to control and contain the Native-American population. In their role as soldiers in the military, African-American men were instrumental in patrolling the Great Plains, the Rio Grande, and areas of New Mexico, Arizona, Colorado, and the Dakotas. Under acts of Congress, four segregated regiments were established in 1866 to use the services of African-American soldiers. Two were cavalry regiments and two were infantry units. Black cavalry regiments consisted of the 9th and 10th Cavalry, and the infantry units included the 24th and 25th Infantry divisions.

The exploits and experiences of the Buffalo Soldiers, a term used by the Native Americans to describe the black troops, are described in a comprehensive account by William H. Lick in *The Buffalo Soldiers: A Narrative of the Negro Cavalry in the* West (Norman: University of Oklahoma Press).

12. What is the main idea of this passage?   ELAALRL1, NF

A   After the Civil War, many African Americans moved to the West.

B   The Buffalo Soldiers lived among the Native Americans.

C   After the Civil War, many African-American soldiers worked and patrolled on the frontier.

D   Native Americans coined the term "Buffalo Soldiers."

13. Which of the following is NOT true, according to the passage?   ELAALRL1, NF

A   Buffalo Soldiers was a name Native Americans gave African-American soldiers after the Civil War.

B   African-American soldiers were patrolling the Great Plains before 1866.

C   The 9th and 10th Cavalry units were working to contain Native-American populations after the Civil War.

D   The 24th and 25th Infantry divisions were comprised of African Americans.

GO ON

14. From the passage, one can infer that the writer   ELAALRL1,NF
    A   Admired the African-American soldiers.
    B   Thought that African Americans should not live with Native Americans.
    C   Thought that African Americans should not move to the West.
    D   Was neutral toward the African-American soldiers.

15. According to the passage, who established the segregated regiments in 1866?   ELAALRL1,NF
    A   Native Americans
    B   the United States Army
    C   Congress
    D   African Americans

16. What does the word "comprehensive" mean, as it is used in the passage?   ELAALRC3
    A   complete
    B   limited
    C   brief
    D   intelligent

---

excerpt from *This Side of Paradise* by F. Scott Fitzgerald

This Side of Paradise, *a novel with many autobiographical elements, follows the life of Amory Blaine from childhood to early adulthood. In this passage, Amory, a senior at Princeton, is talking with his friend Burne Holiday. Amory will soon find himself enlisting in the Army as America enters World War I.*

Then Amory branched off and found that Burne was deep in other things as well. Economics had interested him and he was turning socialist. Pacifism played in the back of his mind, and he read The Masses and Lyoff Tolstoi faithfully.

"How about religion?" Amory asked him.

"Don't know. I'm in a muddle about a lot of things—I've just discovered that I've a mind, and I'm starting to read."

"Read what?"

"Everything. I have to pick and choose, of course, but mostly things to make me think. I'm reading the four gospels now, and the 'Varieties of Religious Experience.'"

"What chiefly started you?"

"Wells, I guess, and Tolstoi, and a man named Edward Carpenter. I've been reading for over a year now—on a few lines, on what I consider the essential lines."

"Poetry?"

"Well, frankly, not what you call poetry, or for your reasons—you two write, of course, and look at things differently. Whitman is the man that attracts me."

"Whitman?"

"Yes; he's a definite ethical force."

"Well, I'm ashamed to say that I'm a blank on the subject of Whitman. How about you, Tom?"

Tom nodded sheepishly.

"Well," continued Burne, "you may strike a few poems that are tiresome, but I mean the mass of his work. He's tremendous—like Tolstoi. They both look things in the face, and, somehow, different as they are, stand for somewhat the same things."

"You have me stumped, Burne," Amory admitted. "I've read 'Anna Karenina' and the 'Kreutzer Sonata' of course, but Tolstoi is mostly in the original Russian as far as I'm concerned."

"He's the greatest man in hundreds of years," cried Burne enthusiastically. "Did you ever see a picture of that shaggy old head of his?"

They talked until three, from biology to organized religion, and when Amory crept shivering into bed it was with his mind aglow with ideas and a sense of shock that some one else had discovered the path he might have followed. Burne Holiday was so evidently developing—and Amory had considered that he was doing the same. He had fallen into a deep cynicism over what had crossed his path, plotted the imperfectability of man and read Shaw and Chesterton enough to keep his mind from the edges of decadence—now suddenly all his mental processes of the last year and a half seemed stale and futile—a petty consummation of himself . . . and like a sombre background lay that incident of the spring before, that filled half his nights with a dreary terror and made him unable to pray. He was not even a Catholic, yet that was the only ghost of a code that he had, the gaudy, ritualistic, paradoxical Catholicism whose prophet was Chesterton, whose claqueurs were such reformed rakes of literature as Huysmans and Bourget, whose American sponsor was Ralph Adams Cram, with his adulation of thirteenth-century cathedrals—a Catholicism which Amory found convenient and ready-made, without priest or sacraments or sacrifice.

He could not sleep, so he turned on his reading-lamp and, taking down the "Kreutzer Sonata," searched it carefully for the germs of Burne's enthusiasm. Being Burne was suddenly so much realler than being clever. Yet he sighed . . . here were other possible clay feet.

He thought back through two years, of Burne as a hurried, nervous freshman, quite submerged in his brother's personality. Then he remembered an incident of sophomore year, in which Burne had been suspected of the leading role.

Dean Hollister had been heard by a large group arguing with a taxi-driver, who had driven him from the junction. In the course of the altercation the dean remarked that he "might as well buy the taxicab." He paid and walked off, but next morning he entered his private office to find the taxicab itself in the space usually occupied by his desk, bearing a sign which read "Property of Dean Hollister. Bought and Paid for." . . . It took two expert mechanics half a day to dissemble it into its minutest parts and remove it, which only goes to prove the rare energy of sophomore humor under efficient leadership.

17. Fitzgerald writes: "Being ELAALRL5
**Burne was suddenly so much
reReader than being clever. Yet he sighed .
. . here were other possible clay feet."
Based on the context, the expression
"clay feet" MOST likely refers to**

A Burne's hidden flaws.

B Burne's sense of humor.

C Burne's evil nature.

D Burne's intelligence.

18. Throughout much of *This* ELAALRL3
***Side of Paradise*, Amory
expresses a strong desire to pursue self-
knowledge. Although F. Scott Fitzgerald
is an author of the Modern Period,
Amory's pursuit is characteristic of
which earlier literary movement?**

A The Revolutionary Period

B The Colonial Period

C Native American Period

D Romanticism and Transcendentalism

19. In the sentence, "It took two ELAALRC3
**expert mechanics half a day
to dissemble it into its minutest parts
and remove it..." the word "minutest"
MOST nearly means**

A strongest.　　C significant.

B smallest.　　D cleanest.

20. Which universal theme of ELAALRL2
**American literature is MOST
apparent in this passage?**

A individualism

B tolerance

C cultural diversity

D American dream

21. Which of Burne's statements ELAALRL2
**below does NOT illustrate the
same theme as the others?**

A "I've just discovered that I've a mind, and I'm starting to read."

B "I have to pick and choose, of course, but mostly things to make me think."

C "He's the greatest man in hundreds of years."

D "I've been reading for over a year now—on a few lines, on what I consider the essential lines"

22. Which word BEST ELAALRL1, F
explains how Amory feels
after his discussion with Burne?

   A   neutral and uninterested
   B   energized and inspired
   C   confused and troubled
   D   weak and defeated

Good Hours

I HAD for my winter evening walk—
No one at all with whom to talk,
But I had the cottages in a row
Up to their shining eyes in snow.

And I thought I had the folk within: *5*
I had the sound of a violin;
I had a glimpse through curtain laces
Of youthful forms and youthful faces.

I had such company outward bound.
I went till there were no cottages found.   *10*
I turned and repented, but coming back
I saw no window but that was black.

Over the snow my creaking feet
Disturbed the slumbering village street
Like profanation, by your leave,   *15*
At ten o'clock of a winter eve.

Robert Frost

23. What type of rhyme ELAALRL1, P
scheme does this poem
use?

   A   slant rhyme
   B   internal rhyme
   C   end rhyme
   D   near rhyme

24. The "shining eyes" in ELAALRL1, P
line 4 refers to

   A   the eyes of the villagers.
   B   the windows of the cottages.
   C   the street lights.
   D   the narrator's eyes.

25. This is an example of what type of poem?   ELAALRL1, P

A   sonnet

B   lyric poem

C   ballad

D   narrative poem

26. Which of the following lines is an example of personification?   ELAALRL1, P

A   "I saw no window but that was black"

B   "Disturbed the slumbering village street"

C   "I had the sound of a violin"

D   "Over the snow my creaking feet"

27. What does the word "form" mean in the context of this poem (line 8)?   ELAALRL5

A   substance

B   figure

C   material

D   paper

The House with Nobody in It

Whenever I walk to Suffern along the Erie track

I go by a poor old farmhouse with its shingles broken and black.

I suppose I've passed it a hundred times, but I always stop for a minute

And look at the house, the tragic house, the house with nobody in it.

I never have seen a haunted house, but I hear there are such things;   *5*

That they hold the talk of spirits, their mirth and sorrowings.

I know this house isn't haunted, and I wish it were, I do;

For it wouldn't be so lonely if it had a ghost or two.

This house on the road to Suffern needs a dozen panes of glass,

And somebody ought to weed the walk and take a scythe to the grass.   *10*

It needs new paint and shingles, and the vines should be trimmed and tied;

But what it needs the most of all is some people living inside.

If I had a lot of money and all my debts were paid

I'd put a gang of men to work with brush and saw and spade.

I'd buy that place and fix it up the way it used to be   *15*

And I'd find some people who wanted a home and give it to them free.

Now, a new house standing empty, with staring window and door,

Looks idle, perhaps, and foolish, like a hat on its block in the store.

But there's nothing mournful about it; it cannot be sad and lone

For the lack of something within it that it has never known.   *20*

But a house that has done what a house should do, a house that has sheltered life,

That has put its loving wooden arms around a man and his wife,

A house that has echoed a baby's laugh and held up his stumbling feet,

Is the saddest sight, when it's left alone, that ever your eyes could meet.

So whenever I go to Suffern along the Erie track   *25*

I never go by the empty house without stopping and looking back,

Yet it hurts me to look at the crumbling roof and the shutters fallen apart,

For I can't help thinking the poor old house is a house with a broken heart.

Joyce Kilmer

28. The author uses personification in the fifth stanza to help the reader   ELAALRL1, P

   A   hear the house.

   B   visualize the house.

   C   sympathize with the house.

   D   understand the history of the house.

29. What is the meaning of "tragic" in line 4 of the poem?   ELA11RC4

   A   unpleasant

   B   disastrous

   C   full of mistakes

   D   marked by sorrow

30. The reader can conclude that the author MOST likely believes   ELAALRL4

   A   people should not buy new houses.

   B   every house should have a family.

   C   all abandoned houses are haunted.

   D   every family should have a house.

31. What is the main idea of the third stanza?   ELAALRL1, P

   A   The house should be returned to its original appearance.

   B   The speaker wants to repair the house and give it a family.

   C   The speaker wants more money.

   D   Many people would be needed to repair the house and yard.

32. The phrase "like a hat on its block" is an example of   ELAALRL1, P

   A   metaphor.

   B   simile.

   C   onomatopoeia.

   D   personification.

33. Which of the following statements BEST reflects the theme of this poem?   ELAALRL2

   A   Houses must be repaired, or else they will fall apart.

   B   The inside of a house is more important than the outside.

   C   Some people like old houses.

   D   A house is not a home without a family in it.

34. Which of the following is the BEST summary of this poem?   ELAALRL1, P

   A   The speaker feels sad about an old, abandoned house and wants to repair it and give it what it really needs— a family.

   B   Older abandoned homes require a great deal of work and money to make them livable again.

   C   It would be better to give away older homes than to leave them empty.

   D   Although some empty farmhouses may be haunted, others are not.

excerpt from President William J. Clinton's Second Inaugural Address, Washington, D.C., January 20, 1997

America demands and deserves big things from us—and nothing big ever came from being small. Let us remember the timeless wisdom of Cardinal Bernardin, when facing the end of his own life. He said:

"It is wrong to waste the precious gift of time on acrimony and division."

Fellow citizens, we must not waste the precious gift of this time. For all of us are on that same journey of our lives, and our journey, too, will come to an end. But the journey of our America must go on.

And so, my fellow Americans, we must be strong, for there is much to dare. The demands of our time are great and they are different. Let us meet them with faith and courage, with patience and a grateful and happy heart. Let us shape the hope of this day into the noblest chapter in our history. Yes, let us build our bridge. A bridge wide enough and strong enough for every American to cross over to a blessed land of new promise.

May those generations whose faces we cannot yet see, whose names we may never know, say of us here that we led our beloved land into a new century with the American Dream alive for all her children; with the American promise of a more perfect union a reality for all her people; with America's bright flame of freedom spreading throughout all the world.

35. As it is used in the first paragraph, the word "acrimony" MOST nearly means ELAALRC3

A   fear, anxiety.

B   diplomacy.

C   bitterness, harshness.

D   tact.

36. The main purpose of this speech is to ELA11SV2

A   inspire.

B   entertain.

C   inform.

D   tell a story.

37. From this speech, you can infer that President Clinton ELA11SV2

A   is fearful about the future.

B   thinks that the present time is peaceful.

C   thinks that America shouldn't interfere with other countries.

D   wants to preserve the American Dream for future generations.

38. What is the spread of American freedom compared to in the passage? ELA11SV2

A   a journey

B   a bridge

C   a river

D   a flame

39. The Preamble to the United States Constitution begins with: "We the People of the United States, in Order to form a more perfect Union…" When President Clinton echoes these words with "the American promise of a more perfect union," this is called a(n) ELAALRC4
ELA11LSV2

A   allusion.

B   metaphor.

C   analogy.

D   conceit.

40. Which of the statements below do NOT support the purpose of this speech as effectively as the others? ELA11LSV2

A   "Let us shape the hope of this day into the noblest chapter in our history."

B   "Let us meet them with faith and courage, with patience and a grateful and happy heart."

C   "The demands of our time are great and they are different."

D   "A bridge wide enough and strong enough for every American to cross over to a blessed land of new promise."

SECTION 2

DO NOT TURN PAGE UNTIL INSTRUCTED TO DO SO

SCENE—*Two days out. A section of the promenade deck. MILDRED DOUGLAS and her aunt are discovered reclining in deck chairs. The former is a girl of twenty, slender, delicate, with a pale, pretty face marred by a self-conscious expression of disdainful superiority. She looks fretful, nervous and discontented, bored by her own anemia. Her aunt is a pompous and proud—and fat—old lady. She is a type even to the point of a double chin and lorgnettes. She is dressed pretentiously, as if afraid her face alone would never indicate her position in life. MILDRED is dressed all in white.*

The impression to be conveyed by this scene is one of the beautiful, vivid life of the sea all about— sunshine on the deck in a great flood, the fresh sea wind blowing across it. In the midst of this, these two incongruous, artificial figures, inert and disharmonious, the elder like a gray lump of dough touched up with rouge, the younger looking as if the vitality of her stock had been sapped before she was conceived, so that she is the expression not of its life energy but merely of the artificialities that energy had won for itself in the spending.

MILDRED. [*Looking up with affected dreaminess.*] How the black smoke swirls back against the sky! Is it not beautiful?

AUNT. [*Without looking up.*] I dislike smoke of any kind.

MILDRED. My great-grandmother smoked a pipe—a clay pipe.

AUNT. [*Ruffling.*] Vulgar!

MILDRED. She was too distant a relative to be vulgar. Time mellows pipes.

AUNT. [*Pretending boredom but irritated.*] Did the sociology you took up at college teach you that— to play the ghoul on every possible occasion, excavating old bones? Why not let your great-grandmother rest in her grave?

MILDRED. [*Dreamily.*] With her pipe beside her—puffing in Paradise.

AUNT. [*With spite.*] Yes, you are a natural born ghoul. You are even getting to look like one, my dear.

MILDRED. [*In a passionless tone.*] I detest you, Aunt. [*Looking at her critically.*] Do you know what you remind me of? Of a cold pork pudding against a background of linoleum tablecloth in the kitchen of a—but the possibilities are wearisome. [*She closes her eyes.*]

AUNT. [*With a bitter laugh.*] Merci for your candor. But since I am and must be your chaperone—in appearance, at least—let us patch up some sort of armed truce. For my part you are quite free to indulge any pose of eccentricity that beguiles you—as long as you observe the amenities—

MILDRED—[*Drawling.*] The inanities?

AUNT. [*Going on as if she hadn't heard*.] After exhausting the morbid thrills of social service work on New York's East Side—how they must have hated you, by the way, the poor that you made so much poorer in their own eyes!—you are now bent on making your slumming international. Well, I hope Whitechapel will provide the needed nerve tonic. Do not ask me to chaperone you there, however. I told your father I would not. I loathe deformity. We will hire an army of detectives and you may investigate everything—they allow you to see.

MILDRED. [*Protesting with a trace of genuine earnestness*.] Please do not mock at my attempts to discover how the other half lives. Give me credit for some sort of groping sincerity in that at least. I would like to help them. I would like to be some use in the world. Is it my fault I don't know how? I would like to be sincere, to touch life somewhere. [*With weary bitterness*.] But I'm afraid I have neither the vitality nor integrity. All that was burnt out in our stock before I was born. Grandfather's blast furnaces, flaming to the sky, melting steel, making millions—then father keeping those home fires burning, making more millions—and little me at the tail-end of it all. I'm a waste product in the Bessemer process—like the millions. Or rather, I inherit the acquired trait of the by-product, wealth, but none of the energy, none of the strength of the steel that made it. I am sired by gold and darned by it, as they say at the race track—damned in more ways than one [*She laughs mirthlessly*].

AUNT. [*Unimpressed—superciliously*.] You seem to be going in for sincerity to-day. It isn't becoming to you, really—except as an obvious pose. Be as artificial as you are, I advise. There's a sort of sincerity in that, you know. And, after all, you must confess you like that better.

MILDRED. [*Again affected and bored*.] Yes, I suppose I do. Pardon me for my outburst. When a leopard complains of its spots, it must sound rather grotesque. [*In a mocking tone*.] Purr, little leopard. Purr, scratch, tear, kill, gorge yourself and be happy—only stay in the jungle where your spots are camouflage. In a cage they make you conspicuous.

–excerpt from Eugene O'Neill's *The Hairy Ape*

41. As it is used in following sen-   ELAALRC3
tence from the passage, the
word *inert* means

> In the midst of this, these two incongruous,
> artificial figures, inert and disharmonious, the
> elder like a gray lump of dough touched up with
> rouge, the younger looking as if the vitality of
> her stock had been sapped before she was
> conceived, so that she is the expression not of its
> life energy but merely of the artificialities that
> energy had won for itself in the spending.

    A   dissimilar.   **C**   agitated.

    B   sluggish.   **D**   wealthy.

42. Which statement from the   ELAALRL1, D
passage is paradoxical?

    A   "Be as artificial as you are, I advise.
There's a sort of sincerity in that, you
know."

    B   "But I'm afraid I have neither the
vitality nor integrity. All that was
burnt out in our stock before I was
born."

    C   "When a leopard complains of its
spots, it must sound rather grotesque."

    D   "She was too distant a relative to be
vulgar. Time mellows pipes."

43. Which of Mildred's state-   ELAALRL1, D
ments below would her
aunt agree with?

    A   "But I'm afraid I have neither the
vitality nor integrity. All that was
burnt out in our stock before I was
born."

    B   "I would like to be sincere, to touch
life somewhere."

    C   "I am sired by gold and darned by it,
as they say at the race track—damned
in more ways than one."

    D   "Purr, little leopard…only stay in the
jungle where your spots are camou-
flage. In a cage they make you conspicuous."

Read the following excerpt from the passage

> **AUNT**. [*With a bitter laugh.*] Merci for your
> candor. But since I am and must be your
> chaperone—in appearance, at least—let us
> patch up some sort of armed truce. For my part
> you are quite free to indulge any pose of
> eccentricity that beguiles you—as long as you
> observe the amenities—
>
> **MILDRED**. [*Drawling.*] The inanities?
>
> **AUNT**. [*Going on as if she hadn't heard.*]

44. What is the significance of   ELAALRL1, D
Mildred's reply?

    A   Mildred cannot understand what her
aunt is trying to say, so she makes a
guess.

    B   Mildred is referring to the sometimes
empty and shallow nature of wealthy
life.

    C   Mildred is mockingly alluding to her
aunt's lack of intelligence.

    D   Mildred is hinting at her aunt's
doughy and unattractive appearance
in an attempt to anger her.

45. The passage indicates that   ELAALRL4
this play is MOST like what
type of dramatic literature?

    A   tragedy   **C**   modern

    B   comedy   **D**   minimalist

46. Which of the following   ELAALRL1, D
words does NOT describe
Mildred, according to the stage directions?

    A   weary

    B   artificial

    C   restless

    D   unintelligent

Read the following sentence and then answer questions 47 and 48.

> Thomas is preparing a persuasive speech for his high-school class about the importance of keeping music programs in schools.

47. Which visual or audio aid would be the LEAST effective in persuading his audience? ELA11LSV2

    A a poster with photos of musical instruments on it

    B PowerPoint slides summarizing the research that highlights the benefits of school music programs

    C audio clips of teachers and administrators expressing their support for school music programs.

    D a sound clip of the school orchestra, band, and chorus performances

48. Thomas now wants to adapt this speech for an audience of elementary school children and teachers, where the music program is in danger of being cut. Which adjustment is the MOST appropriate for his change in audience? ELA11LSV2

    A gathering more quotes from experts on the subject

    B providing more statistics and research to support his points

    C bringing musical instruments for the children to play with, under his guidance

    D playing a recording of a symphony

The following text appeared in an advertisement for shampoo in a women's magazine.

> Everyone wants strong and shiny hair, and that's why women across America are trying our new BelleVitamin Shampoo. Try our new shampoo for 10 days, and we guarantee you'll have the vibrant hair you've always wanted. If you're unsatisfied after 10 days, we will refund your money! Our shampoo has a fresh, clean scent that you'll love. Don't be left in the cold with dull, boring hair. Join the rest of us, and try BelleVitamin Shampoo. We promise others will notice!

49. What is the primary persuasive technique used in the advertisement? ELA11LSV2

    A stereotyping

    B bandwagon

    C card stacking

    D rhetorical questions

50. The advertisement text needs to be cut due to space restrictions. Which sentence would be the BEST choice for removal? ELA11W4

    A Everyone wants strong and shiny hair, and that's why women across America are trying our new BelleVitamin Shampoo.

    B If you're unsatisfied after 10 days, we will refund your money!

    C Don't be left in the cold with dull, boring hair.

    D Our shampoo has a fresh, clean scent that you'll love.

Max Cavitch. *American Elegy: The Poetry of Mourning from the Puritans to Whitman.* Minneapolis: U of Minnesota P, 2007.

Terry Eagleton. *How to Read a Poem.* Oxford: Blackwell, 2007.

Joan Shelley Rubin. *Songs of Ourselves: The Uses of Poetry in America.* London: Belknap, 2007.

51. Which of the following explains a problem with the bibliography shown above?   ELA11C2

A   Only the first word of the book titles should be capitalized.

B   The page numbers are not given.

C   The author's last name should come first in each entry.

D   The city does not need to be listed.

52. Which source would be LEAST helpful when starting a research project that incorporates historical elements of the Jazz Age with the writers and artists of the time?   ELA11W3

A   an encyclopedia

B   an American history textbook

C   F. Scott Fitzgerald's *Tales of the Jazz Age*

D   music from the Jazz age

Michael is writing a paper about Ralph Waldo Emerson's essay "Self-Reliance." He comes across this passage:

But now we are a mob. Man does not stand in awe of man, nor is his genius admonished to stay at home to put itself in communication with the internal ocean, but it goes abroad to beg a cup of water of the urns of other men. We must go alone. I like the silent church before the service begins, better than any preaching. How far off, how cool, how chaste the persons look, begirt each one with a precinct or sanctuary! So let us always sit. Why should we assume the faults of our friend, or wife, or father, or child, because they sit around our hearth, or are said to have the same blood? All men have my blood, and I have all men's.

53. Finding this passage particularly striking, Michael wants to discuss it in detail in his paper. What would be the BEST method for doing so?   ELA11C2

A   copy a few sentences into the paper

B   paraphrase

C   summarize

D   direct quote

54. In the same paper discussed above, Michael wants to add biographical detail about Emerson. What would be the BEST method for incorporating this information?   ELA11C2

A   directly quote a paragraph from a biography of Emerson

B   write a one-page summary about Emerson's life

C   write a brief paragraph that paraphrases information from a biography of Emerson

D   write a sentence about Emerson's college years

55. How should the sentence   ELA11C1
    below be correctly written?

> Although there were more than 500 Native-American languages and tribes in North America when the Europeans first arrived, there was no written literature among them, instead, their stories, legends, and songs were passed down orally through the generations.

A   Although there were more than 500 Native-American languages and tribes in North America when the Europeans first arrived, there was no written literature among them, instead, their stories, legends, and songs were passed down orally through the generations.

B   Although there were more than 500 Native-American languages and tribes in North America when the Europeans first arrived, there was no written literature among them; instead, their stories, legends, and songs were passed down orally through the generations.

C   Although there were more than 500 Native-American languages and tribes in North America when the Europeans first arrived, there were no written literature among them, instead, their stories, legends, and songs were passed down orally through the generations.

D   Although there were more than 500 Native-American languages and tribes in North America when the Europeans first arrived, there was no written literature among them…instead, their stories, legends, and songs were passed down orally through the generations.

56. Maria wants to include a pas-   ELA11C2
sage from Mark Twain's *The Adventures of Huckleberry Finn* in her paper, but it is very long. She thinks she can cut out the middle of the passage and still keep the more important parts. What punctuation does she need to add to her excerpt so that the reader knows she omitted something?

A   parentheses

B   a colon

C   a hypen

D   an ellipsis

57. How should the sentence   ELA11C1
    below BEST be written?

> The often dark and morbid works of Edgar Allan Poe are interesting to me because it differs from what I have read before.

A   change *it* to *they* and *differs* to *differ*

B   change *are* to *is*

C   change *have* to *had*

D   change *from* to *than*

GO ON

Read the following passage. Then answer questions 58–68.

1) With the advent of music-sharing programs and CD burners in the late '90s, the music industry found itself losing money as pirating spread like wildfire. **2)** Some may be surprised, however, to hear that a similar problem with pirating have occurred before, albeit in a much different time. **3)** When the United States was still a young country, a lack of proper, piracy-eliminating copyright laws made it difficult for the American literary world to flourish. **4)** A copyright law was established in 1790, but it allowed the pirating of non-American authors, which ironically impeded the success of early American writers. **5)** Until the mid 1800s, authors had to pay printers to publish their writing. **6)** This made it difficult for anyone other than the incredibly rich (such as Washington Irving) to pursue the life of a writer. **7)** American printers preferred to pirate the best-selling works of English authors. **8)** The printers did not want to waste their time on unknown American authors when there was a much greater wealth of material waiting in England. **9)** One American publisher, named Matthew Carey, paid a London agent to send copies of unbound pages in ships that could sail quickly across the Atlantic. **10)** Then, the pirated books would be printed quickly and sold cheaply. **11)** Sometimes, the American-printed books were ready as soon as the ones in England were! **12)** This caused problems for foreign authors such as Charles Dickens, because their imported, authorized works were more expensive than the pirated copies! **13)** American authors, such as James Fenimore Cooper, suffered an even worse fate because they were paid less and *still* saw their works pirated virtually in front of him. **14)** Piracy was at its high point in 1815: not surprisingly, this was a low period for American writing. **15)** However, in the end, the abundance of pirated classics and foreign books helped educate Americans, eventually causing the emergence of our first great writers in the mid 1800s.

58. Which sentence uses parallel structure? ELA11W2

A sentence 3   C sentence 6

B sentence 10   D sentence 4

59. This passage is

A narrative

B persuasive

C expository

D a literary analysis

ELA11W2

60. This passage needs to be edited. What problem should the author focus on first? ELA11W1

A It lacks coherence.

B There isn't a main idea.

C The sentences are too wordy.

D There aren't enough examples.

61. The claims made in this passage are NOT supported by ELA11W1

A statistics.

B specific examples.

C anecdotes.

D historical facts.

62. What question could the author pose in order to start the writing process for a persuasive essay related to the main idea of this passage? ELA11W1 ELA11W2

A   Is music better today?

B   Do people read enough classic literature?

C   Do American copyright laws need to be changed?

D   What are the differences between American writers and English writers?

63. How can sentences 7 and 8 be combined to improve the flow of the passage? ELA11W4

> 7) American printers preferred to pirate the best-selling works of English authors. 8) The printers did not want to waste their time on unknown American authors when there was a much greater wealth of material waiting in England.

A   Choosing not to waste their time on unknown American authors, American printers preferred instead the great wealth of material in England and pirate the works of English authors.

B   American printers preferred to pirate the best-selling works of English authors because they did not want to waste their time on less profitable and unknown American authors.

C   They did not want to waste their time on unknown American authors when there was a much greater wealth of material waiting in England, so American printers preferred to pirate the best-selling works of English authors.

D   Preferring to pirate the best-selling works of English authors, American printers did not want to waste their time on unknown American authors when there was a much greater wealth of material waiting in England to be printed.

Read sentence 2 from the passage.

> Some people may be surprised, however, to hear that a similar problem with pirating have occurred before, albeit in a much different time.

64. How should sentence 2 be revised? ELA11W4 ELA11C1

A   change *may be* to *maybe*

B   change *hear* to *here*

C   remove the comma before however

D   change *have* to *has*

65. Which two sentences need to be removed? ELA11W4 ELA11W2

A   sentences 5 & 6

B   sentences 12 & 13

C   sentences 2 & 3

D   sentences 9 & 10

66. What would be a good title for the passage? ELA11W2

A   "Piracy in the Music Industry Is Not a New Problem"

B   "Piracy Problems in America"

C   "The Battle Between English and American Authors"

D   "American Printers and Piracy"

67. The purpose of the first sentence of the passage is to ELA11W2

A   show how today's problems with copyrights are unique.

B   engage the reader's interest by making a comparison between the past and present.

C   explain that music piracy should be allowed.

D   make the reader laugh.

 GO ON

68. Which sentence BEST expresses the main idea of the passage? ELA11W1

A sentence 1   C sentence 3

B sentence 2   D sentence 8

Emily is researching John Steinbeck and has found this piece of information in one of her sources:

> *The Grapes of Wrath*, although a successful book, still garnered its share of controversy: many people were angered by Steinbeck's liberal views and his portrayal of the events surrounding the Dust Bowl.

69. Emily wants to paraphrase this information. Which of the following is the BEST paraphrase? ELA11W3

A Steinbeck's *The Grapes of Wrath* garnered its share of controversy because people were angered by his liberal views.

B Despite the popularity of *The Grapes of Wrath*, its success did not come without controversy, as many people were put off by Steinbeck's liberal politics and the creative licenses he took in depicting the events of the Dust Bowl.

C *The Grapes of Wrath*, although a successful book, still garnered its share of controversy: many people were angered by Steinbeck's liberal views and his portrayal of the events surrounding the Dust Bowl.

D Angered at his liberal views and portrayal of the events surrounding the Dust Bowl, many people took part in the controversy surrounding Steinbeck's *The Grapes of Wrath*.

Read the following passage and answer questions 70–75.

1) Spoken language has never been a static or isolated entity, remaining exactly the same over the years. **2)** Instead it evolves and shifts according to the characteristics of its environment. **3)** A wide variety of influences effect the features or evolution of a dialect, such as migration, social status, culture, and even changes in society. **4)** As one of the most noticeable American dialects, people who speak Southern English provides an excellent source for analyzing the effects of environment on a person. **5)** Although it is a fact that our accents are set very early on in life and possibly stay that way, this fact does not completely explain or consider the changes that can occur in a person's speech later in life as a result of environmental change. **6)** People who grow up speaking one dialect may move away to an area where the influence of the new environment causes their accent to be subdued or lost. **7)** However, it has been observed that a return to one's hometown will often result in a speedy recovery of the accent.

70. How should sentence 2 be   ELA11C1
    changed to fix an error?

  A   *according* should be spelled *acording*

  B   *its* should be changed to *it's*

  C   *to* should be changed to *with*

  D   A comma should be placed after *instead*

71. Which sentence contains a mis-   ELA11C1
    placed modifier?

  A   sentence 3   **C**   sentence 4

  B   sentence 5   **D**   sentence 1

72. How should sentence 3 be   ELA11C1
    changed to fix an error?

  A   *effect* should be *affect*

  B   *effect* should be *effects*

  C   the last comma should be removed

  D   a colon should be placed after *dialect*

73. How can sentence 5 be revised   ELA11C1
    to eliminate wordiness and
    confusion?

> **5)** Although it is a fact that our accents are set very early on in life and possibly stay that way, this fact does not completely explain or consider the changes that can occur in a person's speech later in life as a result of environmental change.

  A   Although it is a fact that our accents are set very early on, this fact does not completely explain a person's speech later in life as a result of environmental change.

  B   Although it is a fact that our accents are set very early on in life, this fact does not completely explain or consider the changes that can occur in a person's speech later in life as a result of environmental change.

  C   Although our accents are set in early childhood, this does not completely explain how changes occur in a person's speech later in life.

  D   Although our accents are set in early childhood, environmental changes later in life can still have an effect on the way we speak.

74. Which phrase from the paragraph is a participial phrase? ELA11C1

A   provide an excellent source

B   remaining exactly the same over the years

C   who grows up speaking one dialect

D   analyzing the effects of environment

75. Which sentence has a subject-verb agreement error? ELA11C1

A   sentence 1   C   sentence 6

B   sentence 4   D   sentence 7

Read the following passage and answer questions 76–80.

Although Nabokov's Lolita contains no tidy moral ending, and Humbert does not experience a complete change of values, the evolution of his jealousy at the books conclusion hints at the regret he feels. When Humbert first finds himself in possession of Lolita, his since of ownership and control of her is almost at its peak.

76. What is the proper format for the title of the work in the first sentence? ELA11C2

A   Lolita   C   "Lolita"

B   *Lolita*   D   **Lolita**

77. How should the following excerpt be corrected? ELA11C1

the evolution of his jealousy at the books conclusion hints at the regret he feels

A   change *hints* to *hint*

B   change *feels* to *feel*

C   change *books* to *book's*

D   change *books* to *books'*

78. How should the following excerpt be corrected? ELA11C1

his since of ownership and control of her is almost at its peak

A   change *since* to *sense*

B   change *its* to *it's*

C   add a comma after *ownership*

D   change *her* to *hers*

79. Choose the appropriate correction for the following sentence. ELA11C1

"I really like Hemingway's short stories, especially 'The Snows of Kilimanjaro'," Tim said.

A   the comma after *Kilimanjaro* should go inside the quotation mark

B   the title of the short story should have double quotation marks

C   change *Hemingway's* to *Hemingways'*

D   remove the comma after *short stories*

Read the following passage and answer question 80.

1) Molly Bloom, as one of the three main characters in James Joyce's *Ulysses*, possesses considerable power over the narrative of the book. 2) Although she was physically absent throughout the majority of the episodes until the end, her presence is continually felt through Leopold Bloom's thoughts. 3) Without directly referring to her by name or description Joyce continually finds ways to allude to Molly.

80. What error is contained in sentence 2? ELA11C1

A   subject-verb agreement error

B   misplaced modifier

C   verb tense agreement error

D   incorrect punctuation

GA EOCT in American Literature and Composition
Practice Test 2

The purpose of this practice test is to measure your progress in American literature and composition. This practice test is based on the Georgia GPS standards for American Literature and Composition and adheres to the sample question format provided by the Georgia Department of Education.

General Directions:

1. Read all directions carefully.

2. Read each question or sample. Then choose the best answer.

3. Choose only one answer for each question. If you change an answer, be sure to erase your original answer completely.

Standards covered by each question are indicated next to the question. For standard ELAALRL1, a letter follows the standard number, indicating F = fiction, NF= nonfiction, P = poetry, or D = drama.

SECTION I

excerpt from *Six Months in the Gold Fields* by E. Gold Buffum

An ex-journalist and ex-soldier tells of how he joined the California Gold Rush and with a few companions went to seek his fortune on the Middle Fork River.

The soil of this bar was exceedingly sandy, and the surface was covered with huge imbedded rocks, which required an immense amount of severe manual labor to remove. Below this was a red gravel, which was united with gold, the washing of which turned out about four ounces per day to each man. I was again dreaming of fortune and success, when my hopes were blasted by a terrible scourge which wrought destruction through the northern mines during the winter of 1848. I allude to the land scurvy as opposed to the scurvy you get at sea. The exposed and unaccustomed life of two-thirds of the miners, and their entire subsistence on salt meat, without any mixture of vegetable matter, had produced this disease, which was experienced more or less by at least one-half of the miners within my knowledge.

I noticed its first attack upon myself by swelling and bleeding of the gums, which was followed by a swelling of both legs below the knee, which rendered me unable to walk; and for three weeks, I was laid up in my tent, obliged to feed upon the very food that had caused the disease, and growing daily weaker, without any sign of relief. There were at that time about 800 persons working on the river. Hoping to get some medicine, I set one of my friends one morning, with instructions to get me, if possible, a dose of salts, and to pay for it any price that is asked. He returned at night with the news that he had failed having found only two persons that had brought salts to California with them, and they would not sell it at any price.

I was almost in despair: with only a blanket between myself and the damp, cold earth, and a thin canvas to protect me from the burning sun by day, and the heavy dews by night, I lay one day enduring the most intense suffering from pain in my limbs, which were now becoming more swollen, and were turning completely black. I believed I would have died, had not accident produced the best remedy that could have been produced. In the second week of my illness, one of my friends upon coming down the hill where he had been deer hunting, found near its base, along the foot path, a quantity of beans which sprouted from the ground, and were in leaf.

Someone had probably come down that same path and had dropped them from a bag on his back. My friend gathered them up and brought them to camp. I had them boiled and lived on them for several days, at the same time drinking a tea made of the bark of the spruce tree. These seemed to operate magically, and in a week, I found myself able to walk. As soon as my strength was partially restored I walked to Culoma, and living primarily on a vegetable diet, which I procured by paying three dollars per pound for potatoes, in a very short time I recovered.

1. **What is the purpose of this selection?** ELAALRL1,NF

   A to inform the reader about how to cure swollen legs

   B to describe a mining camp and the value of gold during the California Gold Rush

   C to explain how to find gold in the river

   D to share the experience of one miner in a California gold rush river camp

2. **The document provides the most information on** ELAALRL4

   A deer hunting.

   B the benefits of vegetables.

   C salt meat.

   D the rewards of mining life.

3. **What does *rendered* mean in the phrase "which rendered me unable to walk"?** ELAALRC3

   A found   C made

   B seemed   D limped

4. **The article suggests that miners faced many dangers. Which one of the following dangers was the greatest?** ELAALRL1,NF

   A bear attacks while sleeping in the open

   B food shortages

   C getting sick

   D getting shot while deer hunting

5. **Which of the following sentences from the passage most vividly explains the author's condition?** ELAALRL4

   A ". . . my hopes were blasted by a terrible scourge which wrought destruction through the northern mines during the winter of 1848. I allude to the land scurvy as opposed to the scurvy you get at sea."

   B "Hoping to get some medicine, I set one of my friends one morning, with instructions to get me, if possible, a dose of salts, and to pay for it any price that is asked."

   C "I was almost in despair: with only a blanket between myself and the damp, cold earth, and a thin canvas to protect me from the burning sun by day, and the heavy dews by night, I lay one day enduring the most intense suffering from pain in my limbs, which were now becoming more swollen, and were turning completely black."

   D "In the second week of my illness, one of my friends upon coming down the hill where he had been deer hunting, found near its base, along the foot path, a quantity of beans which sprouted from the ground, and were in leaf."

6. **What does *blasted* mean in the phrase "when my hopes were blasted by a terrible scourge"?** ELAALRC4

   A destroyed   C questioned

   B reconsidered D awarded

7. **What would the writer of the article most recommend bringing along on an extended camping trip?** ELAALRL4

   A dried beef

   B blankets

   C salts

   D vegetables

8. **Which statement below** ELAALRL1,NF
   best illustrates the time
   sequence of the events in the article?

   A   It all takes place on the same day.

   B   It explains events as they happened in order during the winter of 1848.

   C   It begins in the past and then comes forward and than goes back in time again.

   D   It begins in the present, goes back in the past, and then ends in the present.

9. **Based on the author's experi-** ELAALRC4
   ence, which of the following
   best characterizes the period of the
   California Gold Rush?

   A   work   C   hunger

   B   fear   D   friendship

10. **Which of the following is not a** ELA11C1
    correct rewording of the sen-
    tence below?

    > "I allude to the land scurvy as opposed to the scurvy you get at sea."

    A   I am talking about land scurvy.

    B   I mean, of course, the land scurvy, compared to the scurvy you get at sea.

    C   I mention that sea scurvy is just like land scurvy.

    D   I refer to the land scurvy, not sea scurvy.

11. **Which of the following is not a** ELAALRL3
    characteristic of literature
    during the period of Realism?

    A   It attempts to describe life optimistically.

    B   It is most often associated with 19th century France.

    C   It often deals with the lower and middle classes.

    D   It holds that a person's character is determined by environment and social factors.

12. **Which literary device is** ELAALRL1, P
    used in the following sen-
    tence?

    > "I was so tired last night that I slept like a log."

    A   hyperbole   C   metaphor

    B   simile   D   onomatopoeia

13. **Erica must write a bibliogra-** ELA11W3
    phy for a report on a book by
    Maya Angelou. Choose the correct
    MLA form for listing a book by one
    author.

    A   Angelou, Maya <u>I Know Why the Caged Bird Sings</u>, Random House: New York 1970.

    B   Angelou, Maya "I Know Why the Caged Bird Sings," Random House. 1970.

    C   Maya, Angelou. "I Know Why the Caged Bird Sings," Random House. 1970.

    D   Angelou, Maya. *I Know Why the Caged Bird Sings*. New York: Random House, 1970.

14. **The fact that a sweet carbon-** ELA11C1
    ated drink has names like *coke,*
    ***pop, soda,* and *soft drink* suggests differ-**
    ences in

    A   dialect.

    B   spelling.

    C   meaning.

    D   pronounciation.

15. Mark has found a Web site ELA11W3
with helpful information about
career fairs. Choose the correct form for
a Web site source with no author listed.

A   "Meet Top Employers Face to Face."
MSN Careers.
http://msn.careerbuilder.com/Job
Seeker/CareerFairs/default.aspx
(30 June 2007).

B   MSN Careers. "Meet Top Employers
Face to Face." http://msn.career
builder.com/Jobeeker/Careerairs/
default.aspx.

C   "Meet Top Employers Face to Face."
http://msn.careerbuilder.com/
JobSeeker/Career-
Fairs/default.aspx
(30 June 2007).

D   MSN Careers. http://msn.career
builder.com/JobSeeker/
CareerFairs/default.aspx.

16. What does the word *projected* ELAALRC3
mean in the following sen-
tence?

"Projected rates of employment growth are
faster for occupations requiring higher levels
of education or training than for those
requiring less."

A   present   C   future
B   past   D   delayed

17. The English word *museum* ELAALRL5
most likely originated from
which of the following?

A   Mars, the name of the god of war

B   Muses, the name for the goddesses of
art

C   Amuse, the name of the god of entertainment

D   Muscles, the name of the goddess of
strength

GO ON

Read the following poetry selection. Then answer the questions.

excerpt from "The Song of Hiawatha"

by Henry Wadsworth Longfellow

Book VI: Hiawatha's Friends

Two good friends had Hiawatha,
Singled out from all the others,
Bound to him in closest union,
And to whom he gave the right hand
Of his heart, in joy and sorrow;
Chibiabos, the musician,
And the very strong man, Kwasind.

Straight between them ran the pathway,

Never grew the grass upon it;
Singing birds, that utter falsehoods,
Story-tellers, mischief-makers,
Found no eager ear to listen,
Could not breed ill-will between them,
For they kept each other's counsel,
Spake with naked hearts together,
Pondering much and much contriving
How the tribes of men might prosper.

Most beloved by Hiawatha

Was the gentle Chibiabos,
He the best of all musicians,
He the sweetest of all singers.
Beautiful and childlike was he,
Brave as man is, soft as woman,
Pliant as a wand of willow,
Stately as a deer with antlers.

When he sang, the village listened;

All the warriors gathered round him,
All the women came to hear him;
Now he stirred their souls to passion,
Now he melted them to pity.

18. What type of literary device is being used in the following quote? ELAALRL1, P

> "And to whom he gave the right hand/Of his heart, in joy and sorrow."

A hyperbole   C rhyme

B personification   D oxymoron

19. What type of literary device is being used in the following quote? ELAALRL1, P

> "Pliant as a wand of willow,/Stately as a deer with antlers."

A metaphor   C alliteration

B simile   D symbol

20. What is the figurative language of this phrase, "Now he melted them to pity," saying about Chibiabos' singing? ELAALRL1, P

A His magical singing could melt people.

B His singing caused people in local villages to pity him.

C His singing was so awful the village felt sorry for him.

D His singing caused them to feel emotion, such as compassion and pity.

Woman's Political Future

by Frances Harper (1825–1911)

If the fifteenth century discovered America to the Old World, the nineteenth is discovering woman to herself. Little did Columbus imagine, when the New World broke upon his vision like a lovely gem in the coronet of the universe, the glorious possibilities of a land where the sun should be our engraver, the winged lightning our messenger, and steam our beast of burden. But as mind is more than matter, and the highest ideal always the true real, so to woman comes the opportunity to strive for richer and grander discoveries than ever gladdened the eye of the Genoese mariner.

The social and political advancement which woman has already gained bears the promise of the rising of the full-orbed sun of emancipation. The result will be not to make home less happy, but society more holy; yet I do not think the mere extension of the ballot a panacea for all the ills of our national life. What we need today is not more voters but better voters.

21. **What is the main literary device used in this passage?** ELAALRL1,NF

   A onomatopoeia   **C** analogy

   B conflict   **D** irony

22. **What is the meaning of the phrase "the mere extension of the ballot" in the passage?** ELAALRL5

   A adding more candidates to the ballot, giving people more choices

   B granting women the right to vote

   C keeping the polls open longer on election day

   D allowing women to run for public office

excerpt from *The Red Badge of Courage*

by Stephen Crane

Turning his head swiftly, the youth saw his friend, Jim, running in a staggering and stumbling way toward a little clump of bushes. His heart seemed to wrench itself almost free from his body at this sight. His friend made a noise of pain. He and the tattered man began a pursuit. There was a singular race.

When he overtook the tall soldier, he began to plead with all the words he could

find. "Jim—Jim—what are you doing—what makes you do this way—you'll hurt yerself."

The same purpose was in the tall soldier's face. He protested in a dulled way, keeping his eyes fastened on the mystic place of his intentions.

"No—no—don't touch me—leave me be—leave me be—"

The youth, aghast and filled with wonder at the tall soldier, began quavering to question him. "Where yeh goin', Jim? What you thinking about? Where you going?

The tall soldier faced about as upon relentless pursuers. In his eyes there was great appeal. "Leave me be, can't yeh? Leave me be fer a minute."

23. **Based on the passage, the**   ELAALRL1, F
    reader can conclude that

   A   the tall soldier has been wounded.

   B   the youth has been injured.

   C   the youth is trying to arrest the tall soldier.

   D   the tall soldier wants to walk home.

24. **The passage suggests that**   ELAALRL1, F

   A   the youth is angry with the tall soldier.

   B   the youth is trying to help the tall soldier.

   C   the youth is indifferent toward the tall soldier.

   D   the youth is trying to bring the tall soldier back to camp.

excerpt from "In a Far Country" by Jack London

1 As the sugar-pile and other little luxuries dwindled, they began to be afraid they were not getting their proper shares, and in order that they might not be robbed, they fell to gorging themselves. The luxuries suffered in this <u>gluttonous</u> contest, as did also the men.

2 In the absence of fresh vegetables and exercise, their blood became impoverished, and a loathsome, purplish rash crept over their bodies. Yet they refused to heed the warning.

3 Next, their muscles and joints began to swell, the flesh turning black, while their mouths, gums, and lips took on the color of rich cream. Instead of being drawn together by their misery, each gloated over the other's symptoms as the scurvy took its course.

4 They lost all regard for personal appearance, and for that matter, common decency. <u>The cabin became a pigpen</u>, and never once were the beds made or fresh pine boughs laid underneath. Yet they could not keep to their blankets, as they would have wished; for the frost was inexorable, and the fire box consumed much fuel. The hair of their heads and faces grew long and shaggy, while their garments would have disgusted a ragpicker. But they did not care. They were sick, and there was no one to see; besides, it was very painful to move about.

5 To all this was added a new trouble — the Fear of the North. This Fear was the joint child of the Great Cold and the Great Silence, and was born in the darkness of December, when the sun dipped below the horizon for good. It affected them according to their natures.

6 Weatherbee fell prey to the grosser superstitions, and did his best to resurrect the spirits which slept in the forgotten graves. It was a fascinating thing, and in his dreams they came to him from out of the cold, and snuggled into his blankets, and told him of their toils and troubles ere they died. He <u>shrank</u> away from the clammy contact as they drew closer and twined their frozen limbs about him, and when they whispered in his ear of things to come, the cabin rang with his frightened shrieks. Cuthfert did not understand — for they no longer spoke — and when thus awakened he invariably grabbed for his revolver. Then he would sit up in bed, shivering nervously, with the weapon trained on the unconscious dreamer. Cuthfert deemed the man going mad, and so came to fear for his life.

7 His own malady assumed a less concrete form. The mysterious artisan who had laid the cabin, log by log, had pegged a wind-vane to the ridgepole. Cuthfert noticed it always pointed south, and one day, irritated by its steadfastness of purpose, he turned it toward the east. He watched eagerly, but never a breath came by to disturb it. Then he turned the vane to the north, swearing never again to touch it till the wind did blow. But the air frightened him with its unearthly calm, and he often rose in the middle of the night to see if the vane had veered — ten degrees would have satisfied him. But no, it poised above him as unchangeable as fate.

25. **In paragraph 1, the word** *glut-* ELAALRC3
    tonous **means**

    A   sugar coating.

    B   rich cooking.

    C   excessive eating.

    D   expensive dining.

26. **What caused the men's sick-** ELAALRL1, F
    ness?

    A   a poor diet

    B   a purple rash

    C   poor hygiene

    D   cold weather

27. **In paragraph 4, when the** ELAALRC3
    author writes, "The cabin
    became a pigpen," what does he mean?

    A   The men ate only scraps of food.

    B   Pigs moved into the cabin.

    C   The cabin was dirty and messy.

    D   Weatherbee dreamed about pigs.

28. **Which of the following is the** ELA11C2
    correct bibliographic entry for
    this story?

    A   London, Jack. "In a Far Country."
         Overland Monthly June 1899.

    B   Jack London. "In a Far Country."
         Overland Monthly, 1899, June issue.

    C   Jack London. Overland Monthly.
         June 1899. "In a Far Country."

    D   London, Jack. "In a Far Country,"
         June 1899, Overland Monthly.

29. **In paragraph 6, the word** ELAALRC3
    shrank **means**

    A   became smaller.

    B   moved sideways.

    C   pulled back instinctively.

    D   lost substance or weight.

30. **Why did Cuthfert grab a** ELAALRL1, F
    gun when Weatherbee
    shrieked?

    A   He was afraid Weatherbee might kill
         him.

    B   He thought he heard the wind move
         the vane.

    C   He thought someone was breaking
         into the cabin.

    D   He wanted to kill the spirits haunting
         Weatherbee.

31. **What is the main idea of** ELAALRL1, F
    paragraph 7?

    A   The cabin was built by an unknown
         man.

    B   A wind-vane on the house pointed
         north.

    C   Cuthfert checked the vane day and
         night.

    D   Cuthfert is frightened by the lack of
         wind.

A Trip to Remember

My mother has crazy ideas sometimes. One year after having moved to Baltimore, she decided it was time to visit Portland, Maine, again. We couldn't get a plane ticket to Portland for the weekend, but that didn't stop her. She just bought tickets to New York instead. "We'll wing it from there," she said. "Winging it" meant landing in New York, taking a cab, and waiting in the Amtrak station for several hours for a train. Then, for 7 hours, the sleek, silver train took us north. But from the time we had left home, we were not able to get in touch with anyone! We didn't have cell phones in those days; nobody did. The station had no phone, there was no time at the airport, and the train never stopped long enough, not even when we changed trains in Boston, to give us time to find a phone booth, call home and dash back to the train before it departed. My dad didn't know where we were for a whole day. But I knew. I remember sleeping in the passenger car and buying soup in the restaurant car. I vividly recall watching the rising sun outside the window, the passing mountains and glimpses of the ocean. And I especially remember the feeling of secret adventure, of being aware that no one knew where I was. It was the best trip I've ever had.

32. The author MOST likely   ELAALRL1,NF
tells readers that no one
had cell phones when this happened in
order to

   A   convey that the family had little money at the time.

   B   point out that the story took place a very long time ago.

   C   emphasize that the family was out of touch the whole trip.

   D   express how lonely and frightened the narrator was on this trip.

Read this sentence from the story.

> I vividly recall watching the rising sun outside the window, the passing mountains and glimpses of the ocean.

33. In this sentence, the phrase   ELA11C1
"outside the window" modifies

   A   recall.   C   passing.

   B   sun.   D   ocean.

My First (and Last) Horseback Ride

The sun rose brightly over the clear blue skies of Yellowstone National Park. The surrounding mountains reflected the glow of a new morning. Barely 15 years old, I was on a two week vacation out West with my family. We were spending our last day horseback riding in the mountains and valleys near this magnificent park. The night before, I dreamed that my horse was almost flying along the ridges and mountain tops in huge leaps that took us into the clouds and back to earth again. Little did I realize what an incredible day I was about to experience.

Early that morning, my older brother Jes and I jumped out of bed, dressed and ate breakfast in the huge lodge's dining room. First, we had to drive to the stables, so Mom and Dad hurried us along for the short drive there. Before we arrived at the horse stables, I noticed a majestic bald eagle gliding overhead, his screeches sounding an alarm throughout the valley. After we reached the stables, we picked out our horses. I chose a lively brown mare that I nicknamed Hyper. Jes rode a big white stallion named Snowball, and Mom and Dad settled for two gentle older horses called Dolly and Sam.

In a matter of minutes, we were starting to climb the well-worn path along the ridge above the stables. Ahead of us was another higher ridge that led us on to the steeper, more challenging trails above. Eventually, we would be able to reach the top of the mountain where we could view the entire valley and the surrounding mountains.

As we climbed higher, I felt light-headed and dizzy. Meanwhile, Hyper forged ahead, suddenly turning and galloping far off the trail to reach the wild grasses that grew along a gully.

With my family out of sight, Hyper started neighing loudly. I could sense something was wrong, and it was. Ahead of us on a rock ledge was a snarling mountain lion with a menacing look in his eyes. Suddenly, Hyper reared on her hind legs as I hung on her back with all my might. Eyeing those dangerous hooves, the mountain lion howled and screamed but backed away from an attack. At that moment, Hyper quickly pivoted and headed straight down the mountain. Scared and angry, I continued to hang on despite the falling rocks and clouds of dust caused by our quick descent. Hyper was amazing as she bounded over rocks, leapt over gullies and tore through the underbrush. I could tell that her intent was to get back to those stables, and in a short time, we were there. Then, I thought about my dream the night before and how different my ride turned out to be.

About an hour later, Mom, Dad and Jes returned to the stables. "I guess you took the short cut," said Jes. Shaking my head, I told them about the mountain lion.

"We're glad you're safe," Mom said, relieved.

"Well, we went looking for you, Ben, and never got to the top of the mountain," remarked Dad. "Would you like to try again?"

"No, thanks, Dad," I stated firmly. "How about a helicopter ride instead?"

So on that last day, we finally saw the top of that mountain and many other mountains besides and valleys too. And, from now on, I'll stick to horseback riding in my dreams.

34. What word would the narrator MOST likely use to describe his horse's reaction to the mountain lion? ELAALRL1, F

   A terrified   **C** inspired

   B cautious   **D** fearless

35. Which of these words is MOST closely related to the theme of the story? ELAALRL2

   A victory

   B pressure

   C misadventure

   D enlightenment

Use the story "A Trip to Remember" and the essay "My First (and Last) Horseback Ride" to answer question 36.

36. Which statement BEST expresses the theme of both "A Trip to Remember" and the essay "My First (and Last) Horseback Ride?" ELAALRL2

   A Taking risks is only for the brave, and not those who frighten easily.

   B When you begin an adventure, you never know how it might turn out.

   C The most memorable things happen when you are very far from home.

   D When you set out on a journey, always make sure you are in control.

Drive-Thru Theater

The scene opens in a typical quick-serve seafood place. The action takes place at the drive-thru window; the restaurant itself is almost deserted. Deborah, a high school junior, is taking orders, one after another, speaking in quick, clipped tones while Aaron, the assistant manager, keeps food coming from under the kitchen's heat lamps.

DEBORAH [*talking into her intercom*]. Can I take your order, please? [pushing long dark hair from her face and sighing.] [*Aside.*] Please—like sometime tonight!

AARON. [*bringing up an order for the car outside of the window*]. Here's the 10 Tiny Tim Shrimp Meals with hats. Think the kids can tell which is the food? [rolls his eyes comically.]

DEBORAH [*talking to the intercom*]. Can I take your money, please? [*Howls from the car can be heard.*] Oh no! Uh—I mean—can I take your order!

AARON [*he's doubled over trying not to laugh too loudly*]. Well, at least that's honest: Can I take your money . . . Oh man. What's with you tonight anyway? Last Saturday we were busting our—well you know, and you weren't this freaked.

DEBORAH. Yeah, well. I just can't believe I said that. [*She finishes taking the order and hands it out the window grinning sheepishly.*]

AARON [*with dramatic handwaving to her*]. So, whazzup?

DEBORAH. Hold on a second—another order. [*Aaron waits, glancing towards the kitchen area to check on that work. Satisfied, he turns back towards Deborah.*] Well, ya know I've been taking this drama course at school. I'm missing some group practice working here. I'm getting really bugged about it. [*She glares at the intercom as it signals another customer.*] Can I take your order please?

AARON. Listen, why don't you practice here—start acting like you care! [*She does a quick double-take towards him, smiling, eyebrows lifted.*] A-a-about the job I mean . . .

DEBORAH [*to intercom*]. 2 Tiny Tim Meals and 1 Scrooge FishFry ValuNet? OK. Come around to the second window. [*Tilting her head towards Aaron.*] Shouldn't you be, like, fixing something, somewhere? [*then at his direct look*] Oh yeah. Care. Like I'm really going to be deeply committed to this window thing.

AARON [*earnestly*]. Well sure. At least you could act as if you care about the customers.

CHILD IN CAR. Hellooo! Hey lady, you forgot my hat! [*Deborah giggles while Aaron grabs a hat and tosses it like a frisbee through the car's rear window.*]

AARON. Or you know, why don't you try out different characters on the customers. They'll never notice. Oh wait. Leave out, like, any horror characters. [*They hear the signal for another car.*] Leave the scary stuff to THEM!

DEBORAH. Can I take your order please? [*To Aaron.*] So I could act like a character and work at the same time. Yeah, all right. I am supposed to be practicing for . . . [*She stands stiffly, arms folded, and intones heavily and dramatically to the glass window before sliding it open.*] I will not see my people suffer and starve.

AARON [*bowing as he hands her the bagged food*]. Then for God's sake, your worshipfullness, don't let them eat this!

DEBORAH [*extending a hand to Aaron*]. The council is pleased with your words. We offer peace between our peoples and will act accordingly to our subjects. [*Turning with an air of majestic dignity to the intercom.*] I await to be advised of your order.

AARON [*Listening to her practice, admiring yet regretful, as he cleans up the remains of ketchup packets, mutters*]. Man, I blew that scene!

37. **Based on the passage, which** ELAALRL1, D
of the following BEST
describes the relationship between Deborah and Aaron?

   A   Aaron is one of Deborah's customers.

   B   They are co-workers and friends.

   C   Deborah is Aaron's daughter.

   D   They are engaged to be married.

38. **According to the stage** ELAALRL1, D
directions, how does Deborah speak to the customers at the beginning of the play?

   A   She intones heavily and dramatically.

   B   Feeling attracted to Aaron, she speaks in a flirting tone.

   C   Liking her job, she talks earnestly.

   D   She speaks in quick, clipped tones.

39. **Based on the passage, what** ELAALRL1, D
is the only other speaking part, besides Aaron's and Deborah's, in the play?

   A   owner of the restaurant

   B   food bagger

   C   child in car

   D   customer over intercom

40. **Which of the following** ELAALRL1, D
BEST describes the setting of the play?

   A   window of a fast-food restaurant

   B   school drama class

   C   kitchen of a fast-food restaurant

   D   cashier training class

SECTION 2

DO NOT TURN PAGE UNTIL INSTRUCTED TO DO SO

41. Which of the following is the BEST explanation of the dramatic device called a chorus? ELAALRL1, D

A   a device that solves a problem in an unexpected way

B   a "stage whisper" which the audience can hear but the other characters must pretend to not hear

C   a character or group who reveals background or emotional insight about the main character

D   one character speaking alone on stage directly to the audience

42. Which of the following BEST describes the dramatic device of a character foil? ELAALRL1, D

A   a character who provides contrast with another character

B   a person who tells the actors how to play scenes, speak, and react to each other

C   the main character in a play, also called the protagonist or hero

D   a character who drops in unexpectedly into a scene

excerpt from *Ethan Frome* by Edith Wharton

I had the story, bit by bit, from various people, and, as generally happens in such cases, each time it was a different story. If you know Starkfield, Massachusetts, you know the post-office. If you know the post-office you must have seen Ethan Frome drive up to it, drop the reins on his hollow-backed bay and drag himself across the brick pavement to the white collonnade: and you must have asked who he was.

It was there that, several years ago, I saw him for the first time; and the sight pulled me up sharp. Even then he was the most striking figure in Starkfield, though he was but the ruin of a man. It was not so much his great height that marked him, for the "natives" were easily singled out by their lank longitude from the stockier foreign breed: it was the careless powerful look he had, in spite of a lameness checking each step like the jerk of a chain. There was something bleak and unapproachable in his face, and he was so stiffened and grizzled that I took him for an old man and was surprised to hear that he was not more than fifty-two. I had this from Harmon Gow, who had driven the stage from Bettsbridge to Starkfield in pre-trolley days and knew the chronicle of all the families on his line.

"He's looked that way ever since he had his smash-up; and that's twenty-four years ago come next February," Harmon threw out between reminiscent pauses.

43. How do we learn the MOST about Ethan Frome? ELAALRL1, F

A   his actions

B   his thoughts

C   his appearance

D   the comments of Harmon Gow

44. Which is a good description of Ethan Frome? ELAALRL1, F

A   a strong, powerful man

B   an old, weak man

C   a tall, lame man

D   a quiet, striking man

45. This selection is written MOSTLY from what point of view?

ELAALRL1, F

A first person

B second person

C third person omniscient

D third person limited

Sidney Lanier (1842–1841)

Born in Macon, Georgia in 1842, Sidney Lanier, poet, writer, and flutist, received his education from Oglethorpe College in Macon, Georgia. He enlisted as a Confederate soldier as the Civil War started. He served as a private until he was captured four months before the end of the conflict. He was held in federal prison at Point Lookout, Maryland, where he developed tuberculosis. He spent the rest of his life fighting poor health and poverty.

His first published book was the novel *Tiger-Lilies* (1867) about his experiences in the Civil War. His book *Poems* (1877) did not sell well and he earned his living playing the flute in the Peabody Orchestra in Baltimore, Maryland. To support his wife and four sons, he wrote poetry and played music for the rest of his life.

He spent his final years writing some of his best poetry. He died at the age of 39.

His most famous poem, "The Marshes of Glynn" (1878), is about the salt marshes along the sea cost of Georgia. Here is a memorable section from this poem:

As the marsh-hen secretly builds on the watery sod,

Behold I will build me a nest on the greatness of God:

I will fly in the greatness of God as the marsh-hen flies

In the freedom that fills all the space 'twixt the marsh and the skies:

By so many roots as the marsh-grass sends in the sod

I will heartily lay me a-hold on the greatness of God:

Oh, like to the greatness of God is the greatness within

The range of the marshes, the liberal marshes of Glynn.

46. **Based on this selection, which** ELAALRL4 **of the following conclusions can be made about Sidney Lanier?**

   A   Sidney Lanier escaped from prison so he could find a cure for his tuberculosis.

   B   Sidney Lanier believed in God and loved music, poetry, and learning.

   C   Sidney Lanier lived a long and productive life as musician and poet.

   D   Through his music and poetry, Sidney Lanier was able to provide a comfortable life for his family.

47. **Based on the verses you just** ELAALRL3 **read from Lanier's "The Marshes of Glynn," which of the following is not a characteristic of Romanticism?**

   A   a bleak view of the nature world

   B   a reverence for the natural world

   C   a belief in a Supreme Being

   D   a close relationship between nature and the individual

48. **If Sidney Lanier were alive** ELAALRC4 **today, what would be MOST different about his life?**

   A   Lanier probably would not have chosen a career as a musician today.

   B   Lanier would most likely live now near his favorite place, the Marshes of Glynn.

   C   Lanier would seek state assistance now so he could write poetry.

   D   Lanier would likely find a cure today for his tuberculosis and live a healthy life.

49. **The word liberal in the phrase** ELAALRC4 **"the liberal Marshes of Glynn" means**

   A   free.

   B   not conservative

   C   broad.

   D   sacred.

50. **How should you correct the** ELA11W4 **punctuation in the sentence below?**

> His book *Poems* (1877) did not sell well and he earned his living playing the flute in the Peabody Orchestra in Baltimore Maryland

   A   His book *Poems* (1877), did not sell well and he earned his living, playing the flute in the Peabody Orchestra in Baltimore Maryland.

   B   His book *Poems* (1877) did not sell well, and he earned his living playing the flute in the Peabody Orchestra in Baltimore, Maryland.

   C   His book *Poems* (1877) did not sell well, and he earned his living, playing the flute in the Peabody Orchestra in Baltimore, Maryland.

   D   His book *Poems* (1877) did not sell well and he earned his living playing the flute, in the Peabody Orchestra, in Baltimore, Maryland.

Oliver's Rescue

"My cat's in your tree—" gasped the young woman. "He's been gone for six days, and we just heard him meow up there!"

Vera looked up, shading her eyes against the setting sun's rays as the girl pointed to the tallest tree in Vera's yard: a seventy-foot pine.

"Yeah, maybe he'd climb down, but it's been so long already . . . Can I please come here tomorrow with some friends and a ladder to get him down?"

"Of course. Whatever you need to do is fine. I'll put tuna under the tree tonight. Come to think of it, my husband likes buyin' tuna.

The next afternoon, Vera watched out her window as the group of friends assembled under her pine. The ladder they brought was forty feet tall but still didn't reach the first branches, stopping short by five feet.

"Michael, here's the rope. Catch!" The boy in the tree caught it and grinned with bravado at the group below. He was already holding a backpack to carry the cat. He quickly scaled the tree, disappearing into the thick growth of needles and branches.

"Michael's a great rescuer!" enthused one girl. "He's strong like Hercules."

Though she had turned a defenete grey color as snapping sounds came from the tree, Kelly seemed to breath easier.

Then, there came a desperate shout from Michael, "He's coming down!"

Instead of a backpack, everyone saw Oliver being lowered by the neck in a noose.

"My cat's strangling! My cat's strangling!" Kelly's voice rose higher and higher as the cat dropped lower and lower. Jeff, Kelly's boyfriend, stood underneath Oliver, with his arms outstretched to catch him. Vera saw Oliver's tongue hanging out. He looked near death. Then, inches above Jeff's reach, Oliver came to a dead stop.

The whole group began screaming, "Michael! The rope! The rope's stuck!" Everyone, including Vera, stared at Oliver gently swaying at the rope's end, willing him to breath, to fight, to do something to get himself down. Instead, they heard branches crashing. Vera looked up at Michael, suspended between branches, reaching to free the rope.

"Hey!" It was Jeff's turn to yell as Oliver landed in his arms scratching and biting. Laura leaped to Jeff's side to free Oliver from the strangling knot. She freed it quickly and as Oliver bit through Jeff's thumbnail, he let the cat go. Kelly moved for the first time since Michael had gone up the tree. She took off after Oliver, and everyone watched as she let Oliver and herself through the door.

GO ON

Later, Kelly returned after taking Oliver to a nearby vet's office. He was pronounced "100 percent fine and doggone lucky." Laura said that having the best people around was the luck.

Vera got tuna salad ready—"My husband doesn't eat tuna," she said, looking affectionately at her husband sitting quietly on their sofa. "He just likes buying it. Fred has Alzheimer's. We're getting on ok, but Michael, I'd like your phone number, so I could officially hire you for some work we need doing."

The young people were quiet until Michael answered, "Ok, but I do want some of this tuna whenever I'm here. Hercules needs good food for those tough jobs."

Vera gazed around her, listening to the chatter, and thanking the Lord for Oliver's rescue.

51. In which organizational pattern is this passage written? ELA11W1

- A chronological
- B cause effect
- C spatial
- D comparison/contrast

Read this sentence from the selection.

> "Vera gazed around her, listening to the chatter, and thanking the Lord for Oliver's rescue."

52. What does this sentence suggest about the author's perspective in this selection? ELA11W1

- A The author's perspective cannot be determined.
- B The cat's response is closest to the author's perspective.
- C Vera's words come closest to the author's perspective.
- D All of the characters mirror the author's perspective.

53. Based on the references, images, and content, choose the most likely time period for this story. ELAALRC4

- A Colonial Period
- B Romantic Period
- C Naturalistic Period
- D Postmodern Period

54. Which of the following sentences contains dialect that reflects the speaker's background? ELA11LSV2

- A Vera looked up, shading her eyes against the setting sun's rays as the girl pointed to the tallest tree in Vera's yard: a seventy-foot pine.
- B Vera tried hard to sound serious as she stepped over her threshold.
- C "Can I please come here tomorrow with some friends and a ladder to get him down?"
- D "Come to think of it, my husband likes buyin' tuna."

55. The mention of Hercules in the story is an allusion to a famous

ELAALRC4

    A American hero.

    B Greek hero.

    C Native American hero.

    D Biblical hero.

Read this sentence from the passage.

> "…she had turned a defenete grey color as snapping sounds came from the tree…"

56. Then choose the correct spelling for *defenete*.

ELA11C2

    A defenete   **C** definite

    B defenete   **D** definete

57. After Oliver's near-fatal rescue, Kelly decided to learn the correct way to rescue cats in trees. Which source would be most helpful in her research?

ELA11W3

    A AnimalPlanet.com cat safety guide

    B encyclopedia of animals in North America

    C magazine article about caring for pets

    D *Guinness World Records* book

Read the sentence below from the selection.

> He was pronounced "100 percent fine and doggone lucky."

58. Which of the following best describes the diction used in this sentence?

ELA11C1

    A formal English

    B figure of speech

    C analogy

    D dialect

59. Hector is writing a literary analysis of "Oliver's Rescue." He wants to cite the sentence that describes the climax of this story. Which of the following is the BEST choice to quote in his essay?

ELAALRL1, F

    A She took off after Oliver, and everyone watched as she let Oliver and herself through the door.

    B "Looks like it's time we cleaned you up," clucked Vera at Jeff, "so get Michael down, and everyone come in for some tea and tuna."

    C The young people were quiet until Michael answered, "Ok, but I do want some of this tuna whenever I'm here."

    D Everyone, including Vera, stared at Oliver gently swaying at the rope's end, willing him to breathe, to fight, to do something to get himself down.

excerpt from a movie script of M. L. Agnesi's *Adventures at the Ball Park*

[*Four teenagers are at a major league ball park. It is their first trip without parents. They begin to argue among themselves.*]

FILMER. Lighten up, will ya? I got this here thing figured out, see? We can all get a signature on the baseball if we send Peewee over to the dugout and make him faint.

PEEWEE [*nervously*]. Why me and how you goin' do it?

[*The other two boys begin to push and yell at the same time.*]

BERNARD. How come the runt gets ta go! I wanna do it. Let me go, huh, why don't ya, huh?

ROLAND. It's cus the runt's your brother right? Playin' favorites again. If that isn't just like you!

[*Filmer looks skyward as the noise continues around him. He daydreams and thinks to himself.*]

FILMER [*now looking straight at the audience, frowning*]. My own brother, afraid of a little overacting. Just a plain dive is all I'm asking him to take. You know it happens all the time at home—doesn't get his way, and he's on the floor turning blue. The other guys, now, you wouldn't think they'd like want to look as stupid and nerdy as my brother. [*Considers what he has just said and smiles.*] Oh yeah! They want to get in the dugout any way they can. They're planning on cutting me out of the scene. I don't get Cal Ripkin Jr.'s autograph!

[*Filmer's daydream ends with shouting and pushing in the group.*]

FILMER [*Arms up in the air*]. All right, all right ! Pipe down already! Listen, I can take a hint. The real talent around here is me, and I got to do the dive. I'll go to the top of the dugout and fall over the ledge, see? You guys start yelling like you were just now and . . . [*Filmer realizes that the others are looking over his shoulder with fear. He turns slowly to see a stadium official reaching for his notebook. Filmer falls on the ground and turns a very convincing shade of blue but gives the now silent group of boys a huge wink before the officer can see.*]

60. What effect does Filmer's ELA11LSV2
visual technique of winking at
the boys have on the audience?

A The audience realizes that Filmer won't get his signature because he has been caught.

B The audience is disappointed because Filmer wants the glory instead of wealth.

C The audience witnesses Filmer's capture but knows he will still get the signature.

D The audience decides that Filmer is spoiled and reckless.

61. Which of the following correc- ELA11C1
tions would BEST improve this
statement?

My own brother, afraid of a little overacting.

A My own brother, you're so afraid of a little overacting.

B My own brother is afraid of a little overacting.

C Afraid of a little overacting, my own brother is against me.

D no change

62. Choose the example that BEST ELA11C1
joins these two independent
clauses.

They begin to argue among themselves. It is their first trip without their parents.

A They begin to argue among themselves because it is their first trip without their parents.

B It is their first trip without their parents, and they begin to argue among themselves.

C It is their first trip without their parents, so they begin to argue among themselves.

D They begin to argue among themselves, for it is their first trip without their parents.

"The Cop and the Anthem" by O. Henry

Between the years of 1852 and 1935, petty criminals were sent to Blackwell Penitentiary to serve time for various offenses. Blackwell's was a minimum security prison and work house on Roosevelt Island in the New York Harbor.

On his bench in Madison Square, Soapy moved uneasily. When wild geese honk high of nights, and when women without sealskin coats grow kind to their husbands, and when Soapy moves uneasily on his bench in the park, you may know that winter is near at hand.

For years the hospitable Blackwell's had been his winter quarters. Just as his more fortunate fellow New Yorkers had bought their tickets to Palm Beach and the Riviera each winter, so Soapy had made his humble arrangements for his annual hegira to the Island. And now the time was come. On the previous night three Sabbath newspapers, distributed beneath his coat, about his ankles and over his lap, had failed to repulse the cold as he slept on his bench near the spurting fountain in the ancient square. So the Island loomed big and timely in Soapy's mind.

Soapy, having decided to go to the Island, at once set about accomplishing his desire. There were many easy ways of doing this.

At a corner of Sixth Avenue electric lights and cunningly displayed wares behind plate-glass made a shop window conspicuous. Soapy took a cobblestone and dashed it through the glass. People came running around the corner, a policeman in the lead. Soapy stood still, with his hands in his pockets, and smiled at the sight of brass buttons.

"Where's the man that done that?" inquired the officer, excitedly.

"Don't you figure out that I might have had something to do with it?" said Soapy, not without sarcasm, but friendly, as one greets good fortune.

The policeman's mind refused to accept Soapy even as a clue. Men who smash windows do not remain to parley with the law's minions. They take to their heels. The policeman saw a man halfway down the block running to catch a cat. With drawn club, he joined in the pursuit. Soapy, with disgust in his heart, loafed along, unsuccessful.

STORY DELETED

In a cigar store he saw a well-dressed man lighting a cigar at a swinging light. His silk umbrella he had set by the door on entering. Soapy stepped inside, secured the umbrella and sauntered off with it slowly. The man at the cigar light followed hastily.

"My umbrella," he said, sternly.

"Oh, is it?" sneered Soapy, adding insult to petit larceny. "Well, why don't you call a policeman? I took it. Your umbrella! Why don't you call a cop? There stands one on the corner."

The umbrella owner slowed his steps. Soapy did likewise, with a presentiment that luck would again run against him. The policeman looked at the two curiously.

"Of course," said the umbrella man— "that is—well, you know how these mistakes occur—I—if it's your umbrella I hope you'll excuse me—I picked it up this morning in a restaurant—If you recognize it as yours, why—I hope you'll—"

"Of course it's mine," said Soapy, viciously.

The ex-umbrella man retreated. The policeman hurried to assist a tall blonde in an opera cloak across the street in front of a street car that was approaching two blocks away.

Soapy walked eastward through a street damaged by improvements. He hurled the umbrella wrathfully into an excavation. He muttered against the men who wear helmets and carry clubs. Because he wanted to fall into their clutches, they seemed to regard him as a king who could do no wrong.

But on an unusually quiet corner Soapy came to a standstill. Here was an old church, quaint and rambling and gabled. Through one violet-stained window a soft light glowed, where, no doubt, the organist loitered over the keys, making sure of his mastery of the coming Sabbath anthem. For there drifted out to Soapy's ears sweet music that caught and held him transfixed against the convolutions of the iron fence.

And also in a moment his heart responded thrillingly to this novel mood. An instantaneous and strong impulse moved him to battle with his desperate fate. He would pull himself out of the mire; he would make a man of himself again; he would conquer the evil that had taken possession of him. There was time; he was comparatively young yet: he would resurrect his old eager ambitions and pursue them without faltering. Those solemn but sweet organ notes had set up a revolution in him. Tomorrow he would go into the roaring downtown district and find work. A fur importer had once offered him a place as driver. He would find him tomorrow and ask for the position. He would be somebody in the world. He would—

Soapy felt a hand laid on his arm. He looked quickly around into the broad face of a policeman.

"What are you doin' here?" asked the officer.

"Nothin'," said Soapy.

"Then come along," said the policeman.

Three months on the Island," said the Magistrate in the Police Court the next morning.

63. Which genre is MOST clearly ELA11W2
evident in the organizational
patterns of this selection?

A persuasion   C description
B exposition   D narration

64. After reading "The Cop and ELA11W3
the Anthem" Lakisha decides
to write a paper on the homeless in
America. Which of the following
research questions is most relevant to
this story?

A Why do the police arrest homeless persons?

B How does weather affect the homeless?

C How do homeless shelters improve lives?

D Where are homeless persons most likely to congregate?

65. One of the sources Lakisha is ELA11W3
using for her research paper is
a book called *Hope for the Homeless*. To
paraphrase correctly from this source,
she should

A copy down the author's exact words in quotations.

B include the author's ideas in her own words.

C use a quotation from each chapter in the book.

D interview the author and take notes for use in her research paper.

66. The sources for a research ELA11W3
paper should be included in
a(an)

A table of contents.
B title page.
C appendix.
D bibliography.

67. What change should be made ELA11C2
in the sentence below?

> The setting of many of O. Henry's stories is in the northeast, particularly New York City.

A Change *is* to *are*.
B Change *northeast* to *Northeast*.
C Change *many* to *more*.
D Change *Henry's* to *Henrys'*.

68. Which of the following sen- ELA11C1
tences about Soapy show incon-
sistent verb tense?

A He is bad tempered and liked to fight.

B He was religious and went to church every Sunday.

C He was a procrastinator who took each day as it came.

D He wanted to be a policeman.

69. How does the author support ELA11W1
the umbrella man's claim that
the umbrella really belongs to Soapy?

A The umbrella man leaves the scene quietly.

B Soapy refuses to claim the umbrella.

C The umbrella man took the umbrella from someone else in a restaurant.

D The policeman believes neither Soapy or the umbrella man and walks away.

70. Which of the following state- ELA11W2
ments would be considered
informal language?

A People came running around the corner, a policeman in the lead.

B With drawn club, he joined in the pursuit.

C The umbrella owner slowed his steps.

D Why don't you call a cop?

71. **How should the sentence below**   ELA11C1
     be correctly written?

> You's gots' ta be logged in t' post yer comment.
> Man!

   A   You gotta be logged in ta post your
        comment. Man!

   B   You must need to be logged in to post
        the comment, sir.

   C   Log in, man. Then post yer comment.

   D   You have to be logged in to post your
        comment, visitor.

excerpt from essay written in 1903 by W.E.B. DuBois, an African-American essayist

The Negro race, like all races, is going to be saved by its exceptional men. The problem of education, then, among Negroes must first of all deal with the Talented Tenth; it is the problem of developing the Best of this race that they may guide the Mass away from the contamination and death of the Worst, in their own and other races. Now the training of men is a difficult and intricate task. Its technique is a matter for educational experts, but its object is for the vision of seers. If we make money the object of man-training, we shall develop money-makers but not necessarily men; if we make technical skill the object of education, we may possess artisans but not, in nature, men. Men we shall have only as we make manhood the object of the work of the schools—intelligence, broad sympathy, knowledge of the world that was and is, and of the relation of men to it—this is the curriculum of that Higher Education which must underlie true life. On this foundation we may build bread winning, skill of hand and quickness of brain, with never a fear lest the child and man mistake the means of living for the object of life.

If this be true—and who can deny it—three tasks lay before me; first to show from the past that the Talented Tenth as they have risen among American Negroes have been worthy of leadership; secondly to show how these men may be educated and developed; and thirdly to show their relation to the Negro problem.

72. In the context of the passage, which is the best summary of the following quote from the passage? ELA11W3

> [Education's] technique is a matter for educational experts, but its object is for the vision of seers.

A   The purpose of education is to develop people of vision by using the best teachers and strategies.

B   Educational experts are visionaries in the field of "training of men" and imparting of knowledge.

C   There is no point in receiving an education in making money, without vision.

D   It takes visionaries, not experts, to determine the highest purpose of education.

73. This passage can best be classified as persuasive because ELA11W2

A   it discusses details about money makers and artisans.

B   it explains the importance of education for all Negroes at that time.

C   it argues for the education and leadership of the Talented Tenth.

D   it focuses on the problem of finding and training the Talented Tenth.

excerpt from speech by President Reagan

President Ronald Reagan lead the nation in mourning for the seven astronauts killed in the Space Shuttle Challenger Explosion, Washington, D.C., January 28, 1986. That evening, he gave the following speech on television to the people of the United States.

Ladies and Gentlemen:

I'd planned to speak to you tonight to report on the state of the Union, but the events of earlier today have led me to change those plans. Today is a day for mourning and remembering. Nancy and I are pained to the core by the tragedy of the shuttle *Challenger*. We know we share this pain with all of the people of our country. This is truly a national loss.

Nineteen years ago, almost to the day, we lost three astronauts in a terrible accident on the ground. But we've never lost an astronaut in flight; we've never had a tragedy like this. And perhaps we've forgotten the courage it took for the crew of the shuttle. But they, the *Challenger* Seven, were aware of the dangers, but overcame them and did their jobs brilliantly. We mourn seven heros: Michael Smith, Dick Scobee, Judith Resnik, Ronald McNair, Ellison Onizuka, Gregory Jarvis, and Christa McAuliffe. We mourn their loss as a nation together.

For the families of the seven, we cannot bear, as you do, the full impact of this tragedy. But we feel the loss, and we're thinking about you so very much. Your loved ones were daring and brave, and they had that special grace, that special spirit that says, "Give me a challenge, and I'll meet it with joy." They had a hunger to explore the universe and discover its truths. They wished to serve, and they did. They served all of us.

We've grown used to wonders in this century. It's hard to dazzle us. But for 25 years the United States space program has been doing just that. We've grown used to the idea of space, and perhaps we forget that we've only just begun. We're still pioneers. They, the members of the *Challenger* crew, were pioneers.

And I want to say something to the school children of America who were watching the live coverage of the shuttle's takeoff. I know it is hard to understand, but sometimes painful things like this happen. It's all part of the process of exploration and discovery. It's all part of taking a chance and expanding man's horizons. The future doesn't belong to the fainhearted; it belongs to the brave. The *Challenger* crew was pulling us into the future, and we'll continue to follow them.

I've always had great faith in and respect for our space program, and what happened today does nothing to diminish it. We don't hide our space program. We don't keep secrets and cover things up. We do it all up front and in public. That's the way freedom is, and we wouldn't change it for a minute. We'll continue our quest in space. There will be more shuttle flights and more shuttle crews and, yes, more volunteers, more civilians, more teachers in space. Nothing ends here; our hopes and our journeys continue. I want to add that I wish I could talk to every man and woman who works for NASA or who worked on this mission and tell them: Your dedication and professionalism have moved and impressed us for decades. And we know of your anguish. We share it.

There's a coincidence today. On this day 390 years ago, the great explorer Sir Francis Drake died aboard a ship off the coast of Panama. In his lifetime, the great frontiers were the oceans, and an historian later said, "He lived by the sea, died on it, and was buried in it." Well, today we can say of the *Challenger* crew: Their dedication was, like Drake's, complete.

The crew of the space shuttle *Challenger* honored us by the manner in which they lived their lives. We will never forget them, nor the last time we saw them, this morning, as they prepared for their journey and waved goodbye, and "slipped the surly bonds of earth" to "touch the face of God."

74. In the speech, which of the following does Reagan do most effectively? ELA11LSV2

A argues for a change in methods used in space exploration

B compares viewpoints of those who both support and oppose space exploration

C comforts the nation after the *Challenger* disaster

D explains the recent progress made in space exploration because of the *Challenger* crew

75. Which source would probably provide the MOST accurate information on the *Challenger* explosion? ELA11W3

A anovel written about the explosion

B newspaper reports about the explosion

C official records about the explosion

D eyewitness accounts of the explosion

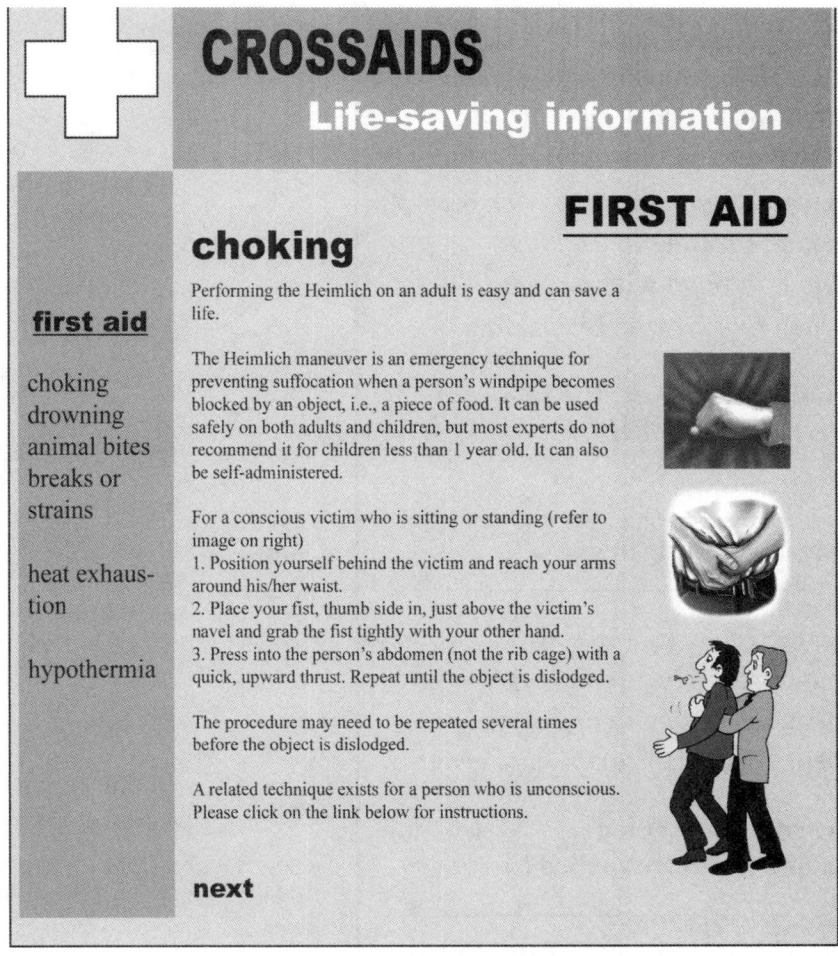

76. How does the author of the Web page simplify the procedure for the Heimlich maneuver?

ELA11LSV2

A The author shows all the techniques on one page.

B The author describes every step using technical language.

C The author explains the procedure with three simple steps aided by pictures.

D The author provides a sidebar that connects to other parts of the web site.

77. Which of the following versions of this sentence from the document is punctuated correctly?

ELA11C1

A The procedure may need to be repeated several times before the object is dislodged.

B The procedure may need to be repeated, several times before the object is dislodged.

C The procedure may need to be repeated several times, before the object is dislodged.

D The procedure may need to be repeated several times; before the object is dislodged.

78. How should the sentence below BEST be written? ELA11C1

> Strolling through the computerized control center, the tool kit carried the technician.

   A   Change *computerized* to *computer.*
   B   Change strolling to *walking.*
   C   Switch *through* with *strolling.*
   D   Switch *tool kit* with *technician.*

79. How would you correct the following error in parallel structure? ELA11C1

> To err is human, forgiving divine.

   A   Change *To err* to *Make errors.*
   B   Change *forgiving* to *the forgive.*
   C   Change *forgiving* to *to forgive.*
   D   Change *To err* to *committing error.*

80. What word in the sentence below is not correctly spelled? ELA11C1

> Our principal praised us for memorizing all of the capitals of the United States.

   A   principal
   B   praised
   C   memorizing
   D   capitals

A

abolitionist 36
act 90
action verb 153
active voice 152
Adams, Samuel 32
aesthetic 65
aesthetic purpose 68
affix 104, 114
African-American
    folklore 38
    literature 43
    novelists 49
alliteration 83
allusion 66, 72, 114
almanac 165
American Revolution 53
analogy 156
Anderson, Sherwood 40
anecdotal scripting, 168
anecdote 148
annotated bibliography 168
antagonist 89
apostrophe
    use of 185
appeal to authority 121
argument 147
aside 92
assonance 83
audience
    appeal 120
    define 131
    mass 123
    targeted 123
author
    audience 120, 123, 140
    choice of words 85
    language 120, 150
    mood 85
    purpose 140
    purpose, types of 120
    style 150
    tone 85, 150
author purpose
    types of 121

B

Baldwin, James 46
ballad 80
bandwagon 121
Beat Generation 47, 53
Beat poetry 48
Bellow, Saul 50
Beverly, Robert 32

bias 166
bibliography 132, 172, 216
    annotated 168
blank verse 81
body paragraph 147
Bradstreet, Anne 32
brainstorming 146
broadside 31
Bryant, William Cullen 36
Byrd, William II 32

C

capitalization 185
Capote, Truman 49
captivity narrative 31
Carver, Raymond 49
Casas, Bartolome de las 31
Cather, Willa 40
cause and effect 99, 144, 207
Chabon, Michael 49
character 89
    development 58, 61
    development of 90
    development, types of 62
Cheever, John 50
chronological order 59, 207
Cisneros, Sandra 50
citation 213
Civil Rights Movement 48, 53
Civil War, post 40
clarity 146
clause
    types of 194
cliché 193
climax 59
cognate 104, 114
coherence 206
Cold War 48
collective noun 188
colon
    use of 182
comedy 88
comma 183
    use of 181, 182
comparing and contrasting 207
comparison 144
comparison and contrast 207
complication 59
compound singular subject 188
concluding sentence 207
conclusion 148
Confessional Poets 48
confidant 89
connotation 102, 114, 193

NOTES

NOTES

NOTES

NOTES